Managing Insecurity

Effective peace building in the aftermath of civil war usually requires the deep reform of security institutions, a process frequently known as security sector reform. Nearly every major donor, as well as a growing number of international organizations, supports the reform of security organizations in countries emerging from conflict and suffering high levels of violence. But how are reform strategies implemented? This collection of nine case studies examines the strategies, methods, and practices of the policy makers and practitioners engaged in security sector reform, and uncovers the profound conceptual and practical challenges encountered in transforming policy aspiration into practice.

This book was previously published as a special issue of *Civil Wars*.

Gordon Peake is a consultant and former associate, International Peace Academy, New York, USA.

Eric Scheye is a consultant on justice and security sector reform.

Alice Hills is professor of conflict and security at the University of Leeds, UK.

Managing Insecurity: Field Experiences of Security Sector Reform

Edited by
Gordon Peake, Eric Scheye and Alice Hills

 Routledge
Taylor & Francis Group

LONDON AND NEW YORK

First published 2008 by Routledge
2 Park Square, Milton Park, Abingdon, Oxon, OX14 4RN

Simultaneously published in the USA and Canada
by Routledge
270 Madison Avenue, New York, NY 10016

Routledge is an imprint of the Taylor & Francis Group, an informa business

© 2008 Gordon Peake, Eric Scheye, Alice Hills

Typeset in Times 10/12pt by the Alden Group, Oxfordshire

British Library Cataloguing in Publication Data
A catalogue record for this book is available from the British Library

Library of Congress Cataloging in Publication Data
A catalog record has been requested

ISBN 10: 0-415-43965-5 (hbk)
ISBN 13: 978-0-415-43965-7 (hbk)

CONTENTS

Introduction

GORDON PEAKE, ERIC SCHEYE AND ALICE HILLS

The reform and reconstruction of state security institutions once civil wars cease is now a central part of the international community's conflict management agenda. As the UN's High Level Panel on Threats, Challenges and Change noted, 'relatively cheap investments in civilian security through police, judicial and rule of law reform...can greatly benefit long-term peacebuilding'[1]

The phrase normally used to describe such projects is 'security sector reform' (SSR). Addressing the wide range of state institutions with a formal mandate to ensure the safety and security of the state and (sometimes) its citizens, SSR's goals are both immediate and long term. In the short-term, it is intended to improve the ability of a country's military, police and intelligence organisations to provide basic security to countries or regions emerging from conflict. Its long-term aims, however, are much more ambitious: it seeks to reconstruct a state's governance so as to ensure that its security institutions serve the interests of society as a whole, rather than those of a political elite. This involves radical changes to the purpose, structure, and values of security organisations that are, moreover, secretive and resistant to change.

Despite the scale of the challenge, many international actors develop and manage SSR programmes. Agencies from the United Nations, regional organisations and development banks fund, design, and implement SSR programming, as do bilateral governments, non-governmental organisations and private contractors. Nationally inspired programmes play an active part too, with or without international assistance.

Much has been written about SSR in relation to peacekeeping, conflict prevention and development, yet the implementation and management of SSR programmes remains an area of benign analytical neglect.[2] Specific aspects of SSR, such as police reform in the western Balkans, have attracted attention, while the experience of countries such as Sierra Leone emphasises the important role that SSR can play in facilitating post-conflict transformation. Yet systematic analyses of SSR in the context of political or socio-economic change are rare, as are accounts of field practice, with the inevitable consequences for conceptual understanding, policy development, and programme refinement.[3]

This collection of articles addresses the resultant theoretical and policy-relevant gap by considering the experiences of policy-makers and practitioners involved in implementing SSR. It relies on the personal reflections and field-based research of individuals who have worked on reform programmes in countries emerging from civil war, or in societies characterised by high levels of communal violence.

As this implies, our approach is, like most work on SSR, positivist in theoretical orientation and is not informed by any specific conceptual or theoretical perspective. We do not, of course, suggest that a positivist approach can provide a full answer to the problems associated with post-conflict change and insecurity. Nor do we dismiss the importance of conceptual insights; it would be informative to analyse SSR from a constructivist viewpoint, but this is not our purpose here. Rather, our intention is to acknowledge the theoretical but emphasise the empirical in order to rebalance the existing debate. As Jentleson has argued, there is a need for praxis, not least because real world issues can enhance our theoretical understanding of why things happen as they do.[4] In this case, real world issues aid understanding of the aftermath of civil wars, the dynamics of transition, and the most effective means of preventing conflict and insecurity.

Nine case studies of the organisational practices typically involved in SSR are presented here. Six concern countries either enmeshed in or emerging from civil war, or experiencing high levels of insecurity and violence: Iraq, Mozambique, Papua New Guinea and Solomon Islands, Serbia and Montenegro, Sierra Leone, and Timor Leste. Three additional case studies supplement the core six, offering comparative and contrasting illustrations of SSR in conditions that while not civil war are sometimes nothing less than localised forms of internecine war. These case studies concern Colombia and Uruguay, Jamaica, and Peru.

To maximize the value of this approach — and to explore the variety of actors and projects involved in SSR — the nine cases are ordered so as to illustrate the following types of programme. First, three examples of foreign countries assuming responsibility for conducting SSR in another state is discussed. These are the Australian operation in the Solomon Islands and Papua New Guinea, the UK-led engagement in Sierra Leone, and the USA's role in Iraq. Second, the role of a range of multi-lateral organisations is represented by the UN Department of Peacekeeping Operations (DPKO)'s work in Timor-Leste, the United Nations Development Programme (UNDP) in Mozambique, and the Organization for Security and Cooperation in Europe (OSCE)'s work in the Republic of Serbia and Montenegro. Third, a case study of Peru is used to illustrate the development of a nationally led SSR programme in which there was very little outside foreign assistance. Admittedly, the brutal war against Maoist rebels that killed up to 69,000 people in the 1980s and 1990s is now ended, but the country still faces entrenched social and economic inequality, and its experience is therefore relevant. Fourth, multi-lateral development banks have recently entered the field, so the Inter-American Development Bank's (IDB) activities in Colombia and Uruguay is offered here as an unusual and compelling case study. Again, Colombia and Uruguay are not in the throes of a civil war, but both experience high levels of violence, crime and insecurity. Similar considerations apply to our last example, Jamaica, which is included here because it illustrates a fifth type of programme arising from the trend for government agencies to hire private contractors to conduct SSR.

Each contributor was asked to consider three sets of questions:

- Foundations of reform

This required contributors to consider what prompted a specific SSR policy, whether a set of policy guidelines were developed or provided, and whether guidance was then disseminated to those implementing the policy. They were asked to compare the theoretical guidance provided (if any) to what actually happened. They were also asked to consider the competences of those involved in the SSR process, for little if any work has been conducted on the composition of staff running SSR programmes.

- Reform Activities

Contributors were asked to assess the extent and relevance of the three major themes widely regarded as crucial for effective SSR: planning, management, and ownership/civil society.

Management was regarded as of special significance because it is usually said that the creation of sustainable, and well-managed institutions is a pivotal element of SSR. By management is meant the creation of a structure that incorporates human resource management, budgeting, financial and asset management, information flows, and internal procedures and policies. It is also a feature that is thought to require leadership, team building, good communications (internal and external), and change management. The authors were specifically asked to examine the importance attached to the creation of institutional structures capable of ensuring consistent, sound and effective management.

Local ownership is now taken to be one of SSR's guiding principles, so contributors were also asked to assess the extent to which this goal was achieved, and identify the relationship between international ideals and those of local stakeholders. We wanted to know the extent to which 'local voices' were considered in the reform process's design, formulation, and implementation.

- Evaluation

Lastly, contributors were asked to identify the factors that accounted for the success or failure of the approach undertaken and, more broadly, what wider lessons could be identified from the approach adopted. Also, they were asked to say what criteria were used to measure achievement and performance, and whether the indicators used proved useful or valid.

This special edition is an outcome of the International Peace Academy (IPA)'s Security-Development Nexus Program, which aims to contribute to a better understanding of the linkages between the various dimensions of conflict and the need for multi-dimensional strategies in conflict management.[5] The IPA's support in facilitating publication is acknowledged.

The IPA Security-Development Nexus Program gratefully acknowledges support from the Rockefeller Foundation and the Governments of Australia, Belgium, Canada, Germany, Luxembourg, Norway, and the United Kingdom (DfID). This IPA program also benefits from core support to IPA from the Governments of Denmark, Sweden and Switzerland, as well as the Ford Foundation and the William and Flora Hewlett Foundation.

ACKNOWLEDGEMENTS

This edited book project forms part of a multi-disciplinary research project of the International Peace Academy called *The Security-Development Nexus*. We are grateful to the help and assistance of our colleagues on the project, Reyko Huang, Agnes Hurwitz, Francesco Mancini and Necla Tschirgi. We are also grateful to Terje Rød-Larsen and Elizabeth Cousens, President and Vice-President of the International Peace Academy, respectively, for their support and encouragement.

Our deep thanks go to our authors, many of whom we no doubt pushed to the limits of their patience with our requests for revisions and additional information. Out interaction with them was always enriching.

We were lucky to have many sharp-eyed friends and colleagues to avail of for reading individual chapters and offering reactions and comments that were always constructive and helpful: Markus Bouillon. Chuck Call, James Cockayne, Graham Day, Matthew Getz, Richard Gowan, Ahmed Hashim, David Hegarty, Claire Howard, David Kendrick, Otwin Marenin, Graham Mathias, Johanna Mendelson-Forman, Andrew Morrison, Eduard Niesten, Rachel Neild, Kevin Rosser, John Roughan, Edward Rees, Graham Thompson, Tor Tanke Holm and Susan Woodward. To each, go our grateful thanks.

Especial thanks go to two people. Francesco Mancini was instrumental in the original design the project and ceaseless in administrative support throughout. Johanna Herman provided valuable research assistance towards the end of the project.

NOTES

1. United Nations High Level Panel on Threats, Challenges and Change, *A more secure world: Our shared responsibility* (New York, United Nations 2004) p. 72.
2. Michael Brzoska 'Introduction: Criteria for Evaluating Post-Conflict Reconstruction and Security Sector Reform in Peace Support Operations' *International Peacekeeping* 13/1 (2006) p. 2. Compare Robin Luckham and Gavin Cawthra (eds) *Governing Insecurity: Democratic Control of Military and Security Establishments in Transitional Democracies* (New York: Zed Books 2003) p. 16; Michael Brzoska, 'Development Donors and the Concept of Security Sector Reform', Geneva Centre for the Democratic Control of Armed Forces (DCAF) Occasional Paper 4 (Geneva: DCAF 2003) p. 2; Jane Chanaa, *Security Sector Reform: Issues, Challenges and Prospects*, Adelphi Paper 344, (Oxford: Oxford University Press 2002); Dylan Hendrickson and Andrzej Karkoszka, 'The Challenges of Security Sector Reform' in *SIPRI Yearbook 2002* (Oxford: Oxford University Press 2002) pp.175-201; Jeremy King, Walter Dorn and Matthew Hodes, *An Unprecedented Experiment: Security Sector Reform in Bosnia and Herzegovina* (London: Saferworld 2002); Tor Tanke Holm and Espen Barth Eide (eds), *Peacebuilding and Police Reform* (London: Cass, 2000).
3. Alan Bryden and Heiner Hanggi 'Reforming and Reconstructing the Security Sector' in Alan Bryden and Heiner Hanggi (eds), *Security Governance in Post-Conflict Peacebuilding* (Munster: Lit Verlag 2005) p.27.
4. Bruce Jentleson, 'The Need for Praxis: Bringing Policy Relevance Back in', *International Security* 26/4 (2002) pp. 169–83.
5. For details see http://www.ipacademy.org/Programs/Programs.htm

Police-Building in Weak States: Australian Approaches in Papua New Guinea and Solomon Islands

SINCLAIR DINNEN, ABBY MCLEOD AND
GORDON PEAKE

This article explores three approaches adopted by Australia towards reforming police in Papua New Guinea (PNG) and Solomon Islands. In PNG, reform efforts over the last 16 years centred on a Royal Papua New Guinea Constabulary (RPNGC) Development Project. Under the project individual consultants (most of whom were former or serving members of Australian or New Zealand police forces) were placed in advisory positions to strengthen the institutional capacity of the police. The second approach, adopted in the troubled Solomon Islands since 2003, was more robust. Policing was a major component in the Australian-led intervention known as the Regional Assistance Mission to Solomon Islands (RAMSI) – that was deployed in July 2003. The strategy had two main components: deploying serving police officers with executive authority to restore law and order following the civil conflict, and simultaneous capacity building intended to endow the local police apparatus, the Royal Solomon Islands Police (RSIP), with the capability of maintaining it. Indeed, so successful did this policing component of RAMSI initially appear to be that it prompted a third – and related – approach called the Enhanced Cooperation Program (ECP) in PNG, the policing component of which lasted from 2004–2005.

This article is composed of four sections. The first three examine the RPNGC Development Project, RAMSI, and the short-lived ECP. The conclusion reflects upon lessons learned and examines the ongoing challenges to Australian involvement in regional police building. It argues that a narrow focus on building formal police structures is untenable, given the resilience of informal systems of conflict resolution in both states, and the limited financial resources available to each government.

THE ROYAL PAPUA NEW GUINEA CONSTABULARY DEVELOPMENT PROJECT

PNG, Australia's nearest neighbour and sole former colony comprises the eastern half of the island of New Guinea, Australia having assumed control of the former British New Guinea in 1905 and the former German colony in the north of the island in 1921. Australia's interest in Papua and New Guinea was primarily strategic. There was minimal interest in development, and its early colonial administration has been described as a 'benevolent type of police rule'.[1]

Government influence was extended incrementally through a system of patrols radiating outwards from newly established district stations. Australian district officers known as *kiaps*, who were accompanied by members of an armed native constabulary, led these. Although Australian and foreign residents were subject to Western laws administered by formal courts, the indigenous population was governed by a paternalistic set of 'native regulations' administered by district officials. There was no discrete system of criminal justice for indigenes. Instead, policing, adjudication and punishment constituted integral parts of an undiffer-entiated system of 'native administration'. In practice, most Papuans and New Guineans continued to rely on customary means for the resolution of everyday disputes and the provision of personal and community security.[2]

The origins of PNG's modern criminal justice system lie in the period of rapid institutional modernisation immediately preceding independence in 1975. With a view to the territory's political future, Australia began to replace the colonial system of district administration with the institutional framework of a modern nation-state. Among other things, this entailed removing the police from the control of the administration, and reforming the judicial system consistent with a separation of powers. This proved slow and difficult, not least because the new system's assumptions and practices often clashed with local perceptions about how disputes should be resolved.[3] For example, the emphasis in formal judicial procedure on due process, individual responsibility, and on punishment rather than restitution, caused confusion and offended local sensitivities.

Not only was state justice not well understood, but it often had limited reach and capacity. For example, the coverage provided by the 'national' police of the RPNGC in 1975 was estimated as extending only to 10 per cent of the new state's total land area and 40 per cent of the population.[4] The reach of the police continues to be limited; the organization — there are currently just under 5,000 sworn officers — has not grown significantly over the past 30 years, despite the population having more than doubled to approximately four and a half million people. At independence, the ratio of police to population was 1:380 whereas it is now 1:1,121. (The UN's recommended ratio is 1:450.[5])

Lawlessness

The transition from a colonial style of policing to a professional and independent constabulary has been slow and painful. Continuing poor performance in modern police work is, in part, a reflection of the RPNGC's colonial origins as a paramilitary institution whose primary role was the extension of government control and only secondarily the control of crime.[6]

The police have been progressively overwhelmed by the scale and diversity of the challenges confronting them.[7] Violent urban crime and rural banditry; periodic outbreaks of serious inter-group conflict in parts of the Highlands and ethnic clashes in the larger towns; a civil war on the island of Bougainville (1989–97); and rising levels of fraud and corruption – all contributed to growing concerns about law and order.[8] So too did the spread of small arms and light weapons.[9] Further, many of the structural factors contributing to violence (these are also evident in PNG's smaller Melanesian neighbours) lie beyond the purview of the police. These include high population growth unmatched by economic growth, poor governance, corruption, deteriorating government services and essential infrastructure, pressures on customary land, internal migration, urbanisation, and highly uneven patterns of development. The weakness of state control, erosion of traditional authority structures, an evolving gun culture, and the spread of HIV/AIDS, accentuate insecurity.[10]

The capacity of the police to respond effectively to lawlessness is extremely limited. The skills of many officers are low, and police appear incapable of undertaking routine criminal investigations, or apprehending suspects. However, this may relate more to cultural issues and resource inadequacies than to lack of skills per se. The powerful pull of kinship loyalty and allegiance to *wantoks*,[11] and a limited sense of public service constitute a serious constraint to police investigations and prosecutions. Likewise, it presents major problems when police are trying to elicit information from members of a particular community or group. While easy to denounce as nepotism, *wantokism* has proven remarkably resistant to efforts to remove it from government and other modern agencies; it is a practice with deep cultural roots that persists in most contemporary social and institutional settings. There are also concerns about the rapid changeover in police leadership (commissioners change with every change of government, which happens frequently), politicisation of senior ranks, and growing levels of police corruption. Charges of ill-discipline and serious human rights abuses are regularly levelled.[12]

A recent review of the constabulary commissioned by the PNG government echoed a widely held view that 'policing was close to total collapse' in many parts of the country.[13] This state of affairs was attributed to a lack of government support and direction; ineffective police leadership; inadequate and unreliable provision of resources to do the job; unpaid allowances and entitlements; inadequate salaries;

a system-wide lack of discipline, accountability and self-respect; and an almost total absence of community trust and respect.[14] Other parts of the criminal justice system are similarly weak. Prosecutions fail for lack of adequate evidence and preparation, while lengthy delays in the processing of court cases result in large numbers of detainees on remand. Mass escapes from the country's under-resourced prison system occur regularly.[15]

Reform

Australia is PNG's largest aid donor. Since 1975, it has provided more than A$14 billion in real terms, with the aid programme amounting to about 20 per cent of the overall Australian aid budget.[16] Assistance has assumed a variety of forms since independence, progressively moving from budgetary support (the primary form of assistance, 1975– 89) to programme aid in the 1990s, with a view to reducing dependency and promoting self-reliance. Aid has focused primarily on building state capacity. Applying a state-centric lens to the country's economic and social problems, Australian policy-makers have long posited governance and institutional capacity constraints as primary impediments to self-reliance, resulting in increased attention to institutional strengthening exercises under the rubric of governance initiatives.

Strengthening the rule of law is perceived as fundamental for reducing poverty and achieving sustainable development. Since independence, Australia has accordingly provided PNG with A$540 million for rule of law activities focusing in particular upon the police.[17] In addition to significant support to the police (outlined in Table 1), assistance has been provided to the courts, prisons, the ombudsman and public legal services.

Reform Initiatives

The RPNGC Development Project was the most substantial of Australian contributions to police reform in PNG, comprising 16 years of project support. As such, it provides insight into the planning and management of Australia's law and justice sector activities in PNG.

The project began in 1989 and followed three years of studies aimed at affecting a shift from the previously ad hoc provision of training and police postings to concerted support to the constabulary. Comprising three separate phases (1989–92, 1993–98 and 2000–2005), the project was a major capacity building and institutional strengthening exercise facilitated by advisers who focused on key areas such as fraud and anti-corruption, prosecutions, community policing (since 1993), corporate planning, information management, human resources, logistics and infrastructure, leadership and management, training, finance, discipline, general duties and gender.

Each phase of the RPNGC Development Project – Phases I, II, III and an interim phase between II and III – involved consultation prior to project design, which was undertaken by a team including design and technical policing specialists. While project design teams included personnel with country experience, local knowledge and the experience of people with ethnographic knowledge of the country such as

TABLE 1
NOTABLE AUSAID PNG LAW AND JUSTICE SECTOR PROGRAMMES

Agency	Project Title	Duration	Cost	Managing Contractor
Department of the Attorney General	PNG Attorney General's Department Institutional Strengthening Project	1999–2003	A$7,673,000	ACIL
Correctional Institutions Services	Correctional Services Development Project	Phase I: 1992–95	A$2.1 million	W. Kidston and Associates
Royal Papua New Guinea Constabulary	RPNGC Development Project	Phase II: 1996– 2002 Phase I: 1989– 92	A$10 million A$29.7 million	Price Waterhouse
		Phase II: 1993–98 Interim: 1999 Phase III: 2000–- 2005	A$79 million A$4 million A$41.2 million	ACIL ACIL ACIL
PNG Ombudsman Commission	PNG Ombudsman Institutional Strengthening Project	1997–2002	A$5.95 million	EDUCO
All law and justice sector agencies	Justice Advisory Group (JAG)	2002–2005	A$4.5 million	EDUCO
All law and justice sector agencies	PNG Law and Justice Sector Program	2002–2009	A$170 million	ACIL

Source: AusAID website, <www.ausaid.gov.au>; ACIL ebsite, <www.acil.com.au>.

anthropologists and sociologists appear to have been underutilised – a deficiency since acknowledged by many of the project's long-term advisers. The nature of project design also affected implementation. Project documents were highly prescriptive, requiring rigid reporting and implementation procedures, meaning that the ability of project personnel to respond to changing local circumstances was severely constrained. However, this weakness has been recognised, and the current Law and Justice Sector Program takes a more flexible and responsive approach to design and implementation.

Strengthening the RPNGC's management capacity has been a central feature of all phases of the project, with adviser assistance provided in the areas of human resource management, finance, corporate planning and internal discipline. During Phase III of the project (2000– 2005), assistance was provided to the constabulary for annual budget preparation and monitoring, a five-year (2002–2007) corporate plan was developed, various units established annual strategic plans, and a monitoring and evaluation framework was created and applied at the provincial level. Additionally, a merit based promotion policy and an equal employment opportunity policy were introduced.

The RPNGC Development Project worked closely with the RPNGC to determine priority needs and areas of concentration. Given the long duration of the project, many RPNGC personnel established enduring professional and personal relationships with advisers working in the constabulary. In the latter phases of the project, a strong emphasis was placed on the facilitating role of advisers, who were instructed to assist rather than do, in an attempt to increase both local ownership and capacity. Keeping to this advice has sometimes proven difficult. Given differences between local and advisers' approaches to task completion, the assistance-through-facilitation model proved frustrating to many advisers, who found it more expedient and effective to complete tasks, rather than assist others to do so. Consequently, the degree to which local ownership reforms occurred was limited and far from uniform. Similarly, the efficacy of foreign advisers with varied socio-linguistic competencies produced different results in different areas of the constabulary. In an attempt to increase local ownership of reform, the follow-on Law and Justice Sector Program places greater responsibility on government agencies to direct their own spending and activities, requiring them to accompany requests for donor support with annual plans that comply with agreed measures (e.g., cross sector impacts, sustainability and specified performance indicators).[18]

Despite the duration of the project, it remained difficult for advisers to communicate the project's aims. By and large, lower ranking members of the constabulary viewed the RPNGC Development Project primarily in terms of monetary support; they had little understanding of its strategic aims. An understanding of the reform agenda was greater in the upper echelons of the Constabulary but operationalising it remained difficult. For example, while there was general consensus about the desirability of reform, problems of internal discipline allowed senior staff with questionable pasts to remain in the force. Furthermore, aspects of the reform programme which were at odds with PNG cultural beliefs (such as the introduction of the Equal Employment Opportunity Policy) were not successfully integrated into local practice, and were explicitly seen as 'something from the West.'

Measurement

The ways in which external assistance was measured changed throughout the various stages of the RPNGC Development Project, beginning with the assessment of efficiency and inputs and moving towards the assessment of outputs and impacts. For the most part, measurement was of outputs (for example, the number of people trained, or the number of fingerprints collected per annum), typically assessed on a numerical basis and usually associated with contractor payment milestones. Advisers working on the project were required to report regularly against these performance indicators, yet constabulary awareness of indicators and their purpose was low, with the exception of the senior managers who worked closely with advisers.

Measuring the impact of specific programme initiatives, or, indeed, the project as a whole, is difficult. Numerical indicators such as the number of officers completing training and the number of planning workshops held were useful for assessing the output of advisers and the breadth of constabulary exposure to particular ideas. However, such indicators did little to demonstrate the actual impact or outcome of such activities, an issue further complicated by the limited availability of benchmark data. Upon the completion of each project, advisers were required to comment on its likely impact, but without research to enable genuine evaluation their comments were highly subjective. This weakness has since been recognised by aid donors, as has the need for greater institutional accountability for expenditure. For example, while previous phases of the development project lacked mechanisms to enforce the constabulary's achievement of agreed goals, future aid to the RPNGC under the follow-on Law and Justice Sector Program will be conditional on the RPNGC's demonstrated performance to mutually agreed standards. It remains unclear as to how Australia will enforce this.

Evaluation

The motto of the RPNGC is 'Securing a Safer Community'. Given PNG's ongoing problems of law and order (which are frequently associated with a lack of social and economic development), some assessments of the RPNGC Development Project have been uncomplimentary, arguing that the 'community' was less safe at the project's end than it was at its beginning. However, such criticism should be tempered, for these perceptions are based upon the limited expectation that a 'good' police 'controls' law and order. In fact, it is not advisable to gauge the success or failure of the project on the presence or absence of law and order problems alone, for the RPNGC is merely one of many actors working towards the creation of an environment conducive to development. Similarly, expectations of what the programme could achieve may have been too high. Even so, it is clear that for many years the development project sustained the RPNGC's basic operations, in addition to increasing its detection of fraud, prosecution of minor cases and corporate planning.

Major problems remain, but they are indicative of the scale of the problem, rather than of failures in the reform project per se. After decades of Australian aid to PNG, a multitude of problems continue to plague the law and justice sector. Indeed, the sector is a 'sector' in name only, for agencies rarely interact with common goals in mind. Certainly, no one could claim that there is an operationally effective security sector in which agencies exhibit good management practice.[19] Nor could one claim that there is accountability of institutions or meaningful civilian oversight of government. To presume that foreign aid alone could rectify this situation is equally problematic.

Non-State Sector

There is also the issue of how efficacious it is to focus on a formal system of policing that is of little relevance to many Papua New Guineans. Thirty one years after independence, the majority of disputes in country are still dealt with by informal means, rather than through resort to an under-resourced formal justice system that remains geographically and socially distant for many. For the ordinary villager, accessing the nearest police post, magistrate, or telephone usually involves a lengthy and difficult journey by foot, truck, or canoe. The villager who wishes to lay a complaint against a neighbour must continue to live alongside that neighbour in the knowledge that external assistance from police and courts is a considerable distance away. In such circumstances, reliance on informal community-based approaches is often the only option for addressing outstanding grievances. Informal mechanisms vary from place to place but are likely to include a combination of methods: negotiation or mediation by kin, traditional leaders or church officials; village moots; or the decisions of local *komitis* (committees).[20]

Dispute resolution of this kind often has a distinct restorative justice flavour, for disputants will have to continue living together in small close-knit communities. Applying restorative solutions to serious infractions raises many issues, including the potential for neglecting the legal (and, perhaps, moral) rights of individual victims, particularly women. The effectiveness of the informal solutions varies significantly in practice and is, in part, a consequence of the degree of social cohesion in the community concerned. Rapid social and economic change has inevitably had a corrosive effect. In the worst cases, these mechanisms have either collapsed completely, or have been appropriated by local elites and used to dominate more vulnerable groups, including women and children. In other cases, high levels of accountability and transparency prevail, and informal mechanisms play an important role in the maintenance of community safety and resolution of minor disputes.

The need to engage with PNG's rich repertoire of informal justice practices is now recognized. A National Law and Justice Policy, endorsed by the PNG government in August 2000, asserted the need to develop crime and conflict prevention and restorative justice strategies involving partnerships between formal agencies such as the police and community-based organisations operating at local levels throughout the country.[21] The significance of the informal justice system is recognised in Australian programming. For example, Australian funding and technical assistance has been provided to a Community Justice Liaison Unit (under the LJSP) that acts as a dedicated mechanism to promote the engagement of community and civil society organisations in the law and justice sector, with a focus on crime prevention, restorative justice and partnerships for change.[22]

AUSTRALIAN INTERVENTION IN SOLOMON ISLANDS

Since mid-2003, there has been a significant change in Australia's strategic thinking and engagement with the Pacific Islands region. This was demonstrated by Australia's agreement to lead a regional intervention mission to assist Solomon Islands in 2003. Operation 'Helpem Fren' was a 'police-first' peacekeeping and reconstruction mission with Australian police officers taking the lead, and soldiers providing mission security.[23] By leading the Regional Assistance Mission to Solomon Islands (RAMSI), Australia reversed its long-standing policy of non-intervention towards internal conflict in its Pacific neighbours.

Intervention

The decision to emphasise policing and the restoration of law and order was consistent with a broader normative shift. This change in Australian approach was precipitated by changes in the international strategic environment following the events of 11 September 2001 and the October 2002 Bali bombings that killed 89 Australians. Elements of Canberra's policy-making community had long been concerned with the slowly expanding 'arc of instability' flanking Australia's northern and eastern shores.[24] Post 9/11, the focus was on the security risks presented to Australia by the region's 'weak' and 'failing' states. These, in turn, were viewed as potential havens for trans-national crime and terrorism.

The dangers allegedly posed to Australian security interests by the collapse of law and order in parts of Solomon Islands were articulated most clearly in an influential report by the Australian Strategic Policy Institute (ASPI), a government-funded but independent think tank. ASPI situated the case for intervention squarely within the emergent 'failed state' paradigm. The report identified Solomon Islands as a 'failing state', and warned of it becoming 'a petri dish in which transnational and non-state security threats can develop and breed' and a 'post-modern badlands, ruled by criminals and governed by violence'. [25]

Given this context, the decision of RAMSI to prioritise the restoration of law and order was unsurprising. In 2003 the police (the main security institution in the country – Solomon Islands has no military) were portrayed, at best, as being incapable of stemming the country's law and order problems and, at worst, complicit in inciting lawlessness.

'Ethnic tensions' between indigenous people from the island of Guadalcanal, where the capital, Honiara, is situated, and 'settlers' from other island provinces (particularly neighbouring Malaita) that had simmered for many years finally boiled over in the late 1990s. However, beneath the rubric of 'ethnic tensions' lay a series of profound challenges of governance and development, including the diverse and dislocative impact of integration into the global economy, demographic factors, land tenure issues, internal migration, and the increasingly dysfunctional and corrupt character of the post-colonial state.[26] Groups of young Guadalcanal militants embarked on a violent campaign of intimidation directed primarily against Malaitans, approximately 30,000 of whom were displaced from their homes in rural Guadalcanal. In response, a Malaitan militia – the Malaita Eagle Force (MEF) – formed in Honiara with the active participation of elements of the Malaitan-dominated police. On 5 June 2000 the MEF and collaborators in the police staged an armed takeover of Honiara, sacking the state armoury and enforcing the resignation of the prime minister. [27]

Australia adopted a hands-off attitude to such problems despite appeals from the Solomon Islands' government that they intervene. Australia had sponsored talks between representatives from the government and militias in 2000 in an effort to halt the violence, but the accord they reached, known as the Townsville Peace Agreement after the Australian coastal town where it was negotiated, had little ultimate effect. Indeed, it resembled a division of spoils between factional groups.[28] Officers from the militias that had incorporated themselves into the Royal Solomon Islands Police (RSIP) were allowed to continue in post, and a 'special constables' programme was established to incorporate even more into the service.[29]

The agreement did not bring order; in many respects it contributed to an instrumentalisation of further disorder. Killings, assaults, forced displacement and looting continued. Members of the police were implicated in 'extrajudicial executions, indiscriminate shootings, deliberate and arbitrary killings, torture, threats and harassment'.[30] External efforts to reform the police during this period proved largely ineffectual too; this was subsequently attributed to the lack of enforcement capability on the part of the increasingly compromised state.[31] Small-scale initiatives, such as a police capacity-building project funded by AusAid, and the appointment of a former British senior police officer to head the RSIP in January 2003, had little lasting impact.[32]

It became clear that the Solomon Islands government lacked the capacity or will to halt the deteriorating security and economic situation.[33] Further, the state had in effect been captured and plundered by a small group of corrupt leaders, armed ex-militants and renegade police officers. With the law and order situation deteriorating further, the collapse of essential government services, and effective bankruptcy and corruption of the state,[34] calls for deeper international involvement increased. Foreign commentators and donors often presented these problems afflicting the Islands as a result of the breakdown of the rule of law, and most of the proposed solutions focused on restoring that state function.[35] The inadequacy of this approach became increasingly apparent, leading to calls for a comprehensive and large-scale intervention.

The Regional Assistance Mission to Solomon Islands (RAMSI) and the Participating Police Force

Canberra reversed its long-standing policy of non-intervention, and on 24 July 2003 Australian Prime Minister John Howard, launched RAMSI. Responding to a formal request from the Solomon Islands government, its initial aim was to restore law and order in light of the "barely functional" criminal justice system and the wholesale collapse in relation to other elements of governance'.[36]

RAMSI was initiated and mobilised as a regional mission under the auspices of the Pacific Islands Forum and, specifically, the 2000 Biketawa Declaration on Mutual Assistance, which authorised Forum leaders to consider collective action in response to a security crisis in a member state. In contrast to most regionally mandated peace operations, police, rather than the military led RAMSI.[37] Although the policing objectives were part of a larger state-building exercise, the Australian-led Participating Police Force (PPF) provided RAMSI's public face, especially in the initial phase.

The PPF contingent of approximately 330 police officers was drawn mainly from the Australian Federal Police, but also included smaller numbers from Australian state and territory forces, New Zealand, Tonga, Samoa, Vanuatu, Fiji, Cook Islands, Tuvalu, Kiribati, and PNG. PPF officers were sworn in as 'line' members of the RSIP, thus legally empowering them with executive authority.[38] Officers were placed with specific responsibilities within the service: investigations, communications, traffic, internal affairs and community policing. In smaller outlying stations they acted as station commanders, but they drove different police vehicles and used different radio communication channels to those of their local counterparts. Their period of service was six months, at which point they returned to their home postings.[39] The policing component of RAMSI also brought resources to the problem far in excess of those available to either the Solomon Islands state or previous international assistance programmes. For example, whereas the RSIP did not have one functioning boat, the PPF could call on airplanes, helicopters and fast boats.

Many of the Australian officers in Solomon Islands had served in previous UN missions, and the experience they brought with them to RAMSI included an awareness of how not to run an international policing mission. Indeed, a substantial proportion had served in Timor-Leste, and were scarred by the manner in which the UN Civilian Police (CIVPOL) mission was organised and managed in that intervention.[40] One officer commented that the RAMSI mission provided a real-time opportunity to remedy many of the failings that Australian officers (like many of their counterparts from other countries) had understood but were structurally powerless to change.[41]

The PPF's approach and operational methods were those used in Australia. The culture was that of Australia, and the fact that most of the officers in Solomon

Islands were based in a camp outside Honiara further embedded a strong *esprit de corps*.[42] This common culture and familiarity of approach – many of the officers knew each other – facilitated a shared understanding of basic goals. The heavy Australian presence within the PPF contributed to a unity of purpose and a shared policing model. RAMSI was thus able to avoid one of the major problems confronting international policing missions: the alien nature of the policing environment, compounded by operating in an unfamiliar bureaucratic structure with foreign operating procedures. Further, the situation was helped by the mission's unusual degree of continuity of funding and organisation.[43]

However, a less positive consequence was the significant gap it generared between the Australian contingent and those they were meant to be working with, namely the RSIP. One reason was because many Australian officers did not have linguistic skills or cultural awareness. In RAMSI, this was offset by the fact that it was a regional mission. Although relatively few in number and peripheral in terms of leadership, officers from New Zealand and, particularly, the smaller Pacific Island contingent, brought with them a doctrine, approach and policing style that were more in tune with the Melanesian culture in Solomon Islands. This greater familiarity with cultural codas and mores, together with the ability of Melanesian contingent members to fluently converse in the Solomon Islands pidgin helped narrow the gap between the non-Australian 'police' and 'the policed' in a way that monolingual English-speakers found considerably more challenging.

Successes and Difficulties

The first part of the mission went remarkably well. Security was quickly restored in Honiara and the police presence extended to other parts of the country. Large numbers of illegally held weapons were taken out of circulation. For example, by the end of a month-long amnesty in August 2003, approximately 3,730 firearms (an estimated 90–95 per cent of the country's stockpile) had been surrendered or collected.[44] The police not only established law and order but also began to address past offences. By the beginning of 2005, more than 5,000 individuals, including senior militia leaders were arrested, and more than 7,300 charges were laid.[45]

The second goal of RAMSI – rebuilding and developing capacity in the police institution, and instilling public trust in it – proved significantly more difficult to achieve. As the following sections discuss, reformers encountered a sceptical and resistant police institution and a public that was not only seared with memories of past practice but also had alternative and proven sources of 'policing'.

Reforming institutional capacity and vetting. One of RAMSI's primary tasks was to rebuild the RSIP's institutional structure. During the conflict many RSIP members failed to provide anything resembling basic police services. Large parts of the country had little or no police presence, training was irregular, officers lost their policing skills, and many stations lacked basics such as pens and paper. There was no dedicated transportation or communications system between headquarters and the field, which was especially serious for a chain of islands. Where there was a police presence, the relationship with headquarters withered completely. Many officers continued to work without guidance, and with irregular pay, but others (finding conditions of work intolerable) simply left their posts.

The structures of the RSIP weakened significantly during the conflict. In Solomon Islands, there were no guidelines for promotion, and advancement in the force was based on political and kin-based connections, rather than performance. Partly as a result of such patronage, the police's senior ranks were bloated, though there was no clear guidance as to what the roles and responsibilities of many senior managers were. Simple mechanisms were missing too. Out-of-date rosters and payrolls made it impossible to know the actual numbers of officers and their location; there were no means of budget monitoring or keeping track of procurement; limited communications capabilities – and the sheer geographic distance between stations – meant that relations between headquarters and the field were weak; and there was no working system of internal or external oversight.

The strategy for rebuilding the institution was twofold. First, the PPF took on an extensive role in directing a process of institutional change, beginning with a thorough vetting, recertification and internal investigation of RSIP personnel, and only then building up new systems. Second, by placing PPF officers in 'line' positions within the RSIP, RAMSI hoped to generate 'look-and-see' learning among local police as to how to conduct police work.

The idea of 'vetting-before-reform' was based on a policy assumption that the force should be 'thoroughly cleaned out' in order that the reform process proceed with uncompromised officers.[46] By February 2004, over 50 police officers (including two deputy commissioners) had been arrested and charged with 285 offences. Over 400 officers (approximately 25 per cent of the total workforce) were dismissed.

Investigators used a variety of sources but relied mostly on witness testimony in determining decisions on prosecution and employment termination. However, international officers were inhibited by a lack of prior written records, and by linguistic and cultural unfamiliarity. One officer observed that 'it was a lot easier to be able to verify the truth of what a witness would tell you in Australia because you'd be able to draw on lots of references to back up their veracity: here it's a lot more difficult to get a feel for whether what is being told as the truth is.' [47]

While this vetting-and-reform approach may be crucial as a means of reclaiming public trust in the service, the combination of daily didactic instruction by 'outside' police officers and an exacting process of recertification brought their own risks. The sheer scale of RAMSI and the well-intentioned desire on the part of many international officers to imbue 'professional practice', coupled with the fact that they were in leadership positions risked undermining the institutions they wanted to build. The management approach that the Australians wished to develop was alien to the working culture of the RSIP. Also, immersion techniques risk overwhelming officers with too much new information, and generating resistance and resentment.

*Overcoming engagement gaps.*The Australians found it difficult to engage the RSIP in the reform process. An oft-heard complaint was that Solomon Islanders did not want to be involved.[48] The array of strategies designed to encourage participation yielded disappointing results; workshops were poorly attended, and requests for written input rarely received substantive responses.

At least two reasons explain the apparent engagement gap. The first relates to the extent to which RSIP personnel were not included by the incoming RAMSI leadership. In large part because of advance planning in Australia, the executive policing segment of the mission was able to get off to a running start and operate efficiently in the field. Planning was inclusive in the sense that it included all the Australian government departments involved. However, there was little inclusion of the RSIP. In some part, this apparent wariness was understandable. That the leadership echelon of the RSIP appeared so complicit in the events that compelled the intervention in the first place forbade prior consultation out of concern about information haemorrhage, particularly important as the primary objective was re-establishment of basic law and order.

A second reason for the continued engagement gap was the profound disconnection in operational culture between the reformers and those they were trying to reform. Members of the RSIP were asked to familiarise themselves with new practices (such as planning), but had little time to absorb them. Australian officers, schooled in a world of systems, reviews and reports, were frustrated by RSIP officers' failure to operate a similar system and quickly become used to them. Impatience with the pace of involvement and the quality of RSIP work (as occurred in the RPNGC Development Project) meant that international officers ended up completing tasks.[49] This fuelled something akin to a dependency culture, and did little to build up capabilities within the RSIP.[50]

Civil society and the informal sector. While Solomon Islanders welcomed the intervention, they had little involvement in its planning, direction or focus;[51] the degree of consultation in shaping policy and implementing it was inadequate.[52] While consultation/ownership did take place at the level of the government elite, it did not reach down much further. Local NGOs noted that while they were consulted, their advice had little discernible effect. In part, this was because the advice and approaches offered by civil society varied so much that it was hard to distil consensus. One figure who leads a network of NGOs in the capital, Honiara, provided an example of such difficulty: 'I was asked to come to the meeting with representatives from "civil society" so I brought about thirty people with me who represented church groups, women's groups and youth groups. It was hard to find a room to fit us all in! We were listened to but we each had different suggestions and views: some thought the police should be doing more patrols in certain parts of Honiara while others thought there should be less.'[53]

One reason why it proved difficult to drum up real interest in the reform process may be that formal police did not conduct much of the 'policing' or conflict resolution that was of relevance to citizens. In Solomon Islands, as in PNG and other emergent states, power and authority are exercised through informal political and legal structures and mechanisms that vary in shape and organization.[54]

As in PNG, Solomon Islands' institutions, including police and courts, tend to be predominantly urban-based, even though approximately 85 per cent of the population lives in rural areas where community-based approaches are often the only option for addressing outstanding grievances. Trying to assert the formal authority of a state police service thus rubs against ingrained allegiance to mechanisms for dispute resolution and restorative justice, which offer solutions that appear more expeditious – and frequently have greater legitimacy – than formal state institutions.[55] It has the effect that in many rural (and also urban) areas, chiefs, elders and other community-based mechanisms with no formal connection to the state often play a more significant role than the police in the settlement of disputes and maintenance of order. Missions and church groups also contribute to the mediation and settlement of disputes in many areas, as well as in the management of young offenders. The gradual expansion of the formal justice system has not supplanted these community-based approaches. Indeed, in some places unofficial mechanisms and responses have increased as the inadequacies of state justice become more pronounced. Attempts to instil public trust in the police become even more complicated when, as was the case in Solomon Islands, the police are profoundly implicated in lawlessness.

The privileging of 'police reform' as 'police institution reform' by RAMSI is in part explained by the rapid turnaround of personnel. Understanding such a layered and ever-moving process is much more difficult than reconstructing the institutions of a formal service as such. Further, the officers concerned not only came from a different background, but also had little time to familiarise themselves with the intricacies of local processes.

ENHANCED COOPERATION PROGRAM (ECP) AND THE AUSTRALIAN ASSISTING POLICE

Australia's leadership of RAMSI marked a significant departure from the Australian government's previous non-interventionist approach. Based on a sensibility to traditional notions of sovereignty, Canberra had previously sought to leave only 'light footsteps' in relations with its Pacific Islands neighbours.[56] RAMSI's early success in restoring law and order also had a significant impact on Australian thinking about how best to proceed in PNG, emboldening policy-makers in Canberra to believe that a similar model could be used to address PNG's crime problem. [57]

After protracted debate, on 30 June 2004, the governments of Australia and PNG signed a treaty establishing the Enhanced Cooperation Programme (ECP), thereby committing an additional A$800 million to PNG over a five-year period. (This figure was additional to the existing A$350 million per annum Australian aid programme to PNG) Under this programme, approximately 230 Australian officers – known as the Australian Assisting Police (AAP) – were to hold 'line' positions in the RPNGC and be deployed initially in the capital, Port Moresby, and the island of Bougainville, subsequently spreading out to other locations around the country.[58]

While there are common threads running through official Australian perceptions about the difficulties facing Solomon Islands and PNG, important differences between the two countries were glossed over. For a start, there was no armed takeover of Port Moresby by an ethnic militia, and no forcible ousting of a democratically appointed Prime Minister as occurred in Honiara in June 2000. Attempts to place PNG in the same category as Solomon Islands and, in particular, to describe it as a 'failed' or 'failing' state were vigorously rejected, especially by sections of the PNG elite.[59] While the deficiencies of the PNG state were manifold, it did not satisfy the broadly defined criteria of a failed or collapsed state. Likewise, its notorious law and order problems are complex in character and uneven in distribution, and did not arise from a single internal conflict. Critics of the 'failed state' thesis in PNG also pointed to the efforts by recent governments to address some of the outstanding governance and economic challenges.[60]

The ECP was beset by difficulties from the outset. Disagreements between the two governments over the conditions of deployment of Australian personnel caused lengthy delays in starting the programme. Canberra insisted that their police and officials receive immunity from potential prosecution under PNG law, while Port Moresby steadfastly refused to grant blanket immunity. Canberra's position stemmed from its concern to protect operational personnel, particularly the police, from vexatious litigation, while PNG opposition to immunity arose, in part, from the implication that its legal system was incapable of providing adequate protection against vexatious actions. The most prominent and consistent PNG critic of the ECP was the governor of Morobe Province and former judge, Luther Wenge. Wenge asserted that the ECP infringed PNG's sovereignty and, in particular, that the immunity provisions breached its constitution. To this end, he initiated a major constitutional challenge in the Supreme Court.[61] Eventually, a compromise between Canberra and Port Moresby on the immunity issue was reached in early July 2004.[62] Later the same month, the PNG parliament passed enabling legislation allowing the deployment of Australian police. Australian police eventually deployed in September 2004.

Approximately 20 officers were sent to Bougainville, while others were deployed in staged phases to Port Moresby. Popular expectations of the Australian police were high, and ordinary Papua New Guineans gave a rapturous reception to the first AAP officers to go on joint patrols with their RPNGC counterparts in Port Moresby. Despite support from the public and key government ministers, other leaders were more guarded. Former prime minister Sir Mekere Morauta welcomed Australia's re-engagement, but also expressed reservations about aspects of the ECP.[63] He pointed out that the programme was widely seen as Australian-imposed and driven. Disagreement over the immunity provisions reinforced this perception. Lack of ownership on the PNG side constituted a potentially fatal weakness.

Some resistance also came from within the ranks of the RPNGC. Complaints by RPNGC members included allegations of poor working relationships with the Australian police, clashes between the different police cultures, and the alleged failure of ECP capacity-building efforts.[64] In addition to these public complaints,

RPNGC officers who participated in focus groups during May and June 2005 claimed that while many of them developed good working relationships with AAP personnel, differences in modes of reporting and access to material resources hampered the formation of meaningful working relationships. Moreover, even where cooperation was apparent, RPNGC members appeared motivated primarily by the promise of material reward, rather than the transfer of skills and capacity building. Tensions between elements of the RPNGC and the AAP also became public in May 2005. A Police Association meeting in Port Moresby resulted in the presentation to the RPNGC Commissioner of an ultimatum demanding the removal of all AAP from PNG within 48 hours.[65]

Although this particular crisis was defused, the policing component of the ECP proved a short-lived assignment. The constitutional challenge initiated by Luther Wenge was upheld; a unanimous panel of five senior judges declared that provisions in the PNG parliament's Enhanced Cooperation Act, including some of those dealing with immunity, were unconstitutional.[66] AAP officers were immediately withdrawn from Bougainville and stood down in Port Moresby prior to repatriation to Australia. The entire deployment lasted less than a year.[67]

CONCLUSION

The approaches taken by Australia to police building in PNG and the Solomon Islands had many differences. Aside from their varying durations, there were important differences in context, with the PNG interventions occurring in a weak state and the Solomons intervention occurring in a post-conflict situation where the state had ceased to operate effectively. There were differences in mandate too, with the RPNGC Development Project limited to a substantial capacity-building exercise, while RAMSI and the ECP were additionally empowered with executive authority. Personnel differed too, with the RPNGC Development Project composed of civilian advisers while RAMSI and ECP were comprised serving police officers. However, the two approaches offered a number of shared lessons that cut across each model of assistance. Further, both models prompted questions regarding the state-centric assumptions underlying Australia's approach.

A key conclusion shared by all three interventions is that context-specific knowledge and expertise is vital for the successful design and implementation of assistance programmes. This played out in at least three ways.

First, hindsight demonstrated the inappropriateness of donor-driven or rigid project design. Over-prescriptive and non-consultative design produced a variety of forms of resistance to institutional and cultural transformation. In Solomon Islands, this resistance was expressed at a micro level, through a lack of engagement. In the ECP in PNG, resistance took a more macro form, through constitutional challenge.

Second, the proposed solutions – whether legal, structural or organizational – required appropriate knowledge about the local context of policing in each country. The RPNGC Development Project demonstrated the need to employ design teams with an in-depth understanding of the country concerned, rather than conceptualising reform as a generic and readily transportable exercise. The failure to understand how social context influenced the form and function of policing and other approaches to dispute resolution risked disconnecting Australian-led reform initiatives from local, community-based initiatives. It is clear that while institutional-strengthening and capacity-building initiatives are important aspects of law and justice sector reform, the strengthening of links between state and society, and the support of informal modes of social control are equally important, a point recognised and reflected in the increased developmental assistance offered to PNG's informal sector.

Third, Australian involvement in the law and justice sector demonstrated the need to employ advisers with cultural sensitivity and a willingness to acquire basic linguistic and social competencies. The absence of such skills makes already difficult police-building projects more difficult, if not impossible.

An evaluation of the approaches adopted in PNG and Solomon Islands also raises difficult questions for Australian policymakers (as well as others working in states with a weak institutional base). These concern the design and implementation of police reform programmes.

The first is whether a reform programme emphasising a formal policing system that may not be culturally appropriate can succeed in the long term. Despite calls from analysts, there is insufficient recognition of the extensive and central role that non-state or sub-national actors play in 'policing' in many weak states. Australia's persistent focus on the strengthening of familiar Western-derived state institutions exemplifies this dissonance.[68]

Australian attempts to assert the 'formal' institutions of law and justice risk being undermined by the strength and resilience of the informal mores and practices of dispute resolution prevailing at local levels, many of which conflict with state notions of law and order. This prompts an important question: Should international assistance concentrate on building a purely formal service in countries where state institutions are weak and compromised, and where alternative, sub-state methods have deeper roots, greater legitimacy, and, in some respects, more proven capabilities? The wider issue of cost is linked to this. For over-reliance on a formal police may not be financially sustainable, especially when funds stop flowing and foreign personnel are withdrawn. With population increase outstripping economic growth in PNG and Solomon Islands, it is questionable whether either country will ever be in a position to provide the support required to operate – let alone expand – expensive and cumbersome justice systems without continuous external assistance.

Given this situation, it is important to consider what other resources might be mobilised to assist the formal sector in building security and justice. This is where the wealth of existing community-based restorative justice resources needs to be recognised and engaged. The way forward, therefore, may be neither reliance on state or community justice, but rather a creative reconfiguration of security governance that integrates the best of both. The recent trend among international donor agencies to explore ways of engaging more effectively with non-state actors is testimony to the growing acknowledgment that a narrow and exclusive focus on state agencies is not the only or, indeed, the best path to enhancing security, governance and development. Such a lesson, gleaned from many years of development assistance in many parts of the world, should hardly need emphasis in countries such as PNG and Solomon Islands where the majority of the population lives beyond the effective reach of the state, and where the foundations of security practice are community-based.

Given the evolving nature of Australia's involvement in police capacity-building initiatives in the region, it is unsurprising that there is significant room for learning and improved engagement. Ongoing evaluations of performance, and the reformulation of approaches to capacity building in keeping with changing local circumstances are clearly central to the success of such missions. Ultimately, however, it is necessary to accept that capacity-building exercises in the Pacific will not – and should not – develop quasi-Australian police organisations. Rather, they should assist local police organisations to develop locally sustainable law enforcement agencies in keeping with international human rights standards.

NOTES

1. Lucy Mair, *Australia in New Guinea* (London: Christophers 1948) p. xvi.
2. See Bernard Brown, 'The State versus Stateless Societies in Papua New Guinea' in Bernard Brown (ed.), *Fashion of Law in New Guinea* (Sydney: Butterworths 1969) pp.15–37.
3. See Marilyn Strathern, *Official and Unofficial Courts: Legal Assumptions and Expectations in a Highlands Community* New Guinea Research Unit, Bulletin 47 (Port Moresby 1972).
4. Sean Dorney *Papua New Guinea: People, Politics and History Since 1975* (Sydney: Random House 1990) p.296.
5. Public Sector Reform Management Unit, Department of Prime Minister and National Executive Council, 'A Review of the Law and Justice Sector Agencies in Papua New Guinea: Opportunities to Improve Efficiency, Effectiveness, Coordination and Accountability', unpublished report (PNG 2002) p.63.
6. Section 197(1) of the PNG Constitution identifies the principal functions of the police force as (i) to preserve peace and good order, and (ii) to maintain and, as necessary, enforce the law in an impartial and objective manner.
7. A predictable outcome of state policing's inadequacy has been a massive growth in private policing and security services. While there are no reliable figures with which to gauge the size of the industry, conservative estimates in the late 1990s put the number of private security employees at twice the number of state police employees. The industry is largely unregulated, although draft legislation has recently been produced. See Sinclair Dinnen, 'Breaking the Cycle of Violence: Crime and State in Papua New Guinea' in Cyndi Banks (ed.), *Developing Cultural Criminology — Theory and Practice in Papua New Guinea* Sydney Institute of Criminology Monograph Series 13 (2000) pp.57–8.
8. For an analysis of PNG's law and order problems and official responses to them see Dinnen (note 7).
9. See Philip Alpers *Gun-running in Papua New Guinea: From Arrows to Assault Weapons in the Southern Highlands* Special Report (Geneva: Small Arms Survey 2005).
10. Ibid.; National AIDS Council Secretariat and Dept. of Health *HIV/AIDS Quarterly Report* (Port Moresby: National AIDS Council Secretariat 2004); Christine Bradley, *Family and Sexual Violence in PNG: an Integrated Long-Term Strategy. Report to the Family Violence Action Committee of the Consultative Implementation and Monitoring Council* (Port Moresby: Institute of National Affairs 2001).
11. The term *wantok* in Melanesian Pidgin means one who speaks the same language (literally, one talk) but is popularly used to describe the relations of obligation binding relatives, members of the same clan or tribal group, and also looser forms of association. In the context of modern institutions, *wantokism* is increasingly used as shorthand for nepotism.

12. See Human Rights Watch, 'Making their own rules': Police beatings, rape, and torture of children in Papua New Guinea', *Human Rights Watch* 17/8 (2005) pp.1–123.
13. Royal Papua New Guinea Constabulary, Administrative Review Committee (ARC). Draft Report (2004) p.40.
14. See, for example, the Human Rights Watch (note 12).
15. See Dinnen (note 7) p.57.
16. AusAID, *The Contribution of Australian Aid to Papua New Guinea's Development 1975–2000: Provisional Conclusions from a Rapid Assessment*, Evaluation and Review Series 34 (Canberra: AusAID 2003).
17. Ibid. pp.xii–xiii.
18. Australian support to PNG's law and justice sector is now channelled through a single programme. the Law and Justice Sector Program (LJSP). Development assistance to the RPNGC, previously provided through the separate RPNGC Development Project, is now delivered through the LJSP. Australia's development assistance has shifted from supporting individual agencies to a sector-wide approach; this is consistent with broader trends in international development assistance. Also, it acknowledges the high level of inter-dependency between agencies like the police, courts, and prisons. The LJSP is designed to work through PNG's own management systems and includes the provision of imprest account funding, technical assistance, infrastructure, training, procurement of materials and equipment, disbursement of grants and support for community-based initiatives.
19. See, for example, Public Sector Reform Management Unit, Department of Prime Minister and National Executive Council, 'A Review of the Law and Justice Sector Agencies in Papua New Guinea: Opportunities to Improve Efficiency, Effectiveness, Coordination and Accountability', Unpublished report (PNG 2002).
20. See Sinclair Dinnen, Anita Jowitt and Tess Newton Cain (eds.), *A Kind of Mending – Restorative Justice in the Pacific Islands* (Canberra: Pandanus Books 2003). See also David Hegarty and Pamela Thomas (eds.), 'Effective Development in Papua New Guinea: Local Initiatives and Community Innovation', *Development Bulletin* 67 (2005) pp.53–66.
21. Dept. of National Planning and Monitoring, Government of Papua New Guinea, *The National Law and Justice Policy and Plan of Action – Toward Restorative Justice 2000–2005* (Port Moresby 2005).
22. Their work includes: training, awareness and advocacy; restorative justice initiatives and research; targeted interventions with women, youth and other vulnerable groups (e.g. sex workers); partnerships for change, and for personal and community development; intervention appraisal, design, monitoring and evaluation.
23. Helpem Fren is Solomon Islands pidgin for 'Helping a friend'.
24. In the same year, Bilateral Counter-Terrorism Memoranda of Understanding (CT MOU) were signed between Australia and several other countries (including PNG on 11 Dec. 2003). They were designed to support increasingly productive intelligence and security relationships, as well as measures to strengthen counter-terrorism capabilities.
25. Ellie Wainwright *Our Failing Neighbour – Australia and the Future of The Solomon Islands* (Canberra: Australian Strategic Policy Institute 2003) p.13.
26. Judith Bennett, 'Roots of Conflict in The Solomon Islands Though Much is Taken, Much Abides: Legacies of Tradition and Colonialism', *State, Society and Governance in Melanesia* Discussion Paper (2002/5) pp.1–16 < http://rspqs.anu.edu.au/melanesia>.
27. Clive Moore, *Happy Isles in Crisis: The Historical Causes for a Failing State in The Solomon Islands, 1998–2004* (Canberra: Asia Pacific Press 2005).
28. 'Engagement of Disciplined Force Members in Militant Groups' in *Townsville Peace Agreement: An Agreement for the Cessation of Hostilities between the Malaita Eagle Force and the Isatabu Freedom Movement and for the Restoration of Peace and Ethnic Harmony in the Solomon Islands* (2000) Part 2.1a/b.
29. Ibid. Part 2.2, 'Restructure of the police force'.
30. Amnesty International, *The Solomon Islands: A Forgotten Conflict, 7 September 2000* (London 2000) pp.6–7.
31. Wainwright (note 25) p.23.
32. Interview with AusAid official, Canberra, 9 July 2004; interview with Commissioner William Morrell, Honiara, 3 July 2004. Funding for this appointment was provided by the European Union.
33. Sinclair Dinnen, 'Winners and Losers: Politics and Disorder in the The Solomon Islands 2000–2002', *Pacific History* 37/3 (2002) pp.285–98.

34. By the end of 2002 the Solomon Islands economy had contracted for the fourth year in a row, having shrunk by around 24 per cent since 1998. Speech by Foreign Minister Alexander Downer at the launch of *The Solomon Islands: Rebuilding an Island Economy* (Brisbane, 20 July 2004) <www.foreignminister.gov.au/speeches/2004/> (All internet sites accessed in Jan. 2006).

35. James Cockayne, 'Operation Helpem Fren: The Solomon Islands, Transitional Justice and the Silence of Contemporary Legal Pathologies on Questions of Distributive Justice', Center for Human Rights and Global Justice Working Paper, Transitional Justice Series 3 (2004) pp.12–14.

36. The Hon. John Howard MP, press conference, Canberra, 22 July 2003 <www.pm.gov.au/news/interviews/Interview382.html>.

37. Around 1,800 regional military personnel (mainly from Australia and New Zealand) provided initial logistical support and security for the police, although this number was significantly reduced as the security situation improved.

38. *Agreement Between The Solomon Islands, Australia, New Zealand, Fiji, Papua New Guinea, Samoa and Tonga Concerning the Operations and Status of the Police and Armed Forces and other Personnel Deployed to The Solomon Islands to Assist in the Restoration of Law and Order and Security* (Townsville, Qld 2003). Available at <www.dfat.gov.au/treaties/news_archive/solomons.html >.

39. The financial package offered to officers made it a lucrative posting; as well as tax breaks and mission allowances, Australian officers were paid a higher basic wage than if they served in Australia. This was on the assumption that it would be difficult otherwise to secure sufficient personnel. It was especially lucrative for officers who came to the PPF from other Pacific police forces. One Fijian officer estimated that he earned more in six months with the PPF than he had done in his previous ten years of service. Interview, Honiara, 29 June 2004.

40. Interviews with Australian PPF officers, Honiara, July 2004.

41. Interviews, Honiara July 2004.

42. The decision to station officers in one camp outside Honiara was informed by security, but also by past experiences of UN missions. The arrival of an influx of 'internationals' with per diems in their pocket increases the cost of housing and living in general, so the hope was that stationing international police outside Honiara would alleviate this. The strategy was partly successful, though the cost of living rose by 6 per cent once RAMSI arrived. See The Solomon Islands National Statistics Office, *The Solomon Islands Consumer Price Index* <www.spc.int/prism/country/sb/stats/Economic/Cpi.htm>.

43. The phrase SSR (and its implications) was alien to most of those involved. Although senior echelons of AusAID were aware of both the concept and Organisation for Economic Cooperation and /Development Assistance Committee guidelines, they were not directly involved in planning. Even if they had, the guidelines would have had little traction. As one official commented, it was 'hard to see how to actually practically use them – we wouldn't know where to start'. Interview with AusAID officials, Canberra, 10 July 2004.

44. C. Nelson, *An Evaluation of Weapons Free Villages in the The Solomon Islands* (Geneva: UN Small Arms Survey 2004).

45. Mick Keelty, 'Challenges to peace and justice in the Asia-Pacific region and the role of the AFP in peacekeeping and responding to these challenges'. Address to the Australian Centre for Peace and Conflict Studies, Univ. of Queensland, 1 April 2005.

46. Interview, Director of Planning for the PPF, Honiara, 2 July 2004.

47. Interview, Honiara, 1 July 2004.

48. Interviews with Head of Strategic Planning, PPF, Brisbane, July 2004.

49. For example, Australian officers wrote the 2003 and 2004 annual reports.

50. Solomon Islands academic, Tarcissius Kabutaulaka, noted that a common saying was *weitem olketa RAMSI bae kam stretem* ('wait for RASMI to come and fix it'). Tarcissius Kabutaulaka, *Failed State and the War on Terror: Intervention in The Solomon Islands* (Honolulu, HI: East-West Center 2004).

51. John Roughan, 'People Speak to RAMSI', *Solomons Star*, 8 March 2004.

52. See Sinclair Dinnen 'Lending a Fist: Australia's New Interventionism in the Southwest Pacific', Discussion Paper 2004/5, State Society and Governance in Melanesia Project (2004) p.4 < http://rspas.anu.edu.au/papers/melanesia/discussion_papers/04_05_dp_dinnen.pdf > ; United Nations Development Program, *The Solomon Islands Peace and Conflict Analysis: Emerging Priorities in Preventing Future Violent Conflict* (Suva, Fiji: UNDP 2004).

53. Interview with John Roughan, Solomon Islands Development Trust, Honiara, 4 July 2004.

54. Robert Rotberg (ed.), *When States Fail: Causes and Consequences* (Princeton UP 2004).

55. Simon Chesterman *You, The People: The United Nations, Transitional Administrations and State-building* (Oxford: OUP 2004) p.243.
56. This pro-active approach emerged soon after the release of the Foreign and Trade Policy White Paper, *Advancing the National Interest* (2003), which, while echoing the conventional non-interventionist stance of previous years, highlighted the increasing interrelatedness of aid and 'regional stability and security'. Eight months after the White Paper release, AusAID called for a more rigorous promotion of good governance. Confronting corruption in the Pacific, and building law, order, peace and stability then became AusAID priorities. To this end, AusAID stated that '[t]o further assist our Pacific partners address their complex development challenges, Australia is adopting a more hands-on approach.' Dept. of Foreign Affairs and Trade, *Advancing the National Interest*, Foreign Affairs and Trade White Paper (Canberra 2003) p.6. Cited online at < www.dfat.gov.au/ani/ > .
57. Doubts were raised as to whether a programme with such a heavy emphasis on policing was the best use of Australian funding, and whether other initiatives addressing underlying causes might not achieve better development outcomes. See Craig Sugden, 'Putting the Enhanced Cooperation Package to the Test', *Pacific Economic Bulletin* 19/1 (2004) pp.55–75. In Sugden's view, the ECP 'may instead be limited to offering temporary relief to their symptoms' (p.55). Moreover, many of its direct benefits were susceptible to capture 'by those already relatively well-off' (p.61).
58. There were to be up to 18 Australians working in non-policing roles in various law and justice agencies. These included the post of solicitor-general, three litigation lawyers in the solicitor-general's office, five prosecutors in the public prosecutor's office, two Correctional Service managers, and four judges, as well as further specialists in other key agencies. Up to 36 seconded Australian public servants were to work in key economic, finance, planning and spending agencies. These were to be drawn largely from Australia's Departments of Treasury and Finance and Administration. Ten Australian officials were to work in PNG's immigration services, border and transport security and management, and aviation security.
59. See Mekere Morauta, 'The Papua New Guinea-Australia Relationship', *Pacific Economic Bulletin* 20/1 (2005) pp.159–61.
60. These included several domestically-driven initiatives aimed at stabilising PNG's parliament and reforming the electoral process. See Ron May, 'Disorderly Democracy: Political Turbulence and Institutional Reform in Papua New Guinea' in *State Society and Governance in Melanesia*, Discussion Paper 2003/3, Australian National University < http://rspas.anu.edu/melanesia>.
61. 'Wenge to Test ECP's Validity in Court', *Papua New Guinea Post-Courier*, 20 July 2004.
62. Under this agreement Australia was to have jurisdiction when one of its officials was alleged to have engaged in behaviour constituting an offence under Australian law but not under PNG law. Where concurrent jurisdiction applied, the choice of jurisdiction was to be decided by a Joint Steering Committee comprising Australian and PNG officials 'Green Light for k2 Billion Aid' *Post-Courier* 28 July 2004.
63. Morauta (note 59).
64. See 'Visiting force faces PNG's old-style policing', *Sydney Morning Herald*, 4–5 Dec. 2004.
65. 'ECP Ultimatum', *Papua New Guinea Post-Courier*, 5 May 2005.
66. 'Focus–ECP's Legal Fallout on Immunity', *Papua New Guinea Post-Courier*, 19 May 2005.
67. Subsequent negotiations between Canberra and Port Moresby resulted in agreement on an ECP Mark II. Under the new agreement, a small number of Australian police members are to deploy to specialist advisory positions in Port Moresby.
68. Dinnen (note 52) p.7.

United Kingdom-led Security Sector Reform in Sierra Leone

ADRIAN HORN AND FUNMI OLONISAKIN WITH
GORDON PEAKE

In May 2000 the United Kingdom (UK) intervened militarily in its former colony of Sierra Leone. Its forces repelled an attack by rebels on Sierra Leone's capital, Freetown, and restored the peace that United Nations peacekeepers had guaranteed since 1999.[1] The UK retained an extensive role in the subsequent process of state reconstruction, with a particular focus on security sector reform (SSR). The reform effort was based on the premise that a professional and accountable security apparatus is a pre-condition for the stable development of state and society. The UK's work in Sierra Leone is widely held to represent an example of successful SSR, and, as such, has been the subject of extensive review, evaluation and plaudits.[2] However, while there has been considerable attention to listing and analysing *what* was done, there has been less attention on *how* it was done, and the practical challenges reform presented.

This article offers the personal impressions and reflections of two individuals actively involved in police and military reform. The article comprises three sections. Following a short historical account of the conflict and an outline of the low operational base of the two institutions prior to reconstruction, the process of police reform since 1998 is charted. A brief assessment is then offered of the UK's efforts to transform the Sierra Leonean military, a process that started in earnest after the 2000 intervention.

Three themes and policy dilemmas emerge from this examination of Sierra Leone's experience. The first is that of disconnection. Despite the UK's heavy

political and financial investment in Sierra Leone, there remained a separation
between policy advice on the conceptual level, and the manner in which it was
actually attempted and implemented.[3] Although UK ministries and academic
institutions developed policy guidance, those engaging in reforms took their cues
from the political environment they were operating in. This raises the question of
how to design and calibrate policy advice in a practical and operational way. A
comparable disconnection arises in relation to the framing and programming of
policy. While the Sierra Leone case is frequently presented as an example of good
practice in SSR, there were no conceptual or substantial linkages between its various
elements.[4] That the various reform elements proceeded independently prompts
debate as to whether SSR programmes can be coordinated.

The second issue is how to manage the complex process of comprehensive
reform. Undertaking fundamental change in organisations with jaundiced public
reputations, steeped in mismanagement, and without the basic tools, policies and
procedures needed to do the job is a monumental task. It becomes even more
challenging when trained personnel capable of managing the institutions are in short
supply. A related managerial issue is how reform can combine short-term work with
long-term goals. For example, although reformers made tangible progress in
improving the basic operational effectiveness of the Sierra Leone Police (SLP) and
the Republic of Sierra Leone Army Forces (RSLAF), the effort expended on this
goal meant that it was impossible to give sufficient attention to longer-term issues of
governance and oversight.

Finally, there is the question of durability, for sustaining the police and military
structures recreated by the UK is beyond the revenue-generating capacity of the
poverty-stricken Sierra Leonean state. The police and military's reliance on donor
funding thus raises the question of how reform gains can be retained in the long term.[5]

POLICE AND MILITARY IN WEAK STATES

Although punctuated by accords, agreements and plans, the 1990s and early 2000s
were a period of almost continual instability and brutal conflict.[6] Out of a
population of six million, 50,000 people were killed, 500,000 became refugees, and
a similar number were internally displaced.[7] The origins of the country's conflicts
are to be found in a complex tangle of poor governance, exclusion, poverty,
ethnicity and the inequitable distribution of resources. In addition, the security
apparatus had always played a role in weakening already frail state structures, thus
exacerbating conflict.[8] From independence in 1961 onwards, but especially since
one-party rule began in 1968, the prime role of the country's police and military
forces was to act in the interests of those controlling the state.[9] Over the decades,
and particularly once conflict erupted, their capacity to do police work or soldiering
shrank significantly.

The authority and reach of the SLP was particularly limited. A review carried out
at the request of the Sierra Leonean government in 1996 by a former foreign
minister, Dr Hastings Banya, was damning in its assessment: 'Over the years the

institution has become a demoralized force, lacking in basic equipment, logistics, accoutrement and resources, inadequate and often neglected accommodation, and a deplorable working environment.'[10]

The historical use of the SLP as a repressive arm of the state, together with its reputation for corruption (though this was often a survival tactic, for wages were irregular) led to deep public mistrust. Many areas of the country had no real police presence. The police had neither serviceable vehicles nor communications equipment, and even functioning police stations were without basic equipment such as pens and paper. Most officers received no training, and were unversed in the basics of their job. Further, the usual system of learning had broken down. Ordinarily, many police skills are learned on the job once basic training is completed, but in Sierra Leone this process of didactic transfer broke down; older officers who knew the skills of policing, and its associated systems and procedures had long since retired.

The RSLAF had also atrophied beyond easy repair. Recruitment, appointment and promotion were heavily politicised.[11] It was, for example, commonplace for relatives of politicians to join the senior ranks regardless of merit, thus giving little or no meaning to the formal command structure.[12] Distrusted by the public, the army was poorly trained, poorly equipped and lacked discipline. The welfare of officers and troops was neglected, and morale within the institution low, meaning that the military was deficient in terms of skills and capability.

By the mid-1990s the army had fallen into complete disarray. Enfeebled by its lack of equipment, sporadic pay and internal divisions, it was incapable of repulsing attacks by rebels from the Revolutionary United Front (RUF). Indeed, some units aligned with the rebels, prompting their name of 'sobels': soldiers by day and rebels by night.[13] As a result, parallel military structures were created to shore up the government. These included bands of tribal fighters amalgamated into the Civil Defence Forces (CDF) under the command of Sam Hinga Norman, a former deputy defence minister. The CDF was often more coherent and organised than the formal military, and President Ahmed Tejan Kabbah's reliance on it reflected the general lack of trust in the competence and capacity of state forces.

Kabbah's lack of faith was warranted. In May 1997, 14 months after the elections that brought him to power, segments of the army colluded with rebels in a coup that ousted the government, and it took the intervention of forces from the Economic Community of West African States (ECOWAS)'s Ceasefire Monitoring Group (ECOMOG) to restore him to office in March 1998. However, Kabbah's reinstatement did not end the conflict. War continued, and in January 1999, the RUF advanced on Freetown. Codenamed Operation 'No Living Thing', their offensive was as dreadful as its name suggests.[14]

Many hoped that the conflict would cease after a power-sharing accord was signed between the government and the RUF in the Togolese capital, Lomé, in 1999. Under the terms of the agreement, to be guaranteed by UN peacekeepers, Kabbah would remain president while RUF leader Foday Sankoh would assume the vice-presidency as well as the portfolio for Sierra Leone's most valuable resource, its diamonds. Also, his fighters were to receive an amnesty, a provision that prompted heavy criticism. The agreement explicitly referred to some aspects of SSR, and stipulated that ex-combatants from the CDF and RUF would integrate into 'new restructured national armed forces'.[15] There was no mention of police reform in the agreement.

Like many previous agreements, the Lomé accord was short lived. The reasons for its rapid unravelling include a questionable commitment to the accord on the part of the RUF, agitation from the Liberian leader Charles Taylor, weak international support, and the general weakness of the United Nations (UN) peacekeeping force. The result was an RUF attack on the capital in early 2000 that attempted to capture unfettered control of the government.[16] The peacekeepers' circumscribed rules of engagement meant that they could do little, and the rebels captured nearly 500 'blue helmets', a major humiliation for the UN.[17] Only the arrival of troops from the UK, Sierra Leone's former colonial power, shored up the city's defence, thereby restoring a semblance of order in which implementation could begin. The expeditionary force (initially tasked with evacuating British nationals) quickly assumed a wider role in restoring basic security in Freetown and the surrounding area. Sankoh was arrested, and the peacekeeping mission began work on restoring the state's basic governance capacity. The UK has remained deeply involved in developing Sierra Leone's security institutions ever since.

EVALUATING SSR PROGRAMMING

Police Reform

The UK became involved in police reform in the period following Kabbah's reinstatement in 1998, and this continued throughout the subsequent conflict. Kabbah's restoration, combined with renewed international interest in what had been a forgotten country, presented an opportunity for police reform. The president requested that the Commonwealth Secretary-General coordinate assistance to improve the effectiveness of the police as a matter of some urgency.[18] A small team of experienced senior police officers from Canada, Sri Lanka, the UK and Zimbabwe was assembled, arriving in country in mid-1998 to conduct an initial assessment and begin work on police reform.

The process of police building can be divided into three phases for analytic purposes. The first (1998–99) saw the development of reform's conceptual foundations and also some practical efforts intended to demonstrate progress to both officers and the public. This work stopped when the RUF attacked in 1999. Much of the tangible progress made during the initial phase was undone, which meant that in the second phase (1999–2002), work had to begin again from scratch. Although the Commonwealth project did not have executive authority to carry out police functions, its members played an instrumental role in leading and directing the reform process. In this period, a new philosophy of policing was introduced and a wide range of initiatives undertaken to build up police capacity and skills. This heavy international involvement gradually receded in the third phase (2002–2006) which was marked by increased Sierra Leonean ownership and direction over the process, and, increasingly, by questions about programme sustainability and the nature of what is being bequeathed.

Phase One: Crisis to Confidence (1998–1999)

Although the Commonwealth team found the Sierra Leone police in an abject state, they also discovered cause for real encouragement. Low ranking officers were especially receptive to reform; they were motivated, educated, and demonstrated a commitment to changing their poor public image. Many officers, for example, took the trouble to handwrite detailed responses and suggestions back to the team, a clear sign of their interest in being involved. The reformers also sought to leverage existing documentation, in particular the Banya committee report of 1999. This report was thorough in its diagnosis of the problems afflicting the institution but suffered a major practicality deficiency: although it identified many of the obstacles, it offered minimal practical guidance on how to conduct police reform and, just as importantly, how to pay for the proposed changes.

From the outset, the reformers were tested by their need to simultaneously manage the short and long-term challenges of police reconstruction. The country was still at war, and while quick fixes were urgently required, it was also necessary to articulate a longer-term vision and strategy. The Commonwealth team thought it unwise to undertake major change without the clear commitment of the relevant Sierra Leonean stakeholders, which included senior political figures, the police leadership and rank-and-file officers. Without their collective engagement, SSR ran the risk of being little more than a useful but ultimately directionless activity. The reformers set out to achieve the necessary support by consulting widely with the SLP. They also sought to secure presidential approval and develop a police mission statement that would serve as a symbol of policing's new beginning.

The team made an effort to confer with as many officers as possible. A 'conceptual overview' based on the findings of the Banya committee was packaged in the form of box diagrams and flowcharts to aid discussions with the SLP. In their discussions, reformers sought to steer the conversation so that it focused on moving forward on 'big picture' issues such as the role of the SLP in relation to the overall aims of the government, and a realistic development plan and time-cycle to deliver these commitments. It was crucial that as wide a range of SLP officers as possible received the briefing in order to offset the generation of misinformation. Reform was resisted in some quarters, and the absence of an internal communications structure meant that rumours regarding the implications of reform were quickly regarded as fact. This was at best disruptive and at worst divisive. In contrast, a clear overview brought clarity to the reformer's work and nullified speculation as to their intent. Wide consultation also served a strategic purpose. Because so many were involved in the consultations, it subsequently made it easier to bring officers who did not agree with the direction of the reform process back on track by reminding them that they had been part of initial discussions.

The second element was securing presidential approval: progress would quickly founder without demonstrated political backing from the highest level. Support was formally secured through the publication of a government policing charter, personally endorsed by President Kabbah in August 1998, a few months after the team's arrival.[19] The document, which was the distillation of conversations between the president and the Commonwealth team, also revealed Sierra Leone's lack of expertise, for it was drafted by the Commonwealth team. The charter set out the government's expectations of the police, its role in developing the institution and affirmed the importance of equal opportunities and human rights, and the rights of the public to have an input into policing. It signified high-level political support and was useful as a means of cutting through potentially difficult situations.

The final conceptual building block was a police mission statement. Formulating such a vision was useful to both symbolically break with the past and articulate a vision for the future. Senior SLP officers with experience of modern, democratic police services elsewhere in the world knew that a proper mission statement was an essential part of the reform process. For it to have credibility and durability, care was taken to ensure that the SLP designed the statement; workshops and meetings were held to discuss and develop the wording. In many ways, the process was as important as the outcome. Facilitated workshops and meetings proved an effective way of enabling top-to-bottom communication, and provided a safe environment for voices that would otherwise have remained silent.

Although aligning the various elements of reform was important, there was a simultaneous need for reform to be visible. Conceptual overviews and mission statements were all very well but their impact could not be easily seen by police officers in dank and ill-equipped stations, or by the public. As part of the emergency response, the task force used their initial budget of US$900,000 to purchase bicycles, vehicles and a basic radio communication system. Buying drugs for the police hospital proved particularly beneficial, for many officers were ill with maladies that relatively cheap medicines such as anti-malarial medicine and vitamins could treat. Caring for officers not only improved health and morale but also improved police effectiveness because it meant that more officers could perform their jobs. Emergency building work to the police training school was undertaken too, enabling refresher training to take place.

Phase Two: Back to Basics (1999–2002)

The RUF attack on Freetown in January 1999 undid many of the achievements of the previous year. Police stations were torched, police files lost and vehicles destroyed. The SLP suffered serious losses. No fewer than 250 SLP officers were murdered during the attacks, together with approximately 375 of their family members.[20]

The task force advisers returned as soon as possible, arriving back in Freetown in April 1999. They were sent by the UK's Department for International Development

(DfID), and tasked with providing an assessment of post-conflict assessment of policing in Sierra Leone, and making recommendations on assistance to the SLP.

Their report starkly summarised the situation:

> Put at its simplest the SLP is not effective and policing has taken a back seat. The streets of Freetown are saturated with soldiers manning checkpoints, armed... Civil Defence Force and youths. ... All mount vehicle checkpoints, which are, all too frequently, independent of each other.

> ...Notwithstanding the GoSL [Government of Sierra Leone's] published position or the desire of the vast majority of Sierra Leoneans, the SLP does not have primacy for the maintenance of law and order and are unlikely to be able to achieve police primacy from the military and paramilitary forces in the near future. ...The GoSL must re-establish the SLP as the primary force for maintaining law and order. It is well appreciated that the country is on a war footing but the impression is one of uncoordinated activity by the security forces exacerbated by all pervasive petty corruption.[21]

An already frail policing institution had become even weaker. Having made an encouraging start to reform in the previous year, the events of January 1999 knocked the SLP back. The physical effects were plain to see, but latent psychological effects were also clear. The situation required careful and sensitive handling to give back officers their confidence and the will to move forward.

In this phase, nothing less than the foundations of a professional police had to be recreated. Although the conceptual documents and agreements from the previous phase proved extremely useful as a foundation for the process, the Commonwealth team had to start from scratch again. It was a daunting undertaking. Organisational structures, policies, procedures and systems had to be updated or, in many instances, crafted for the first time. Communications, transport and other logistics had to be supplied in sufficient quantities to enable effective policing. Simultaneously, new institutions had to be created in order to provide formal external oversight and independent advice to the police. Legislation that had not changed since colonial times had to be updated, and, at the same time, it was necessary to improve the working conditions of police personnel.

The task confronting the newly named Commonwealth Community Safety and Security Project (CCSSP) was ambitious. Although categorised as a Commonwealth mission, and including Commonwealth police officers, the UK's DfID funded the project.[22] As in the previous phase, the reform programme combined conceptual alterations with more tangible steps to improve police capacity. The conceptual centrepiece of the reform programme during this phase was the introduction of a new philosophy of police practice called 'local needs policing' (LNP). The phrase was chosen as the result of a failure to agree on shared terminology. Although the official documentation used the term 'community-based', it proved extremely difficult for the police advisers and members of the UN CIVPOL (civilian police) contingent to agree on what 'community-based' policing entailed.[23] To avoid confusion, a decision was taken to foreswear 'community' and formulate a new phrase with common appeal, and explicitly designed to meet Sierra Leone's policing needs. LNP was described as a 'system of policing that meets the needs and expectations of the local community, and reflects national standards and guidelines'.

Local needs policing was philosophically pivotal to the process of internal organisational change. Its major operational precept – that decisions on police work should devolve to local stations – represented a major change in the context of Sierra Leone. Whereas policing had previously been a highly centralised activity, the role of headquarters now needed to be re-oriented so that it could set out, and oversee, clear policy objectives and standards. This was a significantly new style of management for most SLP officers and demanded much support from the Commonwealth team to make it work. However, the decision to devolve decision-making and establish accountability at the lowest possible level meant that the model also allowed for the flexibility of policing required by the diverse circumstances of post-conflict Sierra Leone. The policy put policing decisions down to the local level, but at the same time ensured that policing was carried out in accordance with national standards and guidelines.

Reform at the policy level was combined with practical steps to improve police capacity. One of the most fundamental elements of the reform process was skills training. As stations reopened and day-to-day policing was reintroduced across the country, the basic ability of officers to do their job became increasingly important. However, police skills, knowledge and ability had been lost, or had never existed in the first place. Learning theme by theme through on-the-job mentoring and monitoring was the chosen way of remedying the situation. As well as the UK-team, the relatively underused UN CIVPOL officers also advised and assisted in the re-introduction of skills. For example, mentors would take a theme, such as maintaining a police notebook. The ability to record activities is crucial for effective police work, but was a basic skill few officers had, so over a period of weeks, Commonwealth and UN CIVPOL officers worked through the theme before moving onto the next area of attention. With all advisers following the same process, it was possible to closely monitor and evaluate activities; progress could be assessed in detail by monitoring the completion or neglect of individual tasks. It was important to resist the temptation to try too much. As officers became skilled, they in turn passed on learning to fellow officers, thereby improving the organisational knowledge and skills base.

Improving the relationship between the police and the media was another plank of the reform process, for the SLP was faced with a tradition of inaccurate and partial reporting in newspapers and radio; sensationalist headlines about police practice were used to sell papers but often had little grounding in fact. On occasions, the media spread unhelpful information about the Commonwealth reform team and their alleged intentions. Reporters rarely checked their facts with the police but creating a new office of public information allowed the media to check stories for factual accuracy before publication. The police themselves began publishing a widely circulated monthly newspaper as a way of meeting internal and external communication problems.

The reform programme made a concerted effort to reach out to parts of communities that had long been alienated from the police. In order to involve the community, police partnership boards comprising representatives of the local community were established at the local level. Special emphasis was placed on the vulnerable and those who had disproportionately suffered during the war, such as women and children; rape and sexual violence were widespread in the war, and domestic violence remained a problem in its aftermath. New institutions were created to deal more sensitively with the issue than had been the case in the past.[24] The establishment of family support units staffed by police officers (many female) and social/medical workers helped improve the standard of service to victims of sexual and domestic abuse.[25]

The reformers created new structures of internal accountability. A department was set up and systems devised to deal with complaints and misconduct, and new disciplinary regulations introduced. New systems and procedures were introduced which drastically reduced the opportunities for corruption and the misuse of resources. One of the biggest areas of corruption was misuse of official fuel, the theft of which may have accounted for approximately 15 per cent of the total budget. Introducing proper systems to manage the supply and use of fuel (e.g., log books for vehicles), together with proper monitoring and checks, stopped a significant amount of the theft.

It was often difficult for the police, with their limited managerial capacity to absorb so many new processes and innovations. A case in point was the difficulties encountered in designing a workable police plan during this period. The SLP had already produced a basic development plan that identified priority areas but it proved difficult for officers to develop it further; that is, so as to take into account the available budget, and ability to sustain initiatives and available infrastructure. Even senior officers found this difficult. It was easy to assume, for example, that everybody in senior position functioned on the same level of planning, managerial and organizational skills, but rank was not always a good guide to competence. Forward planning and thinking managerially had not been part of police culture, and it was difficult for officers to look three to five years ahead. As a result, the Commonwealth team often assumed the task of detailed planning.

Phase Three: Action to Advance (2002–2005)

It was only when new organisational structures, systems and resources were in place that the SLP reached the stage where it could assume primacy for carrying out day-to-day policing; only then had sufficient numbers of senior officers received the management training needed for implementing long-term change.

The process also required less international involvement. The transfer of the highest leadership position in the SLP – that of inspector general – from a British officer, Keith Biddle, to a Sierra Leonean, Brima Acha Kamara, personified the transition from international to national. The changeover necessitated a change of approach by Commonwealth advisers too, whose role became less directive and more supportive. Shifting to a less interventionist role proved difficult for many advisers. While it could be rewarding to see SLP officers take on their responsibilities, it was also frustrating for internationals to see SLP officers labouring for hours over tasks that took internationals minutes to carry out.

Even though improvements were significant, some limitations remained. In particular, it was important to recognise that there was a limit as to how many changes a reformed SLP could absorb, manage and fund. The police had a difficult policing job to do with inadequate resources; finding even simple things like fuel and paper in sufficient quantities remained difficult. Signs of wear and tear in donated capital equipment were also detectable, and many vehicles donated in the early phases broke down due to continual use; the SLP did not have the money in its budget for petrol for those vehicles that worked, never mind the budget for maintaining, replacing or adding vehicles.[26] Moreover, many of the initial training programmes showed signs of wearing down, including, for example, the system of notebook maintenance. A survey of policing in 2005, reported that 'the supply of police notebooks is erratic and many SLP members do not possess them. And even though those who are in possession of police notebooks are generally making good use of such books, very little is being done to inspect these books by the supervisors.'[27]

Gaps between Headquarters and the Field

Guidance on SSR, including some relating specifically to police reform, was developed and written in the UK, either at DfID headquarters or by consultants and researchers hired to provide conceptual guidance. However, little made its way down to the field level. A case in point concerns research developed to provide formal policy guidance on support to policing in developing countries. Although of direct relevance to Sierra Leone, those working in Sierra Leone were oblivious to it.[28]

The limited information flow between London and Freetown can be partly explained by the weak managerial relations existing between headquarters and the field. Communication was sporadic, and DfID's support infrastructure minimal.[29] Rather than learning from formal documents, the police team therefore drew on the operational experience of mission members, many of who had recently retired from senior positions in UK and Commonwealth police forces. There was little in the way of formal coordination with other projects (including the ongoing military reform process), but informal networks proved very effective. Advisers on different projects mixed socially in the evenings, and the friendships that developed proved an effective and expeditious channel for information. Instead of hindering progress, the dearth of formal reporting and the relatively informal nature of decision-making actually proved helpful. It freed advisers from bureaucracy and allowed them get on with the job at hand. However, the success of this approach was heavily reliant on the calibre and experience of advisers, and on their ability to instil confidence and credibility.

When headquarters in London did become involved, it sometimes complicated project implementation, albeit unintentionally. Attempts to provide riot-control equipment to the SLP were a case in point. The Commonwealth team believed the range of options presented to officers was either too light or too heavy for the circumstances, which required less-than-lethal options (including batons, shields, protective clothing, baton guns and training). Finding a way to fund their purchase without contravening UK government regulations was difficult. Eventually these supplies had to be funded from a different source so as to avoid contravening UK legislation and policy.

Military Reform

The UK's involvement in the reform of Sierra Leone's armed forces occurred later than with the police. In the period following Kabbah's re-instatement in 1998, the president initially turned to ECOMOG for assistance in reorganising and restructuring the armed forces, appointing Maxwell Khobe, head of the ECOMOG Task Force, as the country's chief of defence staff.

Direct UK involvement in military reform began in June 1999 with support from the UK's Ministry of Defence Advisory Team (DAT). This launched the first phase of the Sierra Leone Security Sector Reform Programme (SILSEP), which was designed to bring the RSLAF under a democratic form of control based on the UK's model of dual civil/military command. A UK military adviser and a civilian from the UK Ministry of Defence were posted to assist the Sierra Leone government with restructuring.

UK policy emphasised the importance of using professional, well-equipped armed forces to maintain the peace thought to have been secured at Lomé. However, by the time they deployed, the deteriorating political environment, combined with the institutional disarray of the RSLAF, meant that British troops had to take on a more offensive role. Their initial focus was on containing and repulsing the RUF. Short-term training teams (STTT) deployed alongside the three UK infantry companies involved in training Sierra Leoneans to fight the RUF.[30] Such was the lack of capacity within the army that British officers assumed command of the RSLAF in several areas, while other British officers were placed in key command positions in the army and the MoD. The intention was that British officers would to play a mentoring role, and gradually phase out their contribution as their Sierra Leonean counterparts acquired the competence to take over.

The UK maintained a significant role in training and remodelling the army after the intervention, concentrating on training programmes to improve RSLAF effectiveness while at the same time implementing legal and structural reforms, including the creation of new institutions to govern and oversee the military, as well as the development of a national defence policy.[31]

The foundations of a professional military were laid in the five years that followed. The RSLAF has become markedly more professional, and better trained and equipped with the skills and discipline required to carry out basic military missions and tasks. Previously feuding combatants now wear the same uniform, a symbolically powerful sign of progress and non-partisanship. A new Ministry of Defence that works under joint civilian and military management has been created and housed in new headquarters, and new offices of National Security (ONS) and a Central Intelligence and Security Unit (CISU) have been established. A Defence White Paper has been published.

Although much has been accomplished in a relatively short time, it is still too early to offer a definitive judgment on the success or otherwise of the military reform process. Three issues are of particular concern and resonate beyond the military to other security sector initiatives: funding and the sustainability of the armed forces, effective oversight mechanisms, and local ownership of the reform process.

The ambitious nature of the RSLAF project raises questions about whether it is sustainable in the long term. Even with continuing donor funding, the extent to which the Sierra Leonean government can provide the resources necessary for maintaining current capacity and standards (let alone completing the reform process) is doubtful. It is estimated that the UK provided about US$37 million in support of the RSLAF between 2000 and 2002 (covering equipment, uniforms and vehicles), and the ability of the government of Sierra Leone to assume this financial burden when UK assistance ends is in doubt.[32] With greater public scrutiny and external pressures, it will also become increasingly difficult for the government to resort to the traditional resort of hiding defence expenditure in the budgets of social ministries such as health and education.

The second area of concern is oversight. One of the enduring tests of a reformed security sector (in addition to operational effectiveness) is the extent to which the security establishment is democratically governed. It is important that the appropriate ministries such as defence, interior, finance and the National Security Council are able to direct and control the armed forces, the police and intelligence services. Already the management of the MoD (now led by civilians working with their military counterparts) reflects a measure of control over the military. However, this gradual movement toward subordinating the security services to civilian political control through a dual command structure in the MoD remains largely influenced by the UK presence. The newly created oversight institutions have yet to be fully tested and there is serious concern about the ability of many institutions to provide robust oversight given the inexperience of their staff. This is made more important by the creation of the Office of National Security (ONS), which, if properly managed, will support the development of a national security strategy while providing valuable intelligence to deal with current challenges such as the fragile security environment, loss of revenue from mineral resources, and high level corruption. However, if it is not managed appropriately, state security agencies may fall prey to misuse by corrupt and self-serving politicians or members of the ruling elite who could use them to intimidate and hunt their political opponents.

The final issue is the extent to which the process is locally owned. The primary objective of the UK was to provide advice and provide training that would assist in the development of an accountable and operational RSLAF. Emergency conditions compelled IMATT to perform a far greater operational role than initially anticipated but there was an understanding that this role would scale back over time to allow local commanders to take charge of operations, and the local civilian and military leadership to assume control of the MoD. In the event, the delay in transferring authority to Sierra Leoneans within the MoD affected local perceptions and sense of ownership. Differences in management culture also contributed to a gap between trainers and the trained as IMATT used Western-training models that were unknown to many Sierra Leoneans. Delays in phasing in local leadership of the MoD then threatened to widen the gap between MoD's model and other parts of Sierra Leone's public services.

A related issue was the public's perception of the RSLAF. Despite extensive work, trust in the security institutions has yet to develop. To be sure, public confidence has grown with the RSLAF's improved professionalism, better organisation, increased morale and discipline, but suspicion has not disappeared. There remain significant levels of public distrust of the armed forces, coupled with the perception that those complicit in terrorising Sierra Leoneans are receiving rewards (with improved rations, equipment and vehicles for military personnel) rather than punishment for their role in the war.

CONCLUSION

The political, financial, logistical and security support provided by the UK government was, when supplemented by the limited resources of the Sierra Leone government, critical in securing the peace. It provided much needed confidence to people who no longer had faith in their own security institutions, and it created the stable, secure environment in which SSR could take place. Basic capacity and public trust in the police and military have been restored. Given the low level at which reform began, the achievement is praiseworthy.[33]

Although the military and police are no longer politicised and incapacitated forces, reform remains a work in progress, and its future remains an open question. It may be too early for an overall assessment of SSR, but that said, the reflections offered here raise several issues with important implications. The disjuncture between the policy advice proffered and the manner in which reform proceeded raises questions as to how to craft policy advice in a way that will be practically useful. Doubts also remain as to the extent to which the model – which, in part replicates British systems – is appropriate for Sierra Leone.

Finally, the case raises the question of whether SSR can presage wider economic, political and social improvement. The UK government policy sees SSR as a foundational pre-requisite for the achievement of broader development goals, yet the evidence from Sierra Leone is that one does not necessarily lead to the other.[34] Despite extensive and costly reforms, Sierra Leone remains anchored near the bottom of human developmental indicators ranking countries according to life expectancy, educational attainment, and adjusted real income. In the 2005 index,

only Niger ranked below it.[35] The operation may well have been successful but the
patient, for now, remains profoundly weak.

NOTES

1. In 2005 the security situation was judged sufficiently benign to allow the United Nations Assistance
   Mission to Sierra Leone (UNAMSIL) to draw down. A smaller mission, United Nations Observer
   Mission in Sierra Leone (UNOMSIL), replaced it. For an account of the UN's experience in Sierra
   Leone see 'Funmi Olonisakin, *From Reinvention to Renaissance: United Nations Peacekeeping in
   Sierra Leone* (Boulder, CO: Lynne Rienner forthcoming).
2. For a representative range of positive reviews of SSR in Sierra Leone see Roderick Evans, David
   Jones and Graham Thompson, 'Sierra Leone Security Sector Reform Programme II: Output to
   Purpose Review', unpublished report by Defence Advisory Team 2002; Ann Fitz-Gerald, *Security
   Sector Reform in Sierra Leone* (Shivenham, UK: Global Facilitation Network for Security Sector
   Reform 2004); Jeremy Ginifer with Kaye Oliver, *Evaluation of the Conflict Prevention Pools: Sierra
   Leone*, Evaluation Report EV 647 (London: Dept. for International Development 2004); Mark Malan.
   Sarah Meek, Thokozani Thusi, Jeremy Ginifer and Patrick Coker, *Sierra Leone - Building the Road to
   Recovery* (Pretoria, SA: Institute for Strategic Studies 2004); A. Kondeh, 'The Case of Sierra Leone'.
   in Alan Bryden, Boubacar N'Diaye and 'Funmi Olonisakin (eds.), *The Challenges of Security Sector
   Governance in West Africa* (Munster: Lit Verlag 2005).
3. It is difficult to determine exactly what the UK has spent on Sierra Leone, for the money comes from
   different funding sources. However, the figures that exist provide evidence of the strength of
   the financial commitment. Between 2000 and 2006, the UK's Department for International
   Development (DfID) spent US$392 million in Sierra Leone < www.dfid.gov.uk/countries/africa/
   sierraleone.asp > (accessed Feb. 2006).
4. Sierra Leone has been cited as an example of good practice in SSR in the Organisation for Economic
   Cooperation and Development/ Development Assistance Committee (OECD/DAC) documents
   'Security System Reform and Governance: Policy and Good Practice', DAC High Level Meeting,
   15–16 April 2004 < www.oecd.org/dataoecd/40/58/31526562.pdf> ; 'Introduction to Security System
   Reform' Issues Brief (Paris: OECD/DAC 2005) p.5 < www.oecd.org/dataoecd/26/52/ 35785462.pdf >
   (accessed Feb. 2006)
5. International Crisis Group, *Liberia and Sierra Leone: Rebuilding Failed States*, Africa Report No.87
   (Dakar/Brussels 2004) pp.16–17.
6. John Hirsch, *Sierra Leone* (Boulder, CO: Lynne Rienner 2002).
7. King's College London, *A Case for Change* (London: King's College 2003) p.64.
8. See, for example, Arthur Abraham, 'The Quest for Peace in Sierra Leone', in 'Funmi Olonisakin
   (ed.), *Engaging Sierra Leone* (London: Centre for Democracy and Development 2000); A. Abraham
   and Edward Turay, *The Sierra Leone Army: A Century of History* (London: Macmillan 1987).
9. Osman Gbla, 'Security Sector Reform under International Tutelage in Sierra Leone'. *International
   Peacekeeping* 13/1 (2006) pp.78–80.
10. Report of the Dr Banya Committee on the Republic of Sierra Leone Police Force, Freetown,
    Aug.1996. Unpublished document, copy with the author.
11. Kondeh (note 2).
12. Abraham (note 8).
13. David Keen, *Conflict and Collusion in Sierra Leone* (London: James Currey 2005) pp.134–51.
14. Sarah Meek, 'Policing Sierra Leone' in Mark Malan *et al.*, *Sierra Leone – Building the Road to
    Recovery* (Pretoria, ZA: Institute for Security Studies 2003) p.1.
15. Peace agreement between the government of Sierra Leone and the Revolutionary United Front of
    Sierra Leone. Signed in Lomé 7 July 1999. The Lomé Accord, Article XVII, 2.
16. Keen (note 13) pp.253–66.
17. King's College London (note 7) pp.71–73.
18. The UK government had been involved in developing the SLP for some years, mainly through the
    provision of training assistance, but the fraught political situation made more ambitious plans
    unrealistic. A five-year development plan was developed in 1995, but security concerns prevented its
    implementation.

19. Broadcast to the nation on peace and security by His Excellency Alhaji Dr Ahmad Tejan President Kabbah, 2 Sept. 1998 < www.sierra–leone.org/kabbah090298.html>
20. Meek (note 14) p.1.
21. Keith Biddle and Adrian Horn, 'Assessment of the Sierra Leone Police', unpublished document, April 1999. Copy with the author.
22. The CCSSP received substantial funding from DfID to reform and equip the SLP, principally with communications network and vehicles. DfID allocated approximately US $22 million for 2000–2002 and approximately $10 million in each following year. Ylber Bajraktari, Arthur Boutellis, Fatema Gunja, Daniel Y. Harris, James Kapsis, Eva Kaye, and Jane Rhee *The PRIME System: Measuring the Success of Post-Conflict Police Reform* (Princeton, NJ: Woodrow Wilson School 2006) p.8.
23. '[T]o establish an effective community based and accountable police service capable of being a major contributor to the securing of a safe and just society in which the rights of individuals and communities are respected.' Community Safety and Security Project, Project Memorandum, DfID. April 2000.
24. Human Rights Watch,'*We'll Kill You If You Cry*': Sexual Violence in the Sierra Leone Conflict (NY: Human Rights Watch 2003).
25. Christopher Stone, Joel Millar, Monica Thornton and Jennifer Trone, *Supporting Security, Justice and Development: Lessons for a New Era* (London: DfID 2005) p.18.
26. Bajraktari *et al.* (note 22) p.92.
27. UNAMSIL, *Back to Basics Policing* survey, March 2005. Researchers from Princeton University discovered a similar breaking down: 'The police officers we spoke with in Freetown and Bo kept notebooks. However, when asked, none of the officers in Bo were able to produce a single example of an arrest in either their notebooks or logs.' Bajkatarai *et al.* (note 22) p.94.
28. Ian Clegg, Robert Hunt and Jim Whetton, *Policy guidance on support to policing in developing countries* (Swansea: Centre for Development Studies, Univ. of Wales 2000) < www.swansea. ac.uk/cds >.
29. The co-author, for example, spoke to his DfID manager four times in the four years that he worked in Sierra Leone.
30. Fitz-Gerald (note 2) p.11.
31. Gbla (note 9) pp.83–4.
32. See Evans *et al.* (note 2).
33. Despite improved public trust, actors other than the police and military provide most forms of security. See Bruce Baker, 'Who do people turn to for policing in Sierra Leone?' *Contemporary African Studies* 23/3 (2005) pp.371–90; Rita Abrahamsen and Michael Williams, *The Globalization of Private Security: Sierra Leone* (Aberystwyth. Univ. of Wales 2005) available at < http://users. aber.ac.uk/rbh/privatesecurity/country%20report-sierra%20leone.pdf > (accessed March 2006).
34. DfID, *Fighting Poverty to Build a Safer World: A Strategy for Security and Development* (London: DfID 2005).
35. Out of 177 countries surveyed by the UN's Human Development Index in 2005, Sierra Leone ranked 176. UNO, *Human Development Index 2005* (NY: UNDP 2005) < http://hdr.undp.org/reports/global/2005/pdf/HDR05_HDI.pdf > (accessed March 2006).

A Hard Place: The United States and the Creation of a New Security Apparatus in Iraq

CHRISTOPH WILCKE

Security sector reform (SSR) in Iraq in the aftermath of the US-led war of March 2003 against Saddam Hussein's regime was a poorly designed and haphazardly implemented experiment in rapid institutional transformation. A combination of misunderstandings, false assumptions and planning failures on the part of the US-led authorities set the stage for postwar chaos that quickly escalated into lawlessness and insurgency.

The creation of credible and viable indigenous security institutions capable of providing order was essential if a stable and reconstructed Iraq was to be established, and a US exit facilitated.[1] However, the US was largely unprepared for rebuilding the security sector on the scale required and in the timeframe available. The situation was made even more complicated by Iraq's profoundly dangerous environment of criminality, lawlessness and insurgency. Originally intended to be carried out by private contractors, the scale of the task and the insecurity of the situation meant that the bulk of SSR has been carried out by the US military.

This article evaluates two significant aspects of the SSR process that occurred between the overthrow of Saddam's regime in March 2003 and elections for a new Iraqi government in January 2005. Programming continues to evolve and, although subsequent developments are not reflected here, the first two years illustrate the difficulty of creating army, police and auxiliary units on a large scale. Although new security institutions were created, they were extremely weak, dependent on outside help and no match for the challenges they faced. Their loyalty, dependability, capability and discipline remain unproven.

Insufficient pre-planning on the part of the US proved fatal. Emphasis was placed on rushing large numbers of Iraqis through training programmes so that they could assume security functions. Training, however, was too short and often inappropriate for the tasks assigned to the new forces. Although the number of personnel employed and/or trained was the measure most frequently cited as evidence of progress, this was a poor guide to capability and performance. Over-concentration on numbers meant that insufficient attention was paid to constructing appropriate organizational structures, and accountability and oversight mechanisms, and to developing linkages between different institutions in the security sector. As a result, the new services were as fundamentally unaccountable as their Saddam-era predecessors.

Although the scale, complexity and circumstances of SSR in Iraq makes its case appear *sui generis*, the overall SSR scenario may well be repeated in other regions. Further, important lessons can be identified from Iraq's case. The primary lesson is that the reform or establishment of security institutions cannot be treated as an afterthought. In Iraq, the focus was on creating officers in uniform, followed by a command structure, and only then an institution (budget, personnel management), inter-institutional links (military-police collaboration), and, lastly, oversight (ministries, provincial councils) – with the last three steps receiving only cursory attention. The Iraq experience shows the necessity of creating a central hub to coordinate and manage the complex process of institution building in fluid and volatile operating environments. It also emphasizes the necessity for would-be reformers to understand the political and cultural context in which SSR is to be conducted.

REPUBLIC OF FEAR

The security situation in Iraq in early 2003 had a number of important features, of which the following were critical. First, Saddam Hussein had transformed Iraq from a state with a history of endemic coups into a security state with a dense web of police, military and intelligence agencies which he personally controlled.[2] These agencies had no tradition of providing security for Iraqi citizens. Their primary purpose was to preserve and uphold Saddam's personal rule, and this they achieved through individual, collective, and mutual surveillance, repression and violence.[3]

Second, a major element in Saddam's survival strategy was the creation of numerous rival security and intelligence organs. The ruling Ba'ath Party, for example, developed its own intelligence and paramilitary resources, which infiltrated existing security organizations, or staffed new internal intelligence agencies attached to existing security structures. Older officers were bypassed for promotion, placed on distant assignments, dismissed, deported, imprisoned or executed. Ba'ath Party membership was required for senior officers, thus ensuring a loyal if incompetent following in the security apparatus.[4] Intelligence and security organizations reported to and took orders from the Office of the Presidential Palace (OPP), instead of line ministries. Loyalty was created through indoctrination, intimidation and patronage.

Third, Saddam created insulating rings of security agencies around his own position, filling them with members of his own tribe, clan and, at the closest level. immediate family. He also engaged in wholesale tribal bargaining, offering prestige and largesse to tribal groups in return for their loyalty to himself and his entourage.[5] These agents were not committed Ba'athists.

Fourth, the representation of Sunni Arabs in terms of numbers and seniority within the apparatus was disproportionate to their population size. Iraqi Kurds, however, were held in suspicion, and were scrutinized by security and intelligence services. Saddam was dubious about the loyalty of Iraq's Shi'a too, deporting and persecuting them en masse in the 1970s and 1980s. Although they provided the bulk of the Army's foot soldiers, they were rarely promoted to high-ranking positions.

COLLAPSE

Iraqi security agencies quickly disintegrated when US and British troops rolled into Iraq in March 2003. The Iraqi Army put up minimal resistance and, as US troops reached the center of Baghdad on 9 April 2003, 'security officers, intelligence personnel and Ba'ath Party operatives went into hiding, while police officers and members of the regular army took their weapons and went home'.[6]

The swift collapse of what had been an omnipresent system of control unleashed a very different sort of insecurity. Revenge killings escalated quickly in Iraq's newly 'liberated' cities. Looting and banditry was rife as installations were systematically ransacked of their equipment, furniture and files.[7] A combination of the exuberance generated by a quick victory, lack of troops, and unpreparedness meant that US troops stood by and did little to intervene.[8]

Such insecurity and lawlessness was very different to the calm, orderly transition scenario envisioned by Pentagon planners. They foresaw the pullout of all but 30,000 US troops from a stable Iraq within six months. This belief rested on three assumptions: first, military victory would be surgical and decisive; second, Iraqi governance structures, including the police and central ministries, would remain institutionally intact; and, third, international support would materialize after the war. The first was borne out but the latter two were quickly revealed as erroneous and, in hindsight, naïve. In particular, the presumption that a grateful population would embrace democracy revealed a dangerous misunderstanding of the ethnic, religious and political divisions in Iraqi society.

This general unpreparedness was mirrored in the lack of detail on what to do with Iraq's security sector.[9] Despite advice from regional analysts and scholars familiar with previous post-conflict operations, prewar planning did not take into account the possibility of a post-conflict security vacuum, or of clandestine resistance to foreign occupiers, let alone the difficulties of resurrecting and reorienting Iraq's security sector.[10] Additionally, the Pentagon's planning did not incorporate the advice on postwar security governance proffered by other US government institutions.[11] For instance, the Department of State (DoS)'s Future of Iraq project (which was written by exiled Iraqis) set out options for SSR that included transition from a security concept of surveillance and social control to one of law enforcement and rule of law that emphasized civilian oversight.[12] Although widely circulated, the document was routinely ignored inside the Pentagon; few of those who arrived in Baghdad in the aftermath of the invasion were aware of its existence.[13]

What post-conflict planning did take place was predicated on the assumption that Iraq's security apparatus would remain intact and could be remolded. US planners believed that they would only have to abolish Iraqi intelligence and special security services.[14] Although thin on detail, there was some recognition of the need for early vetting to rid the forces of senior Ba'athists by removing them from their positions and prosecuting war criminals. The modalities as to how this would be done, however, were unclear. Ironically, given the amount of money that would subsequently be spent, many of the SSR proposals developed before the war went unfunded on grounds that they were too costly. Even in the immediate aftermath of the war, the reluctance to fund security assistance programs remained. The Pentagon turned down a $628 million plan from the United States Institute of Peace (USIP) for the deployment of 6,200 international police and judicial experts immediately after the war as being too expensive.[15]

POLITICAL AND SECURITY ENVIRONMENT

The security void provoked quick changes in plans for governing Iraq. Originally, the Pentagon intended that a newly established Office of Reconstruction and Humanitarian Assistance (ORHA) would shepherd the country's reconstruction and oversee a quick transition to an Iraqi administration. It quickly became clear that pre-invasion hopes for withdrawal within three to six months were unrealistic, and that ORHA's few hundred staff were wholly inadequate for the task.[16] ORHA's role was subsumed into a larger body called the Coalition Provisional Authority (CPA), headed by Ambassador Paul Bremer, which combined, in theory, the civilian and military tasks of occupation.

The CPA's immediate task was arresting Iraq's chronic insecurity and rebuilding its shattered security institutions. Most agencies had effectively ceased to exist and those that did remain were of little use to the coalition. For example, some police did return to work in April and May 2003, but angry crowds often ran them off the streets, an indication of the size of the task required to improve their reputation.[17] Further, at the same time as the US was trying to create or substantially reform Iraq's security services, it had to deal with insurgency and the presence of militias that commanded significantly more power and authority than state security institutions.

An insurgency began almost immediately President George W. Bush declared the end of combat activities. It was made up of individuals and groups from a variety of backgrounds: Sunni Islamist groups, former Ba'ath and security officials with nothing to lose, and foreign fighters.[18] Although localized and decentralized in its organization, the core aims of the various insurgent groups were to make Iraq ungovernable for the US-led occupation and subsequent Iraqi administration, hence the use of suicide attacks, car bombs, kidnappings, hostage taking and shootings.[19] The attacks often focused on Iraqi 'collaborators' such as members of the new security apparatus, and an estimated 5,050 Iraqi security officers were killed in the period before January 2005.[20]

Iraqi security forces did not have the capability of dealing with the insurgency. Nor were they a match for the numerous Iraqi militias.[21] In some ways, it was the postwar security gap that led to the growth of militias. With no functioning administration or security provision, a range of groups sprang up to fill the gap, operating outside of CPA control and the interim Iraqi government. Some militias were small, paramilitary style brigades formed by local tribes, or in certain geographic areas. Others were more established and organized, and often tied to political parties and religious movements. The peshmerga, for example, are a Kurdish militia beholden to the two main Kurdish political parties, while the Badr Brigade and Mehdi Army are linked, respectively, to the Iranian-backed Supreme Council of the Islamic Revolution in Iraq and the Shia leader, Moqtada al-Sadr. In many parts of the country it was militias and not state institutions that commanded the organized monopoly on violence. Attempts to deal with local militias by the CPA were ineffectual, and there was no political or economic formula that could make demobilization and reintegration attractive to militiamen or their leaders.[22]

The large number of weapons in circulation further complicated the problem.[23] As a result of Saddam's policies, almost every Iraqi was trained in handling weapons and most households owned at least one gun. Prior to the invasion, the regime distributed armaments and munitions to civilian buildings around the country, which the coalition then failed to secure. Although the CPA managed to collect some weapons in localized amnesties, their decommissioning processes barely dented the number of weapons circulating in the country.[24] Widespread insecurity meant that giving up weaponry carried too high a personal risk.

The combination of insurgency and violence meant that throughout the 20 months between the ouster of Saddam Hussein and elections in January 2005, Iraq was one of the most insecure places on earth. Reconstruction and development projects were largely paralyzed because of a lack of security. Many of the Western civilians who came to Iraq in the months following Saddam's fall left because of the increase in kidnapping, which went from zero cases in 2003 to 36 by October 2004.[25] Iraqis suffered even more, with between 19,000 and 37,300 civilians dying violently between the end of the war and the 2005 elections.[26] Although crime figures should be interpreted guardedly because of variance in reporting standards, the Baghdad murder rate of between 70 and 110 murders per 100,000 citizens in the period was over 20 times higher than that other cities in the region, and twice that of cities in the US.[27]

SECURITY SECTOR REFORM, MAY 2003–JANUARY 2005

For analytical clarity, the US attempts to reform Iraq's security sector can be divided into four distinct phases, each marked by adjustments in strategy and implementation.

In the immediate aftermath of the war and the creation of the CPA, the deteriorating security situation meant that an increasingly large proportion of funds – US $3 billion – was appropriated for SSR. However, early decisions during this first phase of SSR (lasting from May to December 2003) only served to worsen the security situation.

As part of its policy of 'de-baathifying' Iraqi institutions, the CPA disbanded the Iraqi Army in May 2003.[28] This proved to be a catastrophic mistake.[29] Some, including Paul Bremer, have suggested good practical and political reasons for the decision; the Army no longer existed in terms of equipment, facilities, command structures and units, for example, and it was necessary to remove suspect Sunni officers from official positions of power. Nevertheless, the decision exacerbated an already volatile situation further, and contributed significantly to fuelling the insurgency.[30]

Steps were admittedly taken to create meaningful new security institutions, and the initial reform strategy expedited training and getting 'boots on the ground'; the goal was to have 145,000 personnel trained and operational by January 2005, with the figure rising to 273,700 by 2006. A CPA decree in August 2003 announced that a new, smaller force would replace the retired Iraqi Army; a new auxiliary force, called the Iraqi Civil Defense Corps (ICDC), was created as an intermediate constabulary force for more immediate deployment; and academies were set up or revived so as to train new police and retrain existing officers. The overwhelming focus was thus on personnel numbers, and there was little consideration given to institutional reconstruction, or to creating linkages between the new agencies.

In line with a trend in the US government towards outsourcing security reform, the original concept was that private contractors would undertake SSR.[31] DynCorp, a company with a history of involvement in US-sponsored police reform, was selected for criminal justice reform; it was to provide up to 500 police, corrections, and judicial advisors, who would work at the 'national, provincial and municipal levels'.[32] Another contracting company, Vinnell, was awarded the contract for army reform. Although these contracts were agreed before hostilities began, there was little detail as to what actual shape reform would take.

The use of private contractors may well have deemphasized the need for coalition officials to help create a national framework for Iraqi security services, but, whatever the case, it rapidly became clear that relying upon contractors was not working.[33] Their initial deployments were delayed which meant training was postponed and, when contractors did arrive, the Army struggled to provide the security required for them to do their work, delaying training further still.[34] When they eventually began work in the fall of 2003, the results disappointed. For example, in December 2003, most of the recruits in a Vinnell-trained battalion of the Iraqi Army deserted before graduation, griping about low pay, lack of equipment and inconsiderate treatment.[35] Major General Paul Eaton, the commander in charge of overseeing military training complained that the contractor-overseen training, 'hasn't gone well. We've had almost one year of no progress.'[36] Although contractors did continue to engage in SSR, the unexpected scale of the task and the hazardous environment meant that the bulk of the work for 'standing up', training, mentoring and deploying the new forces fell on the US military.

The second phase of SSR, lasting from December 2003 to April 2004, saw a further deterioration in the security situation, with few tangible achievements. Work was done at breakneck speed by insufficient numbers of untrained US military officers, but the disorganized nature of reform was also due to the structural failings of the CPA, which was chronically understaffed, often by inexperienced and unqualified individuals.[37] Sequestered in a headquarters in Baghdad, its presence outside the capital was limited, and it control of SSR negligible.[38]

The result was that initiatives proceeded independently of each another, training was not standardized, policies were concocted in isolation – and all these problems were compounded by a rapid staff turnover. A report from the US Army's Center for Lessons Learned noted the absence of standardized procedures: 'The common perception throughout the theater is that a roadmap for the rebuilding of Iraq does not exist. There is not a plan that outlines priorities with short, medium, and long-term objectives. If such a national plan exists with the CPA, it has not been communicated adequately to Coalition forces. Staff at all levels of command have reiterated that there is no clear guidance coming from Baghdad.'[39]

Insecurity worsened with each month, as insurgents targeted coalition soldiers and Iraqi government structures. In April 2004, in a change from the hit-and-run tactics adopted previously, insurgents attempted to take over the cities of Fallujah, Ramadi, Najaf and Nasiriyah, and even parts of Baghdad. Iraqi units ordered to defend their positions or fight alongside the Americans often fled instead.[40] At the same time, the new Iraqi forces complained that they lacked equipment, facilities, and intelligence, prompting the Iraqi minister of the interior to resign in protest.[41]

The US was accused of putting its force protection ahead of the security of Iraqi security personnel by using poorly trained and under-equipped Iraqis to provide the outer security ring at security installations, and by focusing exclusively on offensive operations targeting threats to occupation forces, rather than prioritizing the protection of Iraqi civilians.[42] In truth, coalition tactics did not engender a sense of security. On the contrary, late night house raids and mass detentions alienated the population and probably fuelled the insurgency. Revelations in April and May 2004 of the torture of Iraqi detainees by US troops at Abu Ghraib prison struck a further blow to the coalition's image.[43]

The following months, however, did see a marked increase in US attempts to coordinate SSR in advance of a handover to Iraqi sovereignty. This third phase, which lasted from April 2004 to June 2004, at the end of which Iraq reassumed sovereignty, was marked by a certain managerial consolidation. After a year of relatively disorganized and uncoordinated training programs, the White House signaled an increased readiness to move SSR to the top of its agenda with the promotion and appointment in May 2004 of Lieutenant General David Petraeus as head of the new Office of Security Transition (OST).

The OST offered a means to coordinate training and staffing matters. In late summer 2004 the White House requested, and Congress granted, the redirection of $2 billion in the $18.5 billion supplemental budget from civilian development work to security. Manpower targets were increased, and there was for the first time a real attempt to craft an institutional structure for the security forces, and to create command structures between them. A National Security Council was created as part of the new Iraqi government in order to coordinate the new structures; joint control and command centers were set up to coordinate activities between police, army, and other security agents; and between coalition forces and Iraqi local and national governments. A Directorate of Intelligence was formed to spearhead actions against insurgents. A new policy was adopted of embedding US officers inside Iraqi units in order to provide training advice.[44]

At times, it was hard to reconcile the short-term necessity of providing immediate security with a longer-term vision of what the sector should look like. Security exigencies dictated that a 'quantity over quality' philosophy dominated, thus militating against achieving the long-term vision. With a continuing deterioration in the country's security situation, for example, the CPA opted in June 2004 to increase the Iraqi police force by hiring '30,000 policemen in 30 days',[45] thereby deemphasizing proper vetting, qualification and training – despite the fact that a similar number had been let go only months previously 'for being incompetent or unreliable'.[46]

This move foreshadowed policy under the Iraqi interim government during the next phase, which began in late June as an interim government headed by Prime Minister Iyad Allawi took power, and lasted until the elections of January 2005. The tenor of the interim government's policy and approach was aggressive, as exemplified by its decision to reinstate both the death penalty and emergency laws granting the security institutions powers of arrest and detention.

Changes to the function of the new institutions were also made. The ICDC was renamed the Iraqi National Guard (ING) and its remit was broadened from a defensive organization to one trained, equipped and mandated to carry out offensive anti-insurgent activities. The role of the Iraqi Army was also expanded to encompass internal security tasks. Although still not capable of operating independently without US assistance, the Army and ICDC/ING participated to some degree in the attack on the city of Fallujah (which had been taken over by the insurgency) in November 2004. The Iraqi Army was also commended for performing relatively well with US supervision in securing the elections of 30 January 2005.

Whereas SSR is normally afflicted by a scarcity of monies, in Iraq it was well funded and expensive; in the period from the end of the war up to the January 2005 elections, the costs of the various elements making up the process topped $6 billion.[47] The security situation often caused a discrepancy between what was planned and what could be accomplished, but bureaucratic and accounting regulations also impeded programming, and it was extremely difficult to disburse available funds.

IMPLEMENTATION

Constructing an analytic narrative of security sector reform in Iraq is extremely difficult. As one observer commented, 'governmental structures, political alliances, and surrounding security conditions remain too fluid to mark out a clear picture of evolving civil-military entanglements'.[48]

That said, a detailed look at efforts to train and institutionally reconstruct the Army, the police, and the auxiliary forces reveals four broad themes: first, an over-focus on training and hiring before institution building; second, a gap between policy aspirations to create accountability/oversight and its accomplishment; thirdly, an absence of meaningful Iraqi 'ownership'; and fourthly, a gap between the funds available and their disbursement.

Iraqi Army

The New Iraqi Army was created by a CPA order of August 2003. Discussions on the shape of the institution were conducted with little or no Iraqi input. This trend continued throughout the first year and was symbolized by the head of the CPA, Paul Bremer, taking the role of commander-in-chief until sovereignty was returned to Iraq. [49]

With 27 battalions of 1,000 men each, the Army was significantly smaller than in Saddam's day when it numbered 400,000. Uniquely for the region, recruitment was to be voluntary.. Unlike the prewar army, the ethnic makeup of the military's leadership was to reflect the diversity of the country's population.[50] Ba'ath Party members and Saddam Hussein's security agents were barred from the military, and members of the Army were in turn barred from engaging in domestic political activities.

The original intent for the new Army was minimalist. Its role was to defend Iraq's territory and it was not to be involved in internal operations. The CPA order that created it decreed that 'The New Iraqi Army shall not have, or exercise, domestic law enforcement functions, nor intervene in the domestic political affairs of the nation.'[51] But like many decrees and edicts, it was unclear as to how this could or would be enforced in the face of insecurity and insurgency. The relaxation on the prohibition on Ba'athists is a case in point. Upon his assumption of power, Allawi gradually allowed former Ba'athist officers to join the new security forces in the hope that their experience and knowledge could be leveraged in to counterinsurgency.[52]

Although private contractors continued to perform the bulk of reform-related activities, the unexpected scale of the task, and the hazardous environment, meant that the training and mentoring of the new forces fell primarily on the US military, many of whom were unsuited for the task. Further, the absence of relevant doctrine meant that there were considerable local differences in the quality, aptitude and capability of those conducting the training, and of those trained. Significantly, the 2001 Quadrennial Defense Review Report made no mention of Stability Operations, the US military's term for post-conflict activities.[53]

For some Iraqi cadets, roll call and drilling composed the sum total of their nine-week training, while others were given weapons and even tactical operational training. The best training tended to be conducted by American troops with experience of peace operations in the Balkans. By mid-2004 the US began to redirect its attention to 'train the trainers' programming in order to accelerate training, overcome the bottleneck caused by the limited number of foreign trainers, and reduce attrition by making training more culturally appropriate. Despite the changes, desertions continued and by December 2004 the number of trained soldiers had dropped to fewer than 7,000.

There was a gap between policy aspiration and execution. All forms of oversight and accountability – military codes of conduct, disciplinary procedures, and civilian control of the military – existed on paper as edicts and decrees, but were not implemented in practice. In August 2003, for example, the CPA issued a code of military discipline, but Iraq did not have the civil or military structures required to enforce it. The Army did not even have a legitimate chain of command for imposing discipline.[54]

Iraqi Police

The US strategy towards the police was less radical than the policy of abolition adopted for the military. Although the CPA acknowledged that the existing Iraqi police were 'poorly trained, ineffective, and widely distrusted', the institution was not comprehensively restructured; ranks were kept, and existing police stations reused.[55]

The major difference between the pre- and post-war police was its size. The new police was to have nearly three times the number of personnel it had under Saddam, with a target number of 135,000; this would offset reductions in the Army. Beyond focusing on numbers, however, US planners had no coherent policing model. Indeed, their sole identifiable priority seemed to be the creation of a sizeable police apparatus in the fastest time possible.[56] There was also a political motivation behind the decision to deploy police quickly and in large numbers; uniformed Iraqi police on the streets would be symbolically powerful.

To speed up the training process still further, a dual approach was adopted for 'old' and 'new' police personnel. Saddam-era police were enrolled in three-week Transition Integration Programs (TIP), which were based on courses used in the Balkans; they included instruction on basic human rights, firearms, patrol, and search methods.[57] Three weeks was already an exceedingly short time to reorient officers steeped in an entirely different culture and type of policing, but many TIPs ended up being significantly shorter still. US military commanders, many of whom had no knowledge of policing, had wide latitude in terms of training the police and did not uniformly adopt TIP, being free to establish their own curricula and requirements.[58] Some course lasted just three days.[59]

In contrast, training for the 'new' police took place at a large remote facility in Jordan. The Jordan International Police Training Academy (staffed by retired and active-duty international police trainers) became operational in November 2003, with the aim of rolling out 32,000 fresh graduates a year.[60] That the training had to be based outside Iraq was revealing of the security situation inside the country. It also increased the cost. At $40,000 per recruit, it was an extremely expensive way of training police officers.

The eight-week training program was based on a Balkan curriculum, the applicability of which was often questioned.[61] As one commentator wryly observed, 'the course consists of one week of target practice (at which the average cadet performs execrably), one week of unarmed combat (including with batons, which Iraqi police do not use), and six weeks of absurdly complex instruction – through translation – on human rights'.[62] An instructor at the academy surmised that 'less than 1 percent of the course is relevant'.[63] Despite the short training, achieving the required numbers was impossible. By some estimates, only 30 percent of the police had undergone training by the time sovereignty was handed back to the Iraqi interim administration in June 2004.[64]

The quality of the new police was mixed. Some officers abused their powers by routinely disregarding judicial orders, torturing suspects, disobeying orders from superiors, and failing to report to work, or performing their duties when they did show up.[65] Police were frequently accused of being uninformed about the law, and of privileging local loyalty to family, party or tribe over the institution of which they are members.[66] Public trust in the police was minimal and crime victims were more likely to resort to non-state actors for redress and restitution than to the police.[67]

Minimal attention was paid to reconstructing the institutional system in which individual officers were to work, and lack of coordination mean that many initiatives were meaningless. For example, many police stations were refurbished, but the effect was limited because it was not coordinated with the provision of equipment inside the station. Further, the station concerned was rarely linked to the wider organizational command structure.

As with the Iraqi Army, civilian oversight and internal accountability of the police existed only in the formal sense. An Ombudsman office with investigatory powers over the police was created, but its authority, role, and reach remained unclear. Also, many prosecutors were reluctant to investigate police officers; there was no tradition of doing so, let alone any means for providing redress to victims, or of holding state officials to account.[68]

Civil Defense Corps / National Guard

The Iraqi Civil Defense Corps (ICDC) was founded in September 2003 to serve as 'a bridge between Coalition and Iraqi capability and responsibility'.[69] Its mission was to assist coalition forces in security operations and emergency responses.[70] Its specific duties were set out in the CPA order creating it as including:

> patrolling urban and rural areas; conducting operations to search for and seize illegal weapons and other contraband; providing fixed site, checkpoints, area, route and convoy security; providing crowd and riot control; disaster response services; search and rescue services; providing support to humanitarian missions and disaster recover operations including transportation services;

conducting joint patrols with Coalition Forces; and, participating in other activities designed to build positive relationships between the Iraqi people and Coalition authorities including serving as community liaisons.[71]

Neither the training nor equipment provided to the Corps was adequate for the tasks assigned to it. The necessity of getting its troops onto the streets meant that their two-week training (normally conducted by US units inside Iraq) was perfunctory; many recruits received no training.[72] There are no known assessment indicators of its performance, but the ICDC quickly gained a poor reputation.[73] Coalition spot checks of ICDC operations found low attendance, negligence or refusal of duties, insubordination, lack of accounting for weapons issued, and general indiscipline.[74] When faced with insurgents or overwhelming criminality, local units crumbled or made deals with their adversaries.[75] Relations with the police were strained and there were armed clashes.[76]

In June 2004 one of Prime Minister Allawi's first actions was to broaden the ICDC's mission to include counterinsurgency. The organization, which was re-labelled as the Iraqi National Guard (ING), was to become the primary force for raids on houses suspected of harboring insurgents.

Absence of Ownership

Despite US policy that Iraqis, not Americans, would control Iraq, SSR was further complicated by the absence of Iraqi ownership. When this researcher asked questions regarding Iraqi security institutions at CPA headquarters in Baghdad, for example, the stock answer he received was: 'It's up to Iraqis to decide.' However, this answer was little more than camouflage for the absence of a US strategy, and the capability to implement it. In reality, the CPA gave scant attention to the question of local ownership. Most decisions regarding SSR were made hastily, and without, or even against, Iraqi input.[77]

The reasons for this situation include the fact that robust, quick decision-making was essential in the turmoil of post-Saddam Iraq, and consultation required time that the CPA did not have. Consultation without the certainty of eventual decisions risked widening the already large security gap too. Further, Iraqi officials did not want to assume decision-making control. Taking the initiative was a novel idea for officers who had lived in a police state where individual decision-making was dangerous, and many individuals preferred to receive direct orders.

Attempts at mentorship were often less successful than intended. Due to the shortness of the training programs, the US assumed responsibility for shadowing and mentoring individual recruits. However, although the US placed advisers within ministries, mentorship was uneven and without routine at lower levels. Despite good intentions, many advisers had to act as a locus of control and driver of work, rather than a repository of advice and guidance.[78]

One basic problem was that the US did not know whom to consult, and where to hand authority. It was extremely difficult for the CPA to identify a common voice that could legitimately be called 'Iraqi'. Tribal councils, religious movements and exiled opposition leaders – all claimed to represent Iraq, yet each advocated a different path for the country and role for its security institutions. The coalition was thus unable to start an indigenous political process capable of producing an executive capable of enforcing its decisions, or of generating a representative body to provide oversight of the security sector.

That said, the US rarely attempted meaningful consultation with Iraqis. Careering from issue to issue, the CPA never announced a plan or a set of priorities. Early decrees, such as those abolishing the Army, or 'de-ba'athification', were taken without any substantive consultation.[79] Haphazard implementation of policy compounded the problem. Although streams of decrees were issued, it took months to translate them into an administrative framework, and longer still for Iraqis to know their rights and mechanisms for redress. Additionally, CPA orders and regulations were rarely widely disseminated, limiting awareness of their very existence.[80]

The result was that plans would be designed which bore little relation to Iraqi realities. For example, coalition staff developed a national policing plan from desk-based research, but the plan reflected the US origins of its authors, rather than the world in which Iraqi police worked.[81] It looked exemplary on paper and addressed many structural flaws in the police by formulating managerial relationships between Baghdad and the provinces, establishing quantifiable and qualitative targets to measure progress, and by requiring regular reporting.[82] However, it was a plan designed for a benign environment. As such, it did not work.[83]

Lastly, there was minimal consultation about the purpose and command structures of the new security forces. As a result, the new institutions became as fundamentally unaccountable as their predecessors. The initial US focus on numbers of personnel rather than institutional development meant that the security forces floated in a vacuum of accountability, and were able to forestall the establishment of links between the various agencies. In consequence, security institutions were 'owned' by the leaders of the agency concerned.

CONCLUSION

The SSR experiment in Iraq was poorly sequenced, managed and coordinated. Not only was progress towards the creation of accountable security institutions minimal, but also training failed to equip recruits with the rudimentary skills required to survive the hostile environment confronting them. It was only towards the end of direct US control in June 2004 that the US appeared to have learned lessons and created a coordinating SSR hub. By then it was arguably too little, too late, and the US troops and the interim government under Allawi was confronted by a deepening insurgency, competing security providers, and law and order problems they were unable to cope with.

Lessons Identified

The tasks the US faced in restoring order and bequeathing effective security institutions to the new Iraq were perhaps unique in their scale, yet the basic premise of reconstructing institutions in the aftermath of war – and under direct military occupation – was not. SSR's record in Iraq suggests at least five lessons have yet to be learned.

The first lesson is to come prepared, which is what the US did not do. In the immediate period following victory, the US did not have sufficient troops or civilian experts to provide security, keep public services running, vet institutions, and detain security threats.[84] Their absence was felt particularly strongly in Iraq, where there was no tradition of providing effective public security and services, and a lack of experienced and qualified technocrats.

The second lesson is that the military needs to be adequately trained for the tasks it can expect to confront. In a fluid post-conflict situation, military forces will be the first and perhaps only forces on the ground. However, US troops in Iraq were not trained to keep the peace. With no experience of crowd control, they failed to prevent crime, and demonstrations or volatile gatherings. This experience reaffirmed the need for a rapidly deployable international police capacity, capable of assuming responsibility for maintaining public order, a task for which the military is neither trained nor temperamentally suited to handle.[85]

The third is the need for nuanced vetting of personnel. In Iraq, it was clear that the organs of security needed radical change. There were good moral and strategic reasons for this, including denying Ba'athist supporters access to centers of control. The means by which it was done, however – dissolution by decree – was dangerous and irresponsible. Vetting requires considerable knowledge of the national society, culture, history, people, and institutions. The US military did not have such knowledge, and nor did it attempt to acquire it.

Fourth, SSR needs to pay attention to institution building, and the control of institutions (i.e. civilian oversight) from the outset, not as an afterthought. In Iraq, the first priority for the US was the number of personnel, and only then the creation of a command structure, institutional elements (budget; personnel management), inter-institutional links, and, lastly, oversight. The last three elements were dealt with cursorily, to the potential long-term detriment of the security sector.

Finally, the Iraq experience underscored the need for a central hub to manage a process as complex as the reconstruction of a country's security sector. The appointment of General Petraeus and the creation of the OST reflected a growing awareness of such a need, but it came too late. The establishment of a dedicated hub earlier in the process would have served to coordinate reconstruction, and standardize strategy and implementation policy at local, provincial and national levels. Also, a hub could have proved a useful means for handling the mechanics of transition. In general, such a hub should provide a system for information sharing that can evaluate situational requirements, and plan strategy accordingly while creating confidence in all the relevant institutions. Such a hub must gradually become accessible (in terms of information sharing and decision-making) to the evolving structures of local security governance.

Of course, no matter how prepared and organized the US reform process might have been, creating capable and effective Iraqi security forces was only one part of the program to stabilize Iraq, albeit an important one. The high level of violence in Iraq is political in origin and requires a political solution. Without meaningful political concord, the reconstruction of Iraq's security organizations will remain without solid foundation.

NOTES

1. The US was the major actor in security sector reform in Iraq, but not the only one. The UK, for example, set up security structures in the south of the country.
2. Robert Perito, *Establishing the Rule of Law in Iraq* (Washington DC: US Institute of Peace 2003) pp.3–5; Charles Tripp, *A History of Iraq* (Cambridge: Cambridge University Press 2002); Phebe Marr, *The Modern History of Iraq* (Boulder, CO: Westview 2003).
3. Iraqi exile Kanan Makiya (Samir al-Khalil) wrote that 'published information on the role and purpose of policing agencies does not exist'. Kanan Makiya, *Republic of Fear. The Politics of Modern Iraq* (Berkeley/Los Angeles: Univ. of California Press 1989) p.5.

   For more recent work on Iraq's security sector see Sean Boyne, 'Inside Iraq's security network', *Jane's Intelligence Review* 9/7 (1997) p.300ff.; Amatzia Baram, *Building toward Crisis: Saddam Husayn's Strategy for Survival*, Washington Institute for Near Eastern Policy, Policy Papers 47 (1998); Ibrahim al-Marashi, 'Iraq's Security and Intelligence Network: A Guide and Analysis', *Middle East Review of International Affairs* 6/3 (2002) < http://meria.idc.ac.il/journal/2002/issue3/jv6n3a1.html > (all websites accessed Feb. 2006); Ahmed Hashim, 'Saddam Husayn and civil-military relations in Iraq: The quest for legitimacy and power', *Middle East Journal* 57/1 (2003) pp. 9–41.
4. al-Marashi (note 3).
5. Amatzia Baram, 'Saddam's Power Structure: the Tikritis Before, During and After the War' in Toby Dodge and Steven Simon (eds.), *Iraq at the Crossroads: State and Society in the Shadow of Regime Change*, Adelphi Paper 354 (Oxford: OUP for IISS 2003) pp.93–113.
6. Robert Perito, *The Coalition Provisional Authority's Experience with Public Security in Iraq: Lessons Identified* (Washington DC: US Institute of Peace 2005) pp.3–4.
7. The scale of the looting is evident from the amount of copper stolen from Iraq's electricity network. The world/regional price of copper dropped when looted copper from Iraq's electricity network was sold on the Dubai copper market.
8. John Burns, 'Looting and a Suicide Attack as Chaos Grows in Baghdad', *New York Times* 11 April 2003.
9. James Fallows, 'Blind into Baghdad', *Atlantic Monthly* 293/ 1 (2005) pp.53–74.
10. Anthony Cordesman *et al.*, *Strengthening Iraqi Military and Security Forces* (Washington DC: Center for Strategic and International Studies 2005) p.5. Most independent predictions of post-conflict conditions highlighted the need to secure Iraq's borders. Others stated that 'an occupation force would also have to be large enough initially to discourage neighboring powers, [...] carving out informal areas of interest within Iraq. [...] Coalition troops of some kind may have to be placed directly on the Iranian border to contain Iranian influence.' Conrad Crane and Andrew Terrill, *Reconstructing Iraq: Insights, Challenges, and Missions for Military Forces in a Post-Conflict Scenario* (Carlisle, PA: Strategic Studies Institute 2003) p.33. Compare Graham Day and Christopher Freeman, 'Policekeeping is the Key: Rebuilding the Internal Security Architecture of Postwar Iraq', *International Affairs* 79/2 (2003) pp.299–313; *George Packer, The Assasins' Gate: America in Iraq* (Farrar, Strauss and Giroux, New York: 2005), p.113 ff.
11. For an account of postwar planning see Seymour Hersh, *Chain of Command: The Road from 9/11 to Abu Ghraib* (NY: Harper Perennial 2005).
12. *Future of Iraq Project*, pp.38ff. The US Dept. of State initiated this project in Oct. 2001, bringing together Iraqi émigré scholars and activists to sketch out in over one dozen working group scenarios

for transition in Iraq. Working groups finalized their transition studies around Feb. 2003. United States Department of State, The Future of Iraq Project, Transitional Justice Working Group, Unclassified, Release August 12, 2005, available at http://www.thememoryhole.org/state/future_ of_iraq/future_justice.pdf (last accessed September 7, 2006).

13. George Packer, *The Assassins' Gate: America in Iraq* (NY: Farrar, Strauss & Giroux 2005) p.125.

14. Department of Defense, Contract DABK01-03-R-0012 with Vinnell Corporation, New Iraqi Army Training, June 8, 2003, p.10 (Personnel Screening, which states: "Absolute disqualification, any of the following: Former Regime Security Affiliation (Republican Guard and worse – all SSO [Special Security Organization] and Ba'ath Party security and militia organizations, military and civilian intelligence apparatus)", available at: http://www.publicintegrity.org/docs/wow/Vinnell.pdf (last accessed September 7, 2006) and author's interview with former Office of Reconstruction and Humanitarian Assistance (ORHA) official, Washington DC, Nov. 2004. The former ORHA official said that planning was predicated on the belief that the Kurdish peshmerga (militia) 'would have to demobilize and integrate with the national army'. After 13 years of self-rule and the historic role of the peshmerga, which Kurds viewed as their only protection from a rapacious regime in Baghdad, this policy prescription seemed widely unrealistic.

15. Vernon Loeb and Peter Slevin, 'Plan to Secure Postwar Iraq Faulted: Pentagon Ignored Lessons from Decade of Peacekeeping, Critics Say', *Washington Post*, 19 May 2003.

16. Larry Diamond *Squandered Victory: The American Occupation and the Bungled Effort to Bring Democracy to Iraq* (NY: Henry Holt 2005) pp.30–2.

17. Anthony Cordesman, 'The Current Military Situation in Iraq', Washington DC: Center for Strategic and International Studies, 14 Nov. 2003.

18. Ahmed Hashim, 'The Insurgency in Iraq', *Small Wars and Insurgencies* 14/ 3 (2003) pp. 1–22; Zaki Chehab *Iraq Ablaze: Inside the Insurgency* (London: I.B. Tauris 2005); Lionel Beehner, 'IRAQ: Insurgency Goals', 20 May 2005, available at < www.cfr.org > .

19. International Crisis Group, *In their Own Words: Reading the Iraq Insurgency*, Middle East Report No.50 (2006) pp.15–24.

20. Brookings Institution, *Iraq Index* (18 Feb. 2005) p.5 < www.brookings.edu/fp/saban/iraq/index 20050218.pdf> and <www.brookings.edu/fp/saban/iraq/index20050119.pdf>.

21. Larry Diamond, 'What Went Wrong in Iraq', *Foreign Affairs* 83/5 (Sept./Oct. 2004) pp.219–27 <www.foreignaffairs.org/20040901faessay83505/larry-diamond/what-went-wrong-in-irar.html>.

22. Coalition Provisional Authority (CPA), 'Regulation of Armed Forces and Militias within Iraq', *Order Number 91*, 7 June 2004.

23. Small Arms Survey, *Small Arms Survey 2004: Rights at Risk* (Oxford: OUP 2004). <www.smallarmssurvey.org/publications/yb_2004.htm>.

24. CPA, *Order 3*, 23 May 2003; CPA, *Memorandum 5*, 22 Aug. 2003).

25. Adriana Lins de Albuquerque and Michael O'Hanlon, Op-Chart, *New York Times*, 25 Nov. 2004 <www.nytimes.com/imagepages/2004/11/25/opinion/20041126_opart.html > .

26. Brookings Institution, *Iraq Index* (18 Feb. 2006) p.5.

27. Brookings Institute, *Iraq Index* (7 Feb. 2006) p.12 <www.brookings.edu/fp/saban/iraq/index 20050119.pdf>.

28. Packer (note 13) pp.190–2.

29. David Rieff, 'Who Botched the Occupation?', *New York Times Magazine* 2 Nov. 2003.

30. Walter Slocombe, who was in charge of the Iraqi military for the CPA, repeatedly asserted that 'The entire Iraqi army vaporized. They simply all went home as the fighting went forward. And that meant that a lot of the initial things we would have to do, both good and bad, didn't have to be done because there was no army to deal with.' See 'Interview Walter Slocombe', *PBS Frontline*, 17 Aug. 2004 <www.pbs.org/wgbh/pages/frontline/shows/pentagon/interviews/slocombe.html > . Compare Walter Slocombe,'Iraq's Special Challenge: Security Sector Reform "Under Fire"' in Alan Bryden and Heiner Hänggi (eds.), *Reform and Reconstruction of the Security Sector* (Munster: Lit Verlag 2004) pp.1–26.

31. For a discussion on the trend towards outsourcing of security reform see Francesco Mancini, *In Good Company? The Private Sector and Security Sector Reform* (London: Demos 2005).

32. US Dept. of State, Contract with DynCorp, Section C-Description/Specifications/Work Statement, C2-General Program Description and Overview, S-LMAQM-C-03-0028 (2003) p.6.

33. E. Schmitt, 'Effort to Train New Iraqi Army is Facing Delays', *New York Times*, 20 Sept. 2004.

34. Seth Jones, Jeremy Wilson, Andrew Rathmell and K. Riley, *Establishing Law and Order After Conflict* (Pittsburgh: RAND 2005) p.136.

35. A.E. Cha, 'Iraqi Army Recruits Abandon Battalion, More than Half Quit Days Before Mission', *Washington Post*, 13 Dec. 2003.
36. 'US General: Iraq Police Training a Flop', Associated Press, 10 June 2004 <http://agonist.org/20060303/u_s_general_iraq_police_training_a_flop > .
37. Conrad C. Crane and W. Andrew Terrill, *Reconstructing Iraq: Insights, Challenges, and Missions for Military Forces in a Post-Conflict Scenario* (Carlisle, PA: Strategic Studies Institute, US Army War College, 1 Feb. 2003) p.15.
38. The fact that it was originally unclear whether the CPA was a branch of the US government diminished its say over military affairs, which included training the ICDC. The military-civilian rift came to a head over the question of who should control the billions of dollars in the Wartime Supplemental, which was eventually given to the Pentagon over rival State Department demands. The State Department sought control, arguing that the bulk of the money was for civilian reconstruction projects. The Pentagon countered that the military would inevitably be involved, and that only the Pentagon had the requisite contracting and delivery machinery for projects of this magnitude.
39. Center for Army Lessons Learned (CALL) Newsletter 04-13 'Operation Iraqi Freedom: CAAT Initial Impressions Report' (2004) p.30. Available at <www.globalsecurity.org/military/library/report/call/call_04-13_toc.htm>.
40. Richard Oppel and James Ganz, 'US Officials Say Iraq's Forces Founder Under Rebel Assaults', *New York Times*, 30 Nov. 2004.
41. 'Iraqi minister resigns over failure of security/police forces', WorldTribune.Com 9 April 2004 <www.worldtribune.com/worldtribune/WTARC/2004/ss_iraq_04_09.html > .
42. Walter Pincus, 'An Intelligence Gap Hinders US in Iraq', *Washington Post*, 24 Dec. 2004.
43. 'The scandal of the treatment of detainees at Aqbu [sic] Ghraib has sapped the moral authority of the coalition, inside Iraq and internationally', UK Foreign & Commonwealth Office, *Confidential: Iraq Memo*, undated, after April 2004 but before June 2004. Published in *The Times*, 23 May 2004 <www.timesonline.co.uk/newspaper/0,,176-1120147,00.html > .
44. James Fallows, 'Why Iraq has no Army', *Atlantic Monthly* 296/ 5 (2005) pp.60–77.
45. Personal interviews, Jordan, Nov. 2004.
46. 'Security a shambles ahead of handover', *The Guardian*, 24 June 2004.
47. There were three principal sources of funding for SSR. The Emergency Wartime Supplemental I of 16 April 2003 US Public Law No. 108-11: 2003 made around $2.5bn available for the Iraq Relief and Reconstruction Fund (IRRF). Of this amount, some $136m was spent on planning and implementing SSR activities as of 30 Sept. 2003. Further funds from Iraqi oil revenue and Iraqi funds seized abroad or found in Iraq, brought the total available for SSR to $542m by that date.
    Supplemental II (US Public Law No. 108-6, 6 Nov. 2003) appropriated $18.65bn for reconstruction, of which $4,561bn was earmarked for SSR. The DoS's Bureau of International Narcotics Control and Law Enforcement (INC&LE), which has a roster of international police experts, received $6m. The DoS proposed to spend a further $800m on police academies, chiefly the new facility in Jordan. In late Sept. 2004 the White House asked Congress to reallocate $3.46bn of the $18.65bn to the security sector, of which $1.8bn would be used directly for security and law enforcement. Following this shift, by Nov. 2004, $5,045bn was in the IRRF for security and law enforcement, and $1,122bn for justice, public safety and civil society.
    Another source of funds consists of Iraqi funds, the bulk of which is in the Development Fund for Iraq, administered until 28 June 2004 by the CPA on behalf of Iraq. The CPA put forward a tentative budget for 2003 in July of that year, and a budget for 2004 in Oct. 2003, which was revised in April 2004. Iraqi funds are used primarily to pay ministerial expenses, including salaries for security personnel.
    The CPA's financial accounting did not allow for the source of funds for SSR to be traced, or link to either the activity or the implementer. See White House, *Third Section 1506 Report: 2003*. Reporting for US appropriated funds improved in the second quarter of 2004. See White House, *Third Section 2207 Report: 2004*. However, no accounting exists for the CPA's use of several billion dollars from Iraqi DFI funds. See Iraq Revenue Watch, 'Audit Finds More Irregularities and Mismanagement of Iraq's Revenues', *Open Society Institute*, Dec. 2004 <www.iraqrevenuewatch.org/reports/120604.pdf>; see also: White House, Office of Management and Budget, *Report to Congress* <www.whitehouse.gov/omb/legislative/index.html>. The CPA disbursed DFI funds through the Program Management Office, initially at a very slow rate. It devised strategies and policies, but was unable to implement projects.
48. Barak Salmoni, 'Iraq's Unready Security Forces: An Interim Assessment', *Middle East Review of International Affairs* 8/3 (2004) p.23.

49. CPA Order 22, 'Creation of a New Iraqi Army', 7 Aug. 2003; CPA Order 23, 'Creation of a Code of Military Discipline for the New Iraqi Army', 7 Aug. 2003.
50. 'The New Iraqi Army' <www.globalsecurity.org/military/world/iraq/nia.htm>
51. CPA, Order 22.
52. B. Schweid, 'US Courting Former Baath Party Members', *Associated Press*, 22 April 2004 (available at <580wdbo.com/common/ap/2004/04/22/D82421UO0.html>); Jon Lee Anderson 'Out on the Street', *New Yorker*, 15 Nov. 2004.
53. Wendela Moore, 'Stability Operations: A Core Warfighting Capability?', US National Defense University, National War College, undated (c2003–2004) <www.ndu.edu/library/n4/n03AMoore Stability.pdf>.
54. Steve Cullen, 'Starting Over – The New Iraqi Code of Military Discipline', Center for Law and Military Operations (CLAMO) Report, The Judge Advocate General's Legal Center and School, undated (post June 2004).
55. White House, *Second Section 1506 Report: 2003* <www.whitehouse.gov/omb/legislative/index.html>.
56. Inspectors General, US Depts. of State and Defense, 'Interagency Assessment of Iraq Police Training', 15 July 2005, p.9 available at <http://oig.state.gov/documents/organization/50309.pdf > .
57. Interviews, Amman, Jordan, Oct. 2004. For details of police reform in the Balkans see Gordon Peake, *Policing the Peace: Police Reform Experiences in Kosovo, Macedonia and South Serbia* (London: Saferworld 2004).
58. Anthony H. Cordesman, Cleaning Up the Mess, The Failures of the CPA and the US Effort in Iraq and What Can Be Done to Salvage Them, Center for Strategic and International Studies, July 7, 2004, http://www.csis.org/media/csis/pubs/iraq_cleaningup.pdf (last accessed September 7, 2006).
59. US General Accounting Office, *Rebuilding Iraq: Resource, Security, Governance, Essential Services and Oversight* (Washington DC 2004 GAO-04-002R) p.57.
60. JIPTA is run by DoS, with a mix of DynCorp-contracted police trainers and active police officers seconded from the UK, Austria, Sweden, Canada and Australia.
61. Women are currently trained inside Iraq, because of a lack of separate facilities.
62. 'Training Iraq's police. What they need is gender sensitivity', *The Economist*, 12 May 2005 available at <www.economist.com/displayStory.cfm?story_id = 3968529 > .
63. Ibid.
64. Salmoni (note 48) p.14.
65. Human Rights Watch, *The New Iraq? Torture and ill-treatment of detainees in Iraqi custody* (NY: Human Rights Watch 2005) available at <http://hrw.org/reports/2005/iraq0105/ >
66. Seymour Hersh 'Torture at Abu Ghraib: American soldiers brutalized Iraqis. How far up does the responsibility go?' *New Yorker*, 10 May 2004.
67. Conversations with Jordanian/Iraqi security company providing personal, static and shipment protection, Amman, Jordan, Oct. 2004, and with Iraqis throughout Jordan Jan.–Feb. 2004. The reasons given were lack of faith in their effectiveness, and the belief that security forces were partisan.
68. *Justice Assessment. Southern Iraq: 2004.*
69. Slocombe (note 30) p.241.
70. The CPA organized two other, separate forces – the Force Protection Service (FPS) and the Border Enforcement Agency (BEA) – to fill functional gaps. The FPS was manpower intensive, but required no training. Absorbing militiamen into the force had an economic, but limited security impact. It also brought corruption, with an alleged 20,000 of FPS's 80,000 officers appearing on pay rolls, but not on duty. The BEA included a customs and immigration service among its 14,600 employees.
71. CPA, *Order 3*, 3 Sept. 2003.
72. US Central Command, Headquarters, 'Iraqi National Guard Graduates Basic Training Class', Press Release, Number 04-07-24, 11 July 2004.
73. Salmoni (note 30) pp.18–19.
74. 'Demise of Iraqi Units Symbolic of US Errors: Rebuilding Hindered by Past Mistakes', *Washington Post*, 25 Sept. 2004 p. A01 <www.washingtonpost.com/wp-dyn/articles/A48707-2004 Sep24.html>.
75. 'In Iraq, allegiance to clan, family, tribe, sect, and region often supersedes loyalty to the state. Last Wednesday, coalition troops arrested six members of the Iraqi Civil Defense Corps suspected of involvement in a deadly bomb attack in Ramadi, in the Sunni triangle. Such incidents fuel suspicions that some in the Iraqi police and ICDC cut deals with the insurgents as insurance against assassination

and to honor tribal ties.' 'With handover looming, Iraqis play catch-up with security', *Christian Science Monitor*, 21 June 2004.
76. Salmoni (note 30) p.22.
77. 'Catastrophic Success: Debate Lingering in Decision to Dissolve the Iraqi Military', *New York Times*, 21 Oct. 2004.
78. Personal interviews, Jordan, Oct. 2004.
79. *Justice Assessment. Southern Iraq: 2004.*
80. Often the Internet was the chosen medium for dissemination, a form of communication that not all Iraqis had access to.
81. Interview, Senior British Police Adviser, Coalition Police Advisory Training Team, Nov. 2004.
82. Author's email correspondence with senior police adviser in Baghdad, Nov. 2004.
83. National Policing Plan template:.

Target	Assessment
Restoring National Security	No. of indicted insurgents Casualties from insurgent attacks No. of attacks Volume of drug trade & smuggling
Reducing Fear of Crime	No. of burglaries & robberies Reports of fear of crime or victimization Detection rate of crime
Building an Efficient and Effective Police Service	Training numbers Knowledge of techniques Levels of equipment Quality of reporting, including statistics
Restoring Professionalism, Confidence in Policing,	No. of accusations against police service of Corruption Abuse Public confidence indicators Feeling of bias No. of outreach activities, e.g. to schools

84. Seth Jones *et al.* (note 34) p.1.
85. Perito argues in favor of a US constabulary that could police the immediate aftermath of conflict. Robert Perito, *Where is the Lone Ranger When We Need Him?* (Washington DC: USIP 2004).

Missed Opportunities: The United Nations, Police Service and Defence Force Development in Timor-Leste, 1999–2004

LUDOVIC HOOD[1]

As of July 2006, there were 19 United Nations (UN) peacekeeping operations deployed around the world and of the 73,000 uniformed personnel, approximately 7,300 were UN police officers, usually known as CIVPOLs (Civilian Police). In addition to exercising executive policing authority in Kosovo and Timor-Leste, CIVPOLs have been increasingly called upon to conduct police reform programmes in peace operations.[2] Similarly, many UN peacekeepers are now involved in reforming military forces and/or assisting in the transition of former rebel armies and factions into national defence forces. In cases where UN peacekeeping operations have been mandated to act as transitional administrations (e.g. in Timor-Leste and in Kosovo), UN civil servants have assumed responsibility for the overall development of the security sector, while reform activities have been planned and overseen by the Department of Peacekeeping Operations (DPKO) within the UN Secretariat in New York. For such reasons, the UN is among the most significant global actors undertaking security sector reform.[3]

This article assesses the role of the United Nations Transitional Administration in East Timor (UNTAET)[4] and the United Nations Mission of Support in East Timor (UNMISET)[5] in the establishment and development of the national police service, *Polícia Nacional de Timor-Leste* (PNTL), and the defence force, *Forças de Defesa de Timor-Leste* (F-FDTL). Additionally, it examines UNTAET's role in developing civilian oversight mechanisms and institutions.

The UN's involvement in Timor-Leste is frequently touted as one of the organisation's great success stories: hundreds of thousands of refugees and internally displaced persons were resettled, a rudimentary civil administration was built from scratch, free and fair elections were held, and an independent nation emerged from the ashes after centuries of Portuguese colonial rule, 24 years of brutal Indonesian military occupation, and the devastating violence of 1999.[6] Regrettably, the history of police and defence force development in Timor-Leste is also a story of slipshod UN planning and management, squandered opportunities, and unimaginative UN leadership in Timor-Leste and at UN headquarters in New York. Police development was the remit of an ill-prepared CIVPOL contingent, which was devoid of capacity building, managerial, or institutional development expertise. UNTAET did not engage Timor-Leste's political leaders in the PNTL's establishment. Instead it created a police force lacking strategic vision, coherent identity and institutional loyalty. UNMISET failed egregiously in consolidating the nascent police service, responding to growing international calls for an institutional development approach with interventions that arguably did more harm than good.

In terms of defence force development, the UN was all but negligent: despite acting as the sovereign government, it demurred from playing a formal role in the establishment of a national defence force, and failed outright to establish a modicum of civilian oversight. For almost a year, the UN refused to make any decisions on national defence policy or on the future of FALINTIL (the *Forças Armadas de Liberatação National de Timor-Leste*, or Armed Forces for the National Liberation of Timor-Leste), the venerated guerrilla army of resistance, even though the Security Council 'empowered [UNTAET] to exercise all... executive authority' and mandated the mission to 'establish an effective administration'.[7] Once the size of the defence force was agreed, the UN absconded, handing responsibility to a group of bilateral donors. Hence, the *de jure* government of Timor-Leste divested itself of responsibility for the fledgling state's armed forces, setting a woeful precedent for the development of a national military accountable to civilian oversight.

THE UN AND TIMOR-LESTE

In May 2002, after 24 years of brutal occupation by Indonesia, during which up to 200,000 Timorese were killed, and two and a half years of UN transitional administration, Timor-Leste gained independence.[8] The path to independence had formally begun three years earlier, when the UN brokered an autonomy deal for Timor-Leste with Indonesia and Portugal, to be determined by a 'popular consultation'. Despite considerable intimidation and deadly violence on the part of the Indonesian military and their proxy militias, on 30 August 1999, 78.5 per cent of eligible East Timor voters choose independence.[9] The announcement of the results unleashed a bout of destruction and violence by pro-autonomy militia and elements of the Indonesian armed forces.[10] During the violence, FALINTIL, the armed wing of the resistance movement, remained in cantonment in five locations across the territory on the orders of its commander, Xanana Gusmao.[11] International outrage led to the deployment of an Australian-led, UN-authorised multinational force arrived to restore order and security

On 25 October 1999 the UN Security Council approved the formation of UNTAET, a large transitional administration and peacekeeping operation. Executive, legislative and judicial authority was vested in UNTAET's Brazilian chief, Sergio Vieira de Mello, as head of the peacekeeping mission (known as the Special Representative of the [UN] Secretary-General, or SRSG) and Transitional Administrator. Responding to complaints from East Timorese leaders that they were being excluded from the nation-building exercise, De Mello and his aides appointed a Cabinet of the Transitional Government in East Timor in July 2000, comprising five Timorese and five international 'ministers'. Additionally, an advisory, 33-member National Council was appointed by the Transitional Administrator in the same month.[12]

Elections to a constituent assembly of 88 representatives were held in August 2001. This assembly – which became the National Parliament on independence – debated and prepared a constitution, which was promulgated in March 2002. In the wake of the Constituent Assembly elections, the Transitional Administrator appointed an all-Timorese cabinet, known as the Second Transitional Government, which was headed by the chief of the dominant FRETILIN[13] Party, Mari Alkatiri. While the Transitional Administrator retained ultimate executive authority until independence in May 2002, these Cabinet members took full control of their respective ministries in September 2001. The important exception to this was the fledgling PNTL, control of which remained with UNTAET officials until independence;[14] the East Timorese Minister of the Interior did not assume any responsibility for the PNTL until such time. The Secretary of State for Defence (with responsibility for the military) was not appointed until more than six months after the formation of the Second Transitional Government.

Presidential elections took place in April 2002, with Xanana Gusmao winning 83 per cent of the vote. Five weeks later, Timor-Leste became a sovereign nation. Nevertheless, the post-independence UN peacekeeping operation – the United Nations Mission of Support in East Timor (UNMISET I and II[15]) – retained executive authority over all police functions and operations. Executive authority was only finally turned over to the Timor-Leste government two years later in May 2004.

New Security Services

Prior to the formal establishment of the East Timorese police service and defence force under the auspices of UNTAET in 2001, the country had never possessed an indigenous security structure capable of providing external defence or maintaining internal law and order, despite the fact that thousands of East Timorese had worked for the Indonesian security apparatuses.[16] The events of September 1999 resulted in the departure from East Timor of thousands of the Indonesians that had comprised the bulk of the territory's senior and mid-level administrators. This exodus, combined with the complete collapse of the civil administration, meant that UNTAET faced the enormous challenge of acting as an interim government while simultaneously being responsible for building a Timorese government from scratch.[17] This nation-building challenge extended to the formation of a national police service and defence force.

UN DPKO's Role in Police Development

A critical component of UNTAET's nation-building responsibilities was the establishment of an indigenous police service. CIVPOL officers began recruiting East Timorese for the PNTL[18] on a regional basis in early 2000; this included signing up over 350 East Timorese former officers who had served in the Indonesian police service (POLRI) prior to UNTAET's formation. In March 2000 new recruits began a basic three-month training at the rehabilitated police academy in Dili, while experienced officers were enrolled in a four-week intensive transitional training course.[19] Upon the completion of training at the police academy, all PNTL cadets underwent six months of field training in which they were supposed to receive on-the-job training from CIVPOLs in the district or sub-district police station to which they were assigned. By the time of Timor-Leste's independence, over 1,700 PNTL officers had passed through the police academy. This figure reached approximately 3,000 by the end of the first phase of UNMISET in May 2004.

It was a costly operation – the personnel costs associated with CIVPOL's presence in Timor-Leste during the UNTAET and UNMISET I periods (November 1999 to May 2004) amounted to US$ 173 million. This figure did not, however, include the costs of vehicles, supplies, equipment required for operational activities, communications, administrative support costs and so forth, all of which were amalgamated into the missions' overall administrative costs.[20]

During this period (January 1999 to May 2004), CIVPOL maintained executive authority throughout East Timor. All CIVPOL and PNTL personnel reported to the CIVPOL commissioner, who in turn answered to the deputy SRSG (during UNTAET) or the SRSG (during UNMISET I). During UNMISET I a step-by-step handover of district and departmental operational authority from CIVPOL to PNTL was initiated, although the CIVPOL commissioner retained the right to assume command authority in the event of a crisis.[21]

UNMISET I also comprised 100 civilian advisers to assist various government ministries and the justice sector with service delivery and capacity development. However, none of these advisers were tasked with assisting the government to establish civilian control over the PNTL, or with the institutional and capacity development of the PNTL. Similarly, the 58 civilian advisers assigned to advise government ministries under UNMISET II were not involved in PNTL development. Under UNMISET II, none of the approximately 150 CIVPOL advisors still serving in Timor-Leste had either development experience or were capacity building experts, despite being tasked to 'support the development of law enforcement'.[22]

Mounting concern in mid-2002 led to the organisation of a Joint Assessment Mission (JAM) to examine ways in which police development could be improved and accelerated. The JAM, which included representatives of key donor countries such as Australia, the UK and the US took place in November 2002.[23] The JAM report highlighted critical deficiencies in the PNTL's 'management and administrative support areas such as human resources management and finance', as well as 'planning and policy development,' and called for the urgent formation of an 'institutional strengthening working group' to guide PNTL capacity-building initiatives and programmes. Aspects of the JAM and its findings will be discussed below.[24] Almost half a year later, UNMISET formed a committee in nominal partnership with the government of Timor-Leste and with support from Australia, the UK and UNDP. However, the committee was largely ineffective (as will be discussed below), and was effectively disbanded by the Minister of the Interior after less than six months.

Additionally, UNMISET, with support from the Government of Japan and UNDP, organized two large PNTL institutional capacity-building workshops in 2003. However, these large conferences were of dubious utility in the development of the PNTL.

Other Actors

The UN assumed responsibility for police development for much of the four and a half years of UNTAET and UNMISET I, with other development partners playing a minimal role. During UNMISET I, major donors such as Australia and the UK made it clear that they expected UNMISET and its CIVPOL component to undertake meaningful police-capacity development, but these expectations were never met. In 2003, for example, concerns about the lack of progress prompted Australia and the UK to plan for a major, multi-year programme of support; this began in mid-2004. The highly capable World Bank office in Dili, which played a major role in advising the East Timorese Ministry of Planning and Finance, also became involved in police development issues in the context of budgeting and planning for the Ministry of the Interior. Donor governments and development agencies contributed varying degrees of specialised training and equipment from 2000 onwards, as did international non-governmental organisations (NGOs), such as the US-based National Democratic Institute for International Affairs (NDI).

UN DPKO's Role in Defence Force Development

With astonishing lack of specificity, UN Security Council Resolution 1272 and the 4 October 1999 report of the Secretary-General did not provide guidance to UNTAET on either the disarmament, demobilisation and reintegration (DDR) of FALINTIL, or the possible formation of an East Timorese defence force. Many UN headquarters and UNTAET officials wrongly believed that the UN Charter precluded UN peace operations from actively assisting 'armed groups'. As a result, the UN did not address the issue of disarming and demobilizing the FALINTIL until mid-2000, at which point their inland cantonment in Aileu had deteriorated appreciably, causing the departure of large numbers of armed guerrillas and growing tensions with East Timorese leaders. An independent study on national defence issues took place in mid-2000,[25] and one of the three options developed by the task force was adopted by UNTAET, with donor acquiescence, in November 2000.

Thereafter, UNTAET, and subsequently UNMISET, played a negligible role in the development of the national defence force (the F-FDTL), and in the disarmament, demobilisation and reintegration of FALINTIL.[26] The quasi-independent Office for Defence Force Development (ODFD) – comprising military and civilian defence advisers seconded by their respective governments – was responsible for guiding F-FDTL development. The ODFD provided planning and management assistance to the F-FDTL high command, as well as serving as a coordinator for specialised bilateral military training.[27] Whereas CIVPOL was largely responsible for selecting recruits to the police service, the UN permitted Gusmao and his allies in the FALINTIL high command to decide upon the selection of recruits to the military. The UN made no effort to develop civilian control of the F-FDTL, thereby impeding the prospects of democratic control of armed forces in the fledgling state.

DPKO'S DOCTRINE, STRATEGIES AND APPROACHES IN TIMOR-LESTE

Simply and starkly put, the UN peace operations in Timor-Leste did *not* use or develop any doctrines or strategies in their creation of new police and defence institutions. Virtually all UN field activities were ad hoc; they were conducted without thorough planning or systematic analysis, and no effort was made to acquire the lessons learned in Kosovo, the UN's other transitional authority field operation. Indeed, the lessons learned from UNTAET were essentially ignored by UNMISET. Similarly, lessons learned from UNMISET I were overlooked by UNMISET II.

With nation-building its foremost challenge, UNTAET was primarily concerned with building a police service from scratch, that is, training and deploying as many police as possible in the shortest period of time, ignoring the necessity to build a functional institution and organization. This task was given to an unqualified CIVPOL contingent, which did not adopt a holistic or strategic approach towards building the police, let alone situate it within the wider SSR context. UNTAET's leadership compounded the problem by failing to involve East Timorese political leaders in the PNTL's establishment and early development. Furthermore, no attempt was made to develop democratic civilian oversight of the PNTL.[28]

With regards to defence force development, the UN's institutional refusal to involve itself with 'armed groups' precluded UNTAET from playing any role. As a result, the F-FDTL was established in an uneasy vacuum and without the involvement of the de facto government. Consequently, there was no democratic civilian oversight of the defence force on independence.

UNMISET had an opportunity to rectify UNTAET's failures but did not do so. Instead of formulating and implementing a long-term vision and strategic plan for developing the PNTL, UNMISET's leadership refused to take responsibility for the issue, and its makeshift attempts at capacity building may have done more harm than good. While some CIVPOL officers made an impact on individual PNTL officers by teaching or mentoring through example, UNMISET failed in the task assigned to it by the Security Council of 'assist[ing] in the development of a new law enforcement agency in East Timor'.[29] UNMISET played no systematic role in the development of the F-FDTL, abandoning SSR to informal contacts between individual UN military and F-FDTL officers.

As reports from the Geneva Centre for the Democratic Control of Armed Forces (DCAF)[30] and the Conflict, Security and Development Group of King's College London[31] have shown, UNTAET and UNMISET did not possess an SSR policy or strategy. Further, UNTAET failed to develop effective civilian oversight institutions or mechanisms for either the police or the defence forces. The analysis below is primarily concerned with this shortcoming.

PNTL Recruitment and Training Under UNTAET

In the aftermath of the devastation of 1999, UN CIVPOL's deployment was slow: only 400 officers had arrived in Timor-Leste by the end of January 2000, and by July of that year, nine months after the establishment of UNTAET, the figure was still only 1,270 out of a target 1,640.[32] None of these officers, however, were recruited to be trainers, or were experts in institutional capacity building or organisational development. It was not until mid-2000 that the first CIVPOL officers were even assigned to work in police development. Throughout the UNTAET and UNMISET periods, ad hoc efforts were made locally to place suitably qualified CIVPOL officers at the police academy in Dili, though such initiatives were sporadic at best.[33]

The lack of qualified trainers and institutional development experts compounded the enormous challenges faced by CIVPOL in early 2000 as it started to create an indigenous police service.[34] The overriding objective was to recruit and train a large number of PNTL officers (approximately 2,800) in little more than two and a half years. The combination of tight scheduling and the CIVPOL contingent's lack of expertise meant that there were critical shortcomings in the selection of PNTL cadets, and in their basic and field training.

In terms of police recruitment, the UN did not adequately consult Timor-Leste society, relied excessively on former employees of the Indonesian police forces in East Timor, and used Western procedures for determining candidates' suitability. A select group of Timorese leaders were the only constituency with which the UN consulted on the formation of the PNTL, despite CIVPOL's stated objective of undertaking recruitment in an impartial and apolitical fashion. Over 350 former Timorese officers in the Indonesian police service were recruited into the PNTL by CIVPOL and given only four weeks transitional training instead of the barely adequate three-months training which other cadets underwent, even though in most cases their policing skills were of dubious value given that the vast majority were kept in low-ranking positions in the Indonesian police. The decision to recruit these former officers continues to be a political issue in East Timorese society, particularly since several hold senior positions in the force.[35] Even though the UN's privileged interlocutors approved the selection of these officers, there is a strong argument to be made that the UN should have thought twice about recruiting former members of the previous repressive regime's security apparatus.

Finally, CIVPOL relied on culturally Western interviewing techniques and questionnaires, which made many candidates ill at ease.[36] It should also be noted that the selection system was heavily biased towards those who spoke some English – the value of which is highly dubious in that less than one per cent of the total population has any command of the English language.

The training of the PNTL cadets comprised three months of training at the police academy in Dili and six months of field training. However, not only is three months of basic training an extremely short time for producing an adequately prepared officer, but also this brevity was compounded by the need for all the instruction to be translated, which essentially halved the amount of actual instruction provided. Further, the field-training programme was uneven: there was no coherent, structured strategy, no comprehensive pedagogy, and no uniform, measurable methods of testing the skills learned by the Timorese police, let alone cogent agreement on what those professional skills were in any substantive sense.[37]

The programme wholly depended on the quality and motivation of the CIVPOLs stationed in the PNTL cadet's home district, which, naturally, varied dramatically. While there is no doubt that a relatively small number of dedicated and experienced CIVPOLs had a meaningful impact on the development of many PNTL cadets, the field training program did not enhance the policing skills of PNTL officers overall.

PNTL INSTITUTIONAL DEVELOPMENT UNDER UNTAET

Perhaps even more critical than the shortcomings in training and recruitment was the UN's failure to focus on building the PNTL's institutional capacity. As noted by the Joint Assessment Mission (JAM) of November 2002, the PNTL's most significant weakness lies in the absence of institutional development. CIVPOL's emphasis on recruitment and training in the UNTAET period came at the expense of developing a viable institution with adequate management systems and planning capabilities. The JAM report stated in early 2003, 'there has been little attention paid to strengthening the key management and administrative support areas such as human resources management and finance. Equally, there is little or no planning and policy development capacity within the [PNTL].'[38] In its conclusion, the JAM report quoted an extract from the King's College London assessment of UNTAET:

> The failure [of institutional development] was a direct result of inadequate strategic planning and institution-building know-how at the UN Secretariat and mission level. CIVPOL was left to its own devices to set up an administrative and budgetary framework for the [PNTL]. Lacking the necessary expertise in institution building, strategic planning and budget development (in democratic countries these activities are usually performed by civilian administrators), CIVPOL has produced an institution that is unsustainable and weak... UNTAET would have benefited from an early independent study on police operations. In addition to technical police

expertise, when the mandate includes police development responsibilities, CIVPOL requires civilian experts with project management, administrative, donor mobilisation, human rights and institution-building skills.[39]

As the following sections detail, the UN's failure to develop the PNTL as a meaningful and sustainable institution was primarily the result of three main factors: inadequate planning and deficient mission design; unimaginative and weak leadership; and negligible Timorese ownership of the process.

Inadequate Planning and Deficient Mission Design

The development of the PNTL was plagued by inadequate planning and deficient mission design arising from, among other factors, the dearth of institution-building and organisational development expertise in DPKO, a situation that continues to persist.[40] There was and still is no established personnel or budgetary mechanism within DPKO for a peace operation to conduct discrete organisational development projects, hire project personnel, or hold its personnel accountable for their activities and the results (or lack thereof) they generate. The employment of institutional capacity experts was, and remains, almost non-existent within DPKO, either at the headquarters or field level. The ability of the UN to recruit and select well-qualified CIVPOLs was, and remains, limited, and the selection of police UN commissioners continues to be plagued by political interference to the detriment of quality.

Weak Leadership

CIVPOL's performance was undermined by unimaginative and weak UN leadership across the board, both in Dili and New York, contributing to the UN's failure to produce serious, long-term development programmes for the PNTL. Brief and ill-conceived development plans were produced at various stages but none included a strategic vision for the PNTL's development or, more critically, were project- or programme-based approaches to improving the various elements of the PNTL's administrative and management systems.[41] Such development plans tended to be one-off, short-lived exercises produced for politically expedient reasons. For example, the PNTL development plan circulated at the time of the JAM in November 2002 was not mentioned by CIVPOL when UNMISET's political leadership became involved in PNTL development in early to mid-2003. In another case, a strategy document was lost when a departing CIVPOL officer erased files on a computer's hard drive.[42]

Negligible Timorese Ownership

The development of the Timorese police was beleaguered by the dismal efforts to achieve meaningful East Timorese involvement in – and ownership of – the PNTL's establishment and early growth. Throughout the recruitment process, there was altogether inadequate involvement of the Timorese. The scant dialogue that did take place was essentially confined to ad hoc rubber-stamping by the senior Timorese leadership.[43] The training programme was formulated and implemented without any meaningful collaboration with East Timorese officials, and without reference to the needs of Timorese society, or its values, customs, and traditions. It was, simply put, the imposition of foreign techniques and habits.

Most critical, however, was the UN's failure to involve – or secure the blessing of – East Timorese political leaders, not to mention civil society, in the police's institutional development. Throughout the two and a half years of UNTAET, the police service and its development were left out of the power sharing equation by the UN's senior political leadership. During the first two years of UNTAET, the PNTL was essentially a sub-component of CIVPOL. Indeed, UNTAET did not even promulgate the legislation formally creating the PNTL until August 2001, almost two years after the mission's establishment, and an organic law for the PNTL was not passed in parliament until 2004. Even after the establishment of the Second Transition Government in September 2001, when every nascent Timorese government department was placed under the control of a Timorese minister, the UN continued to hold executive authority and the PNTL reported to the CIVPOL Commissioner and the Deputy SRSG. No East Timorese official had a meaningful say in the PNTL's development until independence on 20 May 2002, when the Minister of the Interior assumed nominal control of the PNTL.[44] Even then, ultimate command and control was retained by the UN and lay with the CIVPOL Commissioner until mid-2004.

This lack of ownership in police development caused problems. No East Timorese officials or civil society representatives played a role in articulating an overriding vision or mission, resulting in a vacuum of purpose and identity for the PNTL, which has led to mounting politicisation of the service since 2003. Such politicisation, combined with the lack of consultation over recruitment and the relatively high proportion of former POLRI officers in the service, contributed to growing mistrust of the PNTL among certain sectors of East Timorese society.[45]

PNTL INSTITUTIONAL DEVELOPMENT UNDER UNMISET

While UNTAET deserves criticism for these shortcomings, UNMISET and its planners in DPKO deserve excoriation for their handling of police development from 2002 to 2004. Despite the benefit of the experiences and lessons learned of 1999–2002 and the blunt words of the JAM, King's College London and other reports, the UN failed to undertake any meaningful institutional development initiatives. Its ham-fisted response to the JAM's recommendations arguably did more to hamper the PNTL's progress rather than cultivate it.[46]

Despite its responsibility to develop the PNTL, CIVPOL's structure did not consider or reflect the realities of capacity building and institutional training. Of an approved complement of 1,250 personnel, only two posts were dedicated to institutional and organisational police service development: a training adviser and an institution and capacity building adviser, who was altogether unqualified for the position.[47] The UNMISET mission included 100 international, civilian advisers to assist and advise key ministries and the justice sector, but not one was assigned to work for or with the PNTL despite the police service's manifest shortcomings.[48] The result was an absence of serious strategic organisational development plans, other than a schedule for handing over day-to-day authority of each district from CIVPOL to PNTL.

The civilian leadership of UNMISET and the UN fared no better. In the aftermath of the JAM's report, the Deputy SRSG's office became involved in PNTL development issues, but had no institution-building expertise and experience among its staff. Furthermore, the UN's civilian leadership made little effort to promote the development of the mechanisms of civilian control and accountability.

Joint Assessment Mission (JAM)

The JAM of November 2003 was the first attempt to address in a systematic manner the PNTL's institutional weaknesses, but the impetus for the JAM originated within the international donor community and UNDP, without the initial concurrence of UNMISET or DPKO. Though the JAM's final report became a much heralded document in 2003–04, the mission itself was undermined by the CIVPOL commissioner, and the failure of DPKO to dispatch a qualified representative from the CPD.[49] Given that these two individuals were the nominal JAM co-team leaders, other mission members were compelled to assume de facto control of the mission's planning, inquiries and deliberations. There was minimal East Timorese involvement; one mid-level PNTL officer served as a full mission member, but there was no attempt to secure meaningful buy-in of, or participation in, the mission by Timor-Leste political leaders. The JAM report's[50] release was further delayed for three months by the Office of the Deputy SRSG in order to debate the wisdom of including an ill-conceived and financially unsustainable and operationally unsound CIVPOL equipment wish list that neither the East Timorese nor the JAM had any role in compiling.[51]

Institution and Capacity Building Committee and Working Group

The JAM report called for the urgent formation of an 'institutional strengthening working group' to guide PNTL capacity-building initiatives, programmes and projects, notably in the 'management and administrative support areas such as human resources management and finance... [and in] planning and policy development'.[52] The report strenuously emphasised the necessity of Timor-Leste government 'buy-in,' noting the critical need for 'ownership rather than imposition'.[53] In response, the Deputy SRSG asked the CIVPOL commissioner to draw up a list of participants to participate in a high-level Institution and Capacity Building (ICB) Committee, and in a striking demonstration of a lack of understanding, the first draft contained approximately ten CIVPOLs and only one East Timorese police officer.[54] A subsequent list prepared by the Office of the Deputy SRSG, with significant input from UNDP, rectified the oversight by including the three relevant East Timorese ministries[55] and representatives of civil society among others.

The process proved to be an outright failure and collapsed within six months. The reasons for this included the setting of politically motivated deadlines to coincide with UNMISET's expected termination in May 2004; the lack of ownership by PNTL and Timor-Leste government officials; micromanagement by UNMISET staff, none of whom possessed institution-building or organisational development knowledge; and the immense pressure put on senior and mid-level PNTL officers who were already trying to cope with an ill-conceived process of change.[56]

In mid-2003, UNMISET and UNDP[57] in nominal partnership with the Timor-Leste government organised two large workshops on institutional development.[58] Despite the participation of several dozen PNTL officers, the workshops were little more than UN public relations exercises, in which ministers and ambassadors gave speeches and all key documentation circulated was in English and Portuguese, languages that most PNTL officers do not understand.[59] Neither workshop produced new PNTL capacity development initiatives, or policy adjustments by the Timor-Leste government.

Broader Context

Throughout UNMISET, donors and the UN spent dozens of millions of dollars on capacity building and institutional development. Almost every ministry, as well as the justice sector, was the recipient of large-scale and carefully planned capacity building and/or institutional development programmes and projects. Most of these projects were multi-year affairs, with detailed work plans, outputs and objectives. The Ministry of Interior and PNTL, however, did not benefit from any such programmes, even though the Ministry's PNTL personnel comprised approximately 27 per cent of the civil servants in Timor-Leste,[60] and consumed 10–15 per cent of the national budget. The primary reason for this was that the UN Security Council specifically tasked UNMISET with PNTL development, leaving bilateral donors, UNDP and other agencies to focus on other areas of public administration.

Role of Other Actors

As in the UNTAET period, donors played a marginal role in PNTL development activities in 2002–2004, engaging only in very modest training programs and equipment provision.[61] By early 2003, key donors such as the UK, Australia, the United States and Portugal had become concerned by the lack of progress in PNTL development.[62] Diplomats made it clear that based on Security Council Resolution 1410 (May 2002) they expected UNMISET to make significant headway on meaningful PNTL development.[63] However, the lack of progress in this regard in 2003 led Australia and the UK to plan for a major programme of support totalling AU$ 40 million over a four and a half year period. The programme, which began in mid-2004, focused on policy development, financial and human resource management, and on police operations, including logistics and communications and training development and delivery. The Australia-UK programme marks the first time that police development in Timor-Leste included a large-scale project with clear objectives, performance benchmarks, work plans and timelines, outputs and detailed activity descriptions.

The World Bank's office in Dili also became substantively involved in the policing sector in the context of its provision of technical assistance to the Timor-Leste Ministry of Planning and Finance. In the process of guiding and monitoring the fledgling government's budget and expenditure, World Bank staff and consultants advised the Ministry of the Interior and the PNTL leadership on planning and budgeting issues. The Timor-Leste government's main planning and monitoring tool, the Transition Support Program (TSP), comprised action matrices which clearly articulated quarterly objectives and milestones for the Ministry of Interior and the PNTL. Embassy officials and UNDP staff working in the sector were appalled to discover in mid-2003 that the UNMISET and CIVPOL officials involved in PNTL development were wholly unaware of the TSP.[64]

DEFENCE DEVELOPMENT

As noted above, the UN played a largely negligible role in the development of the F-FDTL. Qualms about providing assistance to armed groups at UN headquarters and in certain quarters of UNTAET led to a year of inaction vis-à-vis FALINTIL.[65] There was popular dismay in Timor-Leste that the UN could treat the nation's venerated embodiment of armed resistance so shabbily in 1999–2000. An independent study by the Centre for Defence Studies at King's College London in mid-2000 led to UNTAET's acquiescence in permitting the formation of a defence force, the F-FDTL. However, the UN continued to distance itself from the process, even though it was the government of the state for which the military was being developed.

Perhaps the most far-reaching consequence of the UN's refusal to undertake defence force development in Timor-Leste was the dearth of civilian oversight and management of the F-FDTL, a situation that continues to this day. It was irresponsible to tacitly approve the formation of a military force with only the minimal vestige of democratic control, not least in a young nation with no history of controlling its armed forces. This failure by the UN constitutes a serious breach of the most fundamental tenets of democratic governance.

CIVILIAN OVERSIGHT AND MANAGEMENT

The UN did not institutionalise or develop effectual civilian oversight of either the police or defence force in Timor-Leste. As a result, upon independence, only two East Timorese civilians had responsibility for oversight and management of the PNTL and the F-FDTL, the Minister of the Interior and the Secretary of State for Defence, respectively. Even two years later, at the conclusion of UNMISET I, these two Cabinet members had no more than a handful of civilian staff to manage and oversee the two large security services. The National Parliament's Committee B for National Security and Defence was, and continues to be, ill prepared and powerless to monitor effectively the security sector.[66]

The failure to establish effective oversight civilian oversight structures arose from (1) CIVPOL's flawed approach to the PNTL development process, and UNTAET's unwillingness to delegate even a modicum of responsibility for policing matters to East Timorese leaders in 2000–2002, and (2) F-FDTL's ambiguous situation under UNTAET, whereby it had no formal relationship to the *de jure* government, thus preventing the establishment of the relevant government ministry able to manage and oversee the force.

THE UN'S SSR PROGRAMME IN TIMOR-LESTE

By and large, UN operations in Timor-Leste squandered opportunities to build professional security institutions with effective civilian oversight. The UN's misguided approach to PNTL development and UNTAET's unwillingness to assume responsibility for defence force development produced a situation in which the composition and activities of the two security services became highly sensitive and politicised in East Timorese society. Increasingly, both forces are viewed as being loyal to powerful political leaders, rather than to the state or society. The PNTL now stands accused of growing politicisation and human rights violations.[67] There is mounting anger at the inclusion of hundreds of former POLRI officers in the PNTL, particularly among veterans and unemployed urban youth. The F-FDTL, meanwhile, is resentful that the PNTL attracts significantly more government and donor support. Finally, civilian oversight continues to be virtually non-existent, more than six years after the launch of the UN's most significant nation-building exercise.

Other than the goal of recruiting and training 2,800 police cadets in three years, UNTAET and UNMISET did *not* employ any measurement methods to assess progress in the security sector. As noted above, the Australia-UK police capacity-building project which started in mid-2004 was the first large-scale endeavour vis-à-vis PNTL development to include clearly articulated objectives, performance indictors and work plans. Given poor mission design and weak leadership, CIVPOL simply did not possess the institution-building knowledge to formulate and implement capacity-development projects that would methodically build the organisation's management and administrative systems and the capabilities of individual PNTL officers.

The weaknesses of DPKO's planning capabilities, which haunted CIVPOL's performance in Timor-Leste, are well documented. The UN's 2000 Report of the Panel on UN Peacekeeping Operations (known as the Brahimi Report)[68] detailed the many inadequacies of DPKO's mission planning and supporting capabilities, resulting in select reforms such as the expansion of the Civilian Police Division. However, even in late 2004, the Civilian Police Division remained a small, 20-person outfit with a high staff turnover and virtually no capacity development expertise. As a UN official put it in mid-2004, DPKO's core competency seems to be the 'ability to deploy hundreds of low grade personnel'.[69] Indeed, DPKO as a whole continues to lack institution-building knowledge, despite its role in planning for more than a dozen large-scale peace operations which were in essence nation-building exercises.

Leadership

One of the most conspicuous impediments to the UN's effective performance in Timor-Leste's security sector, particularly during the UNMISET period, was the lack of imaginative, proactive and forthright leadership. This was caused partly by the politicised nature of senior appointments. Throughout UNTAET and UNMISET, the appointments of the CIVPOL commissioner and his/her deputies were largely contingent upon the appointees' nationalities, rather than their expertise and experience.[70] Lacklustre or poor performance was rarely censured.[71] DPKO's poor planning notwithstanding, the appointment of capable and dynamic officers to the senior CIVPOL positions might have resulted in superior performance from the contingent as whole, particularly as far as PNTL development was concerned.[72]

UNMISET was plagued by lacklustre leadership, not only within the CIVPOL contingent, but also at the uppermost echelons of the mission itself. The SRSG, a distinguished diplomat, was ill suited to the task at hand, choosing not to rise to the challenge of playing a decisive role in guiding the fledgling government forward in the aftermath of independence. The Deputy SRSG, a long-serving UNDP functionary, was not up to the job.[73] Endowed with ample diplomatic skills, he was, however, bungling in his efforts to oversee the development activities (such as PNTL and justice system development) that the Security Council entrusted to UNMISET. His reliance on unqualified staff compounded the problem.

UN missions are highly centralised and hierarchical and the appointments of SRSGs and DSRSGs can prove critical to their success or failure. Such appointments must be meritocratic, not political. The Secretary-General and member states need to agree on a strategy to reform — and depoliticize — the UN's human resources system so that there is cadre of top lieutenants in the organisation from which the Secretary-General can appoint SRSGs and DSRSGs with the requisite post-conflict experience and forthright personality traits.[74] Member states should desist from pressuring the Secretary-General into hiring their nationals for key positions, instead permitting open and transparent recruitment processes to determine the selection of senior leaders and managers.[75] In this way, egregious shortcomings such as those of UNMISET vis-à-vis PNTL institutional development may be avoided.

CONCLUSION

The development of capable and trustworthy police and defence institutions is one of the most critical areas of any state-building exercise. Timor-Leste represented a great opportunity for the UN to prove its credentials, but the organization was not up to the task. Poor planning by DPKO, CIVPOL's dearth of institution-building expertise, unimaginative and weak leadership both in New York and in Dili, and the failure to secure local leaders' buy-in, all contributed to the UN's meagre performance. As a result, the UN failed to develop a law and order institution with its own institutional prerogatives and loyalty to the state, instead laying the groundwork for a security force that is loyal to political leaders first and foremost. Similarly, the failure to develop civilian oversight of the security sector resulted in a defence force whose loyalties lie with the president, rather than the state.

With member states' support, the UN Secretariat needs to drastically bolster DPKO's capability to plan and support large-scale peacekeeping operations, including building a meaningful peace building expertise in close coordination with other relevant UN departments and agencies. Finally, it is critical that political considerations cease to play the determinant role in the selection of SRSGs, police commissioners and other senior mission personnel: expertise, experience and a proven willingness to implement Security Council mandates in imaginative and vigorous ways must win the day.

EPILOGUE

In May 2006, Timor-Leste's post-independence calm was shattered by the outbreak of violence in Dili and beyond. Lethal clashes between elements of the PNTL and the F-FDTL were followed by widespread rioting and looting in Dili, prompting Australia to form a multinational peacekeeping force to restore order. The PNTL essentially collapsed in the early days of the chaos, confirming some observers' concerns about the police's chronic institutional weaknesses. Similarly, the lethal gun battles between elements of the F-FDTL and the PNTL confirmed suspicions of politicization of the two forces. In August 2006, the UN Security Council established a new peacekeeping mission, the United Nations Integrated Mission in Timor-Leste (UNMIT), the backbone of which will be 1,608 CIVPOL officers. It remains to be seen if the UN will learn from the failings of UNTAET and UNMISET with respect to the development of the PNTL. The fear is that the new CIVPOL will contingent will continue to be devoid of institution-building and capacity-building expertise and that many of the past mistakes will be repeated.

NOTES

1 The author extends his gratitude to Bernice Masterson, Gillian Nevins and in particular Edward Rees for their comments on earlier drafts of this paper. Any errors are those of the author alone. The views expressed in this article are strictly those of the author, and not necessarily those of the US Department of State or the US Government.

2. The country of East Timor became formally known as Timor-Leste on achieving independence on 20 May 2002.

3. The concept of security sector reform (SSR) appears to be little known beyond UN headquarters, Western aid agencies and a handful of think tanks. Despite the international community's considerable involvement in the establishment and development of Timor-Leste's security institutions, an informal poll by the author in 2003–4 found that only a small fraction of those involved were aware of SSR per se, and nobody could define it.

4. UNTAET's mandate derived from Security Council Resolution 1272 of Oct. 1999, and lasted from Oct. 1999 to May 2002 (UNTAET's initial mandate was to 31 Jan. 2001 which the Security Council extended to 19 May 2002).

5. UNMISET's mandate derived from Security Council Resolution 1410 of May 2002. The first phase of UNMISET ended in May 2004, with the second phase concluding in May 2005. UNOTIL, a 'political' mission with a one-year mandate to May 2006, replaced UNMISET.

6. UNTAET's achievements, however, should be understood in the context of other recent post-conflict situations. As Jarat Chopra notes, 'there were conditions for success that are rarely available to peace missions. The belligerent power had completely withdrawn... an effective multinational force could credibly guarantee internal and external security... the local population openly welcomed the UN [and] there was a single interlocutor with which to negotiate – National Council of Timorese Resistance (CNRT) – rather than a myriad of unstable factions.' Jarat Chopra, 'The UN's Kingdom of East Timor', *Survival* 42/3 (Autumn 2000) p. 28.

7. UN Security Council Resolution 1272 (1999), paras. 1 and 2(b).

8. In 1974, as Portugal moved towards democracy, it announced it would grant independence to East Timor. A conflict erupted between pro-Indonesian and pro-independence political parties and in Dec. 1975, Indonesia invaded and occupied East Timor. Following this occupation, an armed wing (FALINTIL) of the leading pro-independence party (FRETILIN) waged guerrilla warfare on the Indonesian forces. After five years of intensive fighting, much of FALINTIL was wiped out in 1979–80. This period also saw enormous suffering on the part of the East Timorese population. Indonesia's heavy-handed occupation continued until the UN-managed popular consultation of Aug. 1999. The United Nations did not recognise Indonesia's annexation of East Timor and continued to consider Portugal as the administering power. The General Assembly passed resolutions between 1976 and 1982 and, while the margin of support was variable, Indonesia was not able to remove East Timor from the UN agenda. The world's attention shifted elsewhere until the infamous Santa Cruz massacre of 1991, the capture of FALINTIL's supreme commander, Xanana Gusmao, by the Indonesian military in 1992, and the awarding of the Nobel Peace Prize to Jose Ramos Horta and Bishop Carlos Belo, two of the leading champions of East Timor's struggle for independence. These events saw renewed and more intense UN interest. This, coupled with political change in Indonesia and Australia, led to a UN-brokered agreements between Indonesia and Portugal in May 1999. See John Taylor, *East Timor: the Price of Freedom* (London: Zed Books 1999).

9. Despite the campaign of intimidation, 98.6 per cent of eligible voters participated in the popular consultation.

10. Ian Martin, *Self-Determination in East Timor* (Boulder, CO: Lynne Rienner 2001) pp.94–101.

11. Gusmao's decision was made in the interests of preventing the Indonesian military from claiming that there was a civil war in the territory.

12. Simon Chesterman, *You, the People: The United Nations, Transitional Administration, and State-building* (Oxford: OUP 2004) pp.138–9.

13. *Frente Revolucionária de Liberatação Nacional de Timor-Leste* (Revolutionary Front for an Independent Timor-Leste).

14. Namely the CIVPOL commissioner and deputy SRSG.

15. Given the significant difference in size and scope of the two phases of UNMISET, the post-UNTAET UN DPKO presence in Timor-Leste is here divided into UNMISET I (May 2002 to May 2004) and UNMISET II (May 2004 to May 2005). A political mission, UNOTIL, succeeded UNMISET with a one-year mandate to May 2006.

16. Several thousand Timorese worked in the junior ranks of POLRI, the Indonesian police during the 24 years of Indonesian occupation. In addition, there were two battalions of East Timorese serving in the Indonesian military (TNI) at various points during the occupation.

17. Security Council Resolution 1272 of Oct. 1999.

18. The PNTL was known for much of the UNTAET period as the ETPS (East Timor Police Service) and was briefly renamed the Timor-Leste Police Service (TLPS) in 2002.

19. Conflict, Security and Development Group (CSDG), *A Review of Peace Operations: the Case for Change* (International Policy Institute, King's College London 2003) paras. 90–91.

20. Information provided by UNMISET DSRSG Atul Khare (Aug. 2004).

21. *Supplemental Arrangement between UNMISET and the Government of the Democratic Republic of Timor-Leste on the Transfer of Policing Responsibilities to the ETPS* (Dili, May 2002).

22. Security Council Resolution 1543 (May 2004), para. 3(ii)

23. The British ambassador participated in the mission, as did officials from the Australian Agency for International Development (AusAid), and a United States ICITAP (International Criminal Investigative Assistance Programme) official. Both UNDP and AusAid funded independent policing experts to participate in the mission.

24. *Report of the Joint Assessment Mission carried out by the Government of Timor-Leste, UNMISET, UNDP and Development Partner Countries for the Timor-Leste Police Service* (Dili, Nov. 2002) pp.8–9.
25. CSDG (note 20).
26. The disarmament, demobilization and reintegration of FALINTIL largely took place through the FALINTIL Reinsertion Assistance Program (FRAP), which was funded largely by the US Agency for International Development (USAID) and the World Bank, and implemented by the International Organization for Migration (IOM). A *Final Evaluation Report* of the FRAP was prepared by John McCarthy under USAID auspices in June 2002.
27. Australia, the USA, UK, Malaysia, Thailand, Portugal and other countries contributed advisers.
28. It should be noted that the first development ideas for the PNTL, which hardly constituted a development plan, were written in 2002 in English and never translated for the benefit of the East Timorese.
29. Security Council Resolution 1410 (May 2002), para. 2(b).
30. Eirin Mobekk, *Law-enforcement: Creating and Maintaining a Police Service in a Post-conflict Society – Problems and Pitfalls* (Geneva: Geneva Centre for the Democratic Control of Armed Forces 2003).
31. CSDG (note 20).
32. Ibid. para. 74.
33. In an interview with the author in Aug. 2004, the PNTL officer in command of the police academy in Dili voiced frustration at the failure of senior CIVPOL officers' to deploy suitably qualified CIVPOLs with training experience at the academy. He said that many unqualified officers (particularly from Portugal) were sent so that they would not have to serve in remote district police stations.
34. CSDG (note 20) paras. 100–101.
35. Edward Rees, *Under Pressure: FALINTIL – Forças de Defesa de Timor-Leste: Three Decades of Defense Force Development in Timor-Leste, 1975–2004* (Geneva Centre for the Democratic Control of Armed Forces 2004) p.53.
36. Mobekk (note 31) pp.8–9.
37. Eirin Mobekk, 'Policing Peace Operations: United Nations Civilian Police in East Timor' (London: King's College 2001) pp.45–9.
38. *Report of the Joint Assessment Mission* (note 25) pp.8–9.
39. CSDG (note 20) para. 101.
40. Former UNMISET and UNTAET senior officials have commented on the poor quality of mission planning by DPKO in late 1999, pointing to the dearth of institution-building expertise in DPKO, the failure to benefit from UNAMET's experiences, and the institutional rivalry between DPKO and the UN's Department of Political Affairs (DPA), which organised the UNAMET mission. See, for example, Ian Martin and Alexander Mayer-Rieckh, 'The United Nations and East Timor: From Self-Determination to State-Building', *International Peacekeeping* 12/1 (Spring 2005) pp.125–45; Chopra (note 7).
41. The 'East Timor Police Service Development Plan' of July 2002, which was presented to the JAM members in November of that year, was a six-page document which discussed the planned handover of districts from CIVPOL to PNTL, the command and control issues pertaining thereto, and three specialised police units. There was no mention of any strategic approach to the PNTL institutional capacity building, or to projects or programmes to build and/or improve the police's management and administrative systems, or policy and planning capabilities.
42. Interview with former Dili-based CIVPOL, now a DPKO Civilian Police Division official, Aug. 2004 (New York).
43. Mobekk (note 31) pp.8–9.
44. Rogerio Lobato, the brother of a resistance era hero killed by the Indonesian military, became Minister of Internal Administration in May 2002, following his involvement in protests by veterans in early and mid-2002. This ministry was later divided into two, and Lobato became Minister of Interior with responsibility for the PNTL and other emergency services. Lobato remains a controversial figure in East Timorese society, with several observers concerned about his tight control of the PNTL. See Rees (note 36).
45. Edward Rees cites UNTAET's failure to adequately consult East Timorese leaders on the PNTL's development as the overriding UN shortcoming in police development. Interview, Dili, Aug. 2004.
46. The reports of Ray Murray (see note 57), senior adviser to the Institution and Capacity Building Committee and the Minister of Interior, allude to the tremendous pressures and distractions imposed

on senior and mid-level PNTL officers by UNMISET's rushed and ill-conceived 'Institution Strengthening Plan of Action'.

47. The individual in question told the author and other members of the JAM in Nov. 2003 that he held the position on account of his friendship with an official in DPKO's Civilian Police Division in New York.

48. These 100 advisors were known as the Civilian Support Group (CSG). UNMISET II had a CSG comprising 58 advisers, none of whom worked with the PNTL.

49. The CIVPOL commissioner spent no time with the mission and its members, and did not appear to want to cooperate with the mission. The UNDP-retained policing consultant did not even have an opportunity to shake hands with him. The CPD representative, in the estimation of the core JAM members, added no value to the inquiries and work of the mission.

50. JAM member Bernice Masterson, a highly experienced AusAid policing consultant, drafted the report with significant input from UNMISET Human Rights Officer John Tyynela and the author. Masterson continues to be heavily involved in PNTL development as part of the 2004–2008 Australia-UK programme of support to the PNTL.

51. The Office of the DSRSG was inexplicably eager to include this equipment wish list (which was one of several such CIVPOL and/or PNTL lists presented to the JAM). JAM members argued that their remit did not include compiling lists of equipment; moreover, they said, it was unwise to throw such wish lists at donors when the police had no strategic vision and minimal capacity to maintain such equipment. Indeed, the very donors which some officials in UNMISET hoped would provide equipment had participated in the mission and believed that the list's inclusion was altogether inappropriate!

52. *Report of the Joint Assessment Mission* (note 25) pp.8–9.

53. Ibid. p. 9.

54. The author was asked to comment on the CIVPOL Commissioner's draft list during a meeting with an Office of the DSRSG staff member in March 2003. The author was critical, and urged that an all-East Timorese committee be formed.

55. Ministry of Interior, Ministry of Planning and Finance, and Ministry of Justice.

56. Ray Murray, *Institutional Strengthening and Capacity Building Advisor to the ICB Committee: Mid-term Monitoring and Review*, July 2003; Ray Murray, *Report to the Minister of the Interior on the Progress of the Current Plan of Action: Polícia Nacional de Timor-Leste*, July 2003; and Ray Murray, *Advisor Report on the Polícia Nacional de Timor-Leste and the Institutional Capacity Building Working Group for the Period 1 June to 31 August 2003*, Sept. 2003.

57. The Government of Japan provided US$90,000 (through UNDP) for these workshops and related activities.

58. The latter workshop took place partly on account of concerns about the performance of the PNTL's riot control police in disturbances in Dili in Dec. 2002 that resulted in two shooting fatalities and several injuries, as well as donors' concerns over the government's plan – with UNMISET blessing – to form a further special, heavily-armed police unit for rural insurgencies.

59. Less than one per cent of East Timorese speak English. Approximately five per cent speak Portuguese. Nevertheless, Portuguese is the working language of the Timor-Leste government. The majority of Timorese speak Tetum and Bahasa Indonesian.

60. As of mid-2004, there were approximately 11,200 civil servants in Timor-Leste, of which approximately 3,050 are PNTL officers.

61. Such donors include Australia, Canada, Japan, Malaysia, New Zealand, Portugal, Singapore, the USA and the UK, as well as the United Nations Development Program (UNDP), the United Nations Children's Fund (UNICEF) and the United Nations Development Fund for Women (UNIFEM).

62. The author engaged in many conversations with numerous embassy officials on this subject throughout 2003.

63. The author was privy to a number of donor meetings with senior UNMISET officials vis-à-vis PNTL development.

64. The author was privy to discussions involving UK and Australian diplomats in 2003 in which shock was expressed at UNMISET officials' ignorance of the TSP process.

65. Several UNTAET officials called for urgent action on the question of FALINTIL's future in 1999–2000, notably John Bevan, the Aileu district administrator.

66. FRETILIN's dominance of both the executive and legislative branches of government prevents the latter from serving as an effective counterweight to the former. Additionally, the National Parliament's members are, for the most part, inexperienced in legislative processes, including oversight.

67. 'Progress report of the Secretary-General on the United Nations Mission of Support in East Timor (for the period from 10 November 2004 to 16 February 2005)', New York 18 Feb. 2005.
68. *Report of the Panel on UN Peacekeeping Operations*, United Nations, Aug. 2000 <www.un.org/ peace/reports/peace_operations> (accessed Nov. 2005).
69. Interview with official, DPKO's Best Practices Unit, Aug. 2004.
70. In interviews with the author in Aug. 2004, three different UNMISET and DPKO officials provided three different explanations for the selection of the head CIVPOL in UNMISET II, all concerning his nationality, the nationality of the other candidates, and/or the nationality of the head of Civilian Police Division at UN HQ. The individual's qualifications and institution-building expertise – or lack thereof – were not a factor. The Australian CIVPOL commissioner in 2003–2004 was the exception to this regrettable rule, though her scope for positive change was handicapped by CIVPOL's dwindling manpower and the Office of the DSRSG's micromanagement of PNTL development.
71. With reference to the UN's inaction regarding the generally recognised lacklustre performance of a CIVPOL commissioner in 2002–3, a senior UNMISET official explained (to the author in an interview in Aug. 2004) that criticism of a senior UN appointee was tantamount to criticism of his/her country, and thus improper. Additionally, observers were stunned to note that the UNMISET CIVPOL institutional and capacity building adviser's contract was renewed in 2003 despite his wholly inadequate performance in 2002–3. See note 50 above.
72. CIVPOL's *operational* capabilities were found to be lacking on 4 Dec. 2002 when Dili was hit by riots during which CIVPOL was unable to stop several hundred students and troublemakers from looting and burning buildings throughout the city for more than seven hours. Scores of off-duty CIVPOLs were not summoned because nobody had their mobile phone numbers. The entire day was marked by indecision by UNMISET senior personnel, with scores of CIVPOLs waiting for hours for orders to deploy in the city.
73. The UN combined the role of UNMISET DSRSG and UNDP Resident Coordinator, a move designed to emphasise sustainable development as a critical focus of UNMISET.
74. See, for example, Ludovic Hood, 'The UN Must Let Talent Rise', *International Herald Tribune*, 13 Aug. 2004.
75. The Outcome Document from the Sept. 2005 world leaders' summit is illustrative of the challenges the UN faces in this regard. The Secretary-General and certain member states (particularly the US) sought to strengthen the Secretary-General's administrative prerogative by reducing the General Assembly's Fifth Committee's de facto micromanagement of the UN Secretariat's operations. However, a coalition of developing states blocked this attempt to strengthen the SG's prerogative in management, hiring, promotions and so forth.

The Difficulties of Donor Coordination: Police and Judicial Reform in Mozambique

ANICIA LALÁ AND LAUDEMIRO FRANCISCO

The United Nations Development Programme (UNDP) is the most prominent of several international actors involved in security sector reform (SSR) in Mozambique. In 1992, following the end of Mozambique's 16-year civil war, it was apparent that the country needed a massive programme of institution-building if peace and economic development were to take hold. Security sector reform was a crucial element of this process. After more than a decade of assistance, Mozambique is the UNDP's longest continuously running SSR programme. For this reason, and because it coincided with the organisation's first attempts to introduce SSR into its development agenda, Mozambique is a particularly important case study from which to draw lessons about devising and implementing SSR programmes.

Wary of involvement in what promised to be highly politicised process, many international donors saw UNDP as a suitable neutral vehicle to advance the cause of SSR in Mozambique. Rather than instigating reform itself, UNDP functioned as a coordinator, 'responsible for the realization of the programme', fronting the reform effort in areas where the government resisted external involvement or outside actors were reluctant to become involved on a bilateral basis.[1] UNDP's multilateral status provided a legitimising platform for propositions that would otherwise have been politically difficult to broach.

Concentrating primarily on the police while looking at similar efforts in the judicial sector, this article traces the UNDP's SSR activities in Mozambique from the organisation's initial involvement during the last stages of the post-civil war demobilization, disarmament, and reintegration (DDR) programme till the beginning of 2005.[2] It explores how UNDP's strategic approach affected the outcome of reforms. It also highlights the crucial role of the country office as it acquired knowledge and experience that exceeded that of UNDP headquarters.

These are crucial aspects that can act either as enablers or disablers of a successful SSR process, especially when UNDP serves as the interface between donors, national government and security institutions.

The article consists of four parts. The first provides the context and rationale for SSR, giving an overview of the police and the judiciary in Mozambique, including the role of UNDP. The second addresses UNDP's doctrine, strategies and approaches to SSR. A third section analysing the reform programmes and initiatives follows this. Finally, the last section evaluates UNDP's programmes and reprises the lessons learned.

An important thread running throughout is the constraints under which Mozambican SSR laboured, from the rationale for initiating the reform to the persistent resistance to change by national institutions. Another key weakness was the failure of the SSR programme to bridge the existing gap between police and judiciary reforms, an omission which ultimately limited the institutional and managerial changes that could be achieved. Some evaluations of UNDP's efforts suggest a general improvement in the sector's performance, pointing to the establishment of strategic plans and ongoing training of personnel. However, more recent reviews of the SSR programmes have called into question the sustainability of the newly reformed institutions and the degree to which reform has been integrated into a coherent whole. This mixed record of success raises difficult questions about what UNDP has learned from almost a decade of experience with SSR in Mozambique.

OVERVIEW OF THE SECURITY CONTEXT IN MOZAMBIQUE

The Security Context Prior to Reform

After Mozambique gained its independence from Portugal on 25 June 1975, the new government dominated by the *Frente de Libertação de Moçambique* (Frelimo) sought to transform the structures of the colonial state into a modern socialist society. At independence, the state justice system catered to the elite urbanised population while a traditional system dealt with the majority of the population. Administration officials mediated conflicts that fell through the cracks. The post-colonial government disbanded this dual system, imposing a socialist, one-party government model. In practice, the state's limited capacity meant that justice continued to be served by formal courts in the urban areas while the communal dwellers experienced the creation of newly instituted politicised structures such as neighbourhood watch groups *(grupos dinamizadores)*, and community courts.[3]

The post-colonial civil war prohibited the establishment of a new security apparatus in Mozambique as former Frelimo fighters were called upon to defend the new state against external and internal foes. The neighbouring apartheid regimes of South Africa and Rhodesia perceived newly independent Mozambique as a threat to regional security and sought to undermine the government through their support of the *Resistência Nacional Moçambicana* (Renamo) rebellion.[4] The civil war reinforced the government's determination to impose a socialist unification of party and state. From the beginning of Mozambique's existence as an independent state the security apparatus was explicitly subordinated to politics.

In the late 1980s Mozambique backed away from Marxist-Leninism and in 1990 adopted a new constitution, which transformed the political system and oversight of the security sector. Compelled by economic necessity to streamline its security forces, the government unilaterally demobilised thousands of soldiers with financial support from Switzerland. By the time peace came to Mozambique in 1992, the war had shattered the state's limited capacity to provide security and justice to its people. The armed forces were devastated; the police were effectively confined to maintaining a presence in the provincial capitals and even then barely had the capacity to perform their duties. The formal justice system, which even in the best of times had never reached the entire territory, was in need of complete restructuring.

The General Peace Agreement was supervised and guaranteed by a United Nations peacekeeping force (UNOMOZ). This initial effort accomplished little with respect to reform of the security sector.[5] Fundamental questions about the role and capability of the new Mozambican military remained unaddressed, including the key issue of civilian control. More problematically, UNOMOZ was considered dangerously out of touch with the rapidly changing political climate. Faced with the downsizing of its military, the Mozambican government relied on the police as its major security force, transferring weaponry and personnel from the military to the police services and defining its police service as a 'paramilitary force'.[6] These actions quickly undermined confidence in the SSR process.

Although UNOMOZ had a civilian police component, its mandate was limited. Its small training and technical assistance programme served mainly highlight the extent of Mozambique's needs. A study by the Spanish *Guardia Civil* described the police as an operational and managerial shambles. It found that the Ministry of the Interior directly interfered with police operations and uncovered many flaws within the organisation. The police performed reactively rather than proactively. The general level of education in the force was low, with the result that officers' knowledge and respect for citizens' rights was limited. Poor equipment hampered the force's capabilities.[7]

The peacekeeping mission accomplished even less with respect to judicial reform. It was recognised that judicial institutions had be overhauled in line with the 1990 Constitution, but there was limited capacity for a nationally directed transformation. In part this was because the government could not secure significant external financing due to its refusal to embrace a restorative justice process, a key international demand in post-conflict peace building.

The Current Police Context

Although the *Defense and Security Act* (17/97)[8] established a basic legal and institutional framework for the military, police, and intelligence services, no similar legislation has been promulgated for the *Polícia da República de Moçambique* (hereafter, 'the police' or 'PRM'). Notwithstanding this legislative vacuum, the government in May 2003 approved basic regulations and a strategic plan for the PRM. Currently the PRM falls under the Ministry of Interior, which in turn is responsible to the parliament's Defense and Public Order Committee. The PRM is composed of several units: the National Police, the Criminal Investigation Police (PIC), the Special and Reserve Forces (Rapid Reaction Police), the immigration and border police, and the previously independent traffic police. In a country of 18 million inhabitants and 800,000 square kilometres of territory, the PRM consists of just 20,000 persons.[9]

In general, the problems highlighted by the *Guardia Civil* report remain. Deep managerial deficiencies at the ministerial and police levels and other institutional weaknesses continue to impede the implementation of the May 2003 strategic plan. Operationally, the PRM has limited human and material capacity to confront the proliferation of organised crime networks related to drug trade and trafficking, money laundering, trafficking of human body parts, smuggling of goods, vehicle theft and bank robberies. The public perceives the PRM to be inefficient and corrupt. It is widely seen as unable to cope with an increase in the rate and violence of crime, especially in and around the capital Maputo. Major problems exist in personnel and financial management and a general absence of clear rules and regulations.

The Current Judicial Context

Several of the problems that hamper the effectiveness of the police are mirrored in Mozambique's judicial system. The existence of overlapping formal and informal judicial systems is partially due to the lack of trained public prosecutors in the Public Prosecution Office (PPC), judges and court clerks, most of whom reside in urban centres. Together with the high costs of legal advice, the formal judicial system is simply not an option for a majority of people. Many rely on informal justice mechanisms comprised of a variety of institutions such as the community courts, traditional authorities, civil society institutions, and the recently established Centre for Arbitration. The ad hoc nature of the judicial environment calls for a harmonisation and coordination between and among these mechanisms so that more Mozambicans can access the formal system.

One main area of particular concern is the criminal justice system, which is marred by a lack of capacity and corruption. Particularly problematic is the interface between the PIC and the PPC. Police investigations consistently fail to meet to prosecutorial requirements and standards.[10] Police procedures also tend to ignore the prosecutor's dominant authority, further undermining a smoothly functioning system by giving rise to bureaucratic infighting. The idea of creating a new judiciary police unit with investigative powers, the *Polícia Judiciária*, has been proposed, but resistance from the police has blocked progress so far.[11]

One of the repercussions of these deficiencies is an overwhelmed penal system.[12] The country's prisons are overcrowded, particularly the prisons managed by the Ministry of Interior.[13] A UNDP study shows that, although the legal limit for pre-trial time incarceration is 150 days, in practice individual cases of pre-trial detention can last as long as two years. Coupled with judicial bottlenecks, approximately 73 per cent of the total prison population is awaiting trial. The imposition of lengthy sentences for minor offences further aggravates the situation.[14] Additionally, the penal infrastructure is in a dilapidated state and the widespread misuse of prison funds underscores a persistent problem of corruption.

UNDP'S REFORMING ROLE

The UNDP's role in Mozambique's SSR programme was largely confined to coordinating the activities of others. Its involvement arose not as a result of its own initiative but because of pressure from international donors. UNDP was more valuable for its politically neutral position within Mozambique than for its expertise in managing security sector reform, a field in which at the time it had little direct experience.

Police Reform Phases

The perception that crime rates had skyrocketed since the end of the civil war, particularly in urban areas, led a group of international donors to form the Police Donor Group (PDG) in 1996. With political direction from the Spanish and Dutch governments, the PDG sought UNDP assistance to start and manage the SSR process.[15] After studying the issue, the PDG, working through the UNDP, presented the government of Mozambique with a proposed police reform agenda.[16] The PDG made an initial commitment of several million dollars of assistance to be managed through UNDP in two three-year project tranches. Eventually a third phase was designed to correct weaknesses in the earlier two phases.

Phase I (1997–2000) had a budget of approximately US $11 million and concentrated on retraining existing officers to begin to transform the PRM into an accountable service in the context of the transition to multi-party democracy.[17] A new police academy (ACIPOL) was to be the linchpin of a modernised police service, as police officers would undergo a four-year course. Candidates for entrance into ACIPOL were to be selected from a public competitive entry exam.[18] At the same time, a police academy Training Centre for rank and file police personnel was constructed to train new recruits. New equipment such as vehicles, motorbikes and computers were acquired.[19] Basic physical infrastructure at provincial police commands buildings were also rehabilitated, as were police headquarters in Maputo. However, little was done with respect to the development of an overall policing strategy or vision. Even though basic police regulation was established, the managerial structures of the organisation were left untouched. This tended to undermine the notion that Phase I was primarily concerned with building the institution of the police.

Phase II (2000–2003) was a continuation of Phase I with a budget of US$ 15.7 million.[20] Although most activities were devoted to training and retraining as ACIPOL welcomed its first class of cadets, more attention was paid to structural issues with the writing of a *Strategic Plan for the Police (PEPRM), 2003–2012.*[21] In addition, the concept of 'model units' was devised with the aim of integrating the 'old' PRM police with the newly trained ACIPOL cadets, whose first class was scheduled to graduate in 2004.

Only with the advent of *Phase III* (2004–2007) has an effort made to tackle the professionalism and management of the PRM head-on. With a budget of US \$7 million, the key theme of the phase is management modernisation. The phase envisages improvements in planning, financial management, procurement, logistics, and human resource management. It is also expected that the PRM will be integrated into a new system of public order and security, with the restructuring of criminal investigations as one key element.[22] What integration means in practice has not been fully defined, and as of January 2005 no actual work had yet taken place.[23]

Judicial Reform

At the same time as the UNDP entered into police reform it launched a parallel judicial and penal reform initiative. The programme had three objectives. Initially, it was meant to strengthen the Centre for Legal and Judicial Training (CFJJ), the national institution designed to train and retrain all judicial personnel. Within three years, however, judicial reform projects were stepped up to address the sector's systemic weaknesses.[24] While judicial training has remained the primary focus of judicial reform, court infrastructure has been rehabilitated and essential equipment provided. The third goal of the UNDP reform project was to assist in developing an integrated strategic plan for the justice sector. This objective was dropped as it was seen to duplicate an existing programme run by the Danish International Development Agency (DANIDA).

UNDP'S SSR DOCTRINE, STRATEGIES AND APPROACHES

It is hardly surprising that UNDP had little strategic vision at the outset of the programme in Mozambique for reforming security sector institutions. The concept of SSR was still in its infancy. What is more remarkable is that by 2002 little knowledge about the five-year-old Mozambique SSR programme existed within UNDP Headquarters. As a result, lessons learned have not been fully incorporated into UNDP's attempts to formulate a SSR corporate practice.[25]

It was not until November 2002 that the Bureau of Crisis Prevention and Recovery (BCPR) first produced a written UNDP corporate approach to security sector reform.[26] Defining SSR as a development programme for crisis and post-conflict countries, the approach emphasised the importance of changing institutional and managerial behaviours rather than concentrating exclusively on the modernisation of legal and administrative procedures.[27] BCPR's strategic approach also presented practical actions grouped around several themes – such as access, due process, effectiveness and efficiency – in order to highlight the interdependencies among the various security and justice institutions. BCPR's formulation of an SSR strategy did not seem to have an effect on the UNDP

Country Office in Mozambique. In fact, the Country Office appears not have been cognisant of the document at all. But as the Country Office's role in Mozambique's reform process was largely limited to being a passive coordinator of other donors' activities, SSR policy documents would have been operationally irrelevant to UNDP's activities as policy formulation was not within its mandate.[28]

REFORM ACTIVITIES AND INITIATIVES

The Police Sector

Although discussions between Mozambique and UNDP began in 1995 when the first Spanish *Guardia Civil* officers arrived in country, it took two years before an SSR programme was signed and work initiated. The delay in implementation was partly attributable to resistance within the Mozambican police. Although some senior police officers recognised the need for reform as a means of investing in their organisation's future, others feared that reform would mean a loss of jobs for serving personnel.[29]

Because of the political context in which police reform was to take place, including allegations of corruption and organised crime penetration in the police ranks, perceived allegiance to Frelimo, and a persistent culture of secrecy, the arrival of the Spanish *Guardia Civil* officers as technical advisers was at first regarded with deep suspicion by the Mozambique police. The police cadres did not fully cooperate in the development of the reform plan in its initial stages and it was not until personal bonds of trust had been created that cooperation started to take place. The international community understood the resistance to be tacitly supported by the minister of interior.[30] It was only after the minister's removal (partly due to international pressure), that reform efforts made better progress, albeit in limited ways. Nevertheless, the *Guardia Civil* were instrumental in building a modicum of support and demand for police reform within the ministry and police; it provided the assistance the Mozambican government needed to develop its chosen policing model.[31]

What the Mozambican government wanted was a police based upon a militarized model, similar to the *Guardia Civil*.[32] The justification was that the police were needed to maintain law and order in rural areas that had witnessed the greatest fighting during the civil war and where illegal armed bands had since taken root. For PRM officers, a militarised model of policing had a natural appeal. Many officers came from a military background, having received Tanzanian police training after independence in their transformation from a liberation guerrilla army to a police service. Subsequently, police officers were recruited from the armed forces when those forces were downsized. Indeed, one of the requirements for entry into the police was completion of military service.[33]

In *Phase I* the basic regulations of the police were overhauled. Among these were the Organic Statute of the PRM, the Statute of the Police Officer (a statement of principles concerning codes of conduct and career development), the salary schedule and the decree creating the police academy.[34] The most important decision made during *Phase I* was to retain the existing police service while a new one was being formed, an essential concession given the seriousness of criminality throughout the country. Consequently reform activities concentrated on basic retraining initiatives, with a six-month programme as the standard period. For instance, 80 police instructors were trained to work at the ACIPOL, which was in the process of being renovated; more than 3,950 officers underwent a general police retraining programme; and specialised training was given to approximately 1,100 officers in areas such as rapid intervention, traffic control and close protection. However, the long-term efficacy of these initiatives, which focused on 'training outputs', is questionable.[35]

The slow progress made during this phase underscores the politically delicate nature of changes in the security sector and in particular the mistrust felt by security actors during such transitions. The fact that the government retained the existing police force reinforced negative perceptions of the service, particularly for Renamo, which was by then the main political opposition to the government. At the same time, this decision also influenced the legitimacy of the reform debate by allowing trust to build up between the national government and the donors.

In contrast to *Phase I*, one of the highlights of *Phase II* was the development of a strategic plan for the PRM, a process that was managed by a special team within the police composed of members of the PRM and headed by the Commissioner.[36] This team also included the UNDP Chief Technical Adviser, a member of the *Guardia Civil*, and representatives of senior officers, the rank and file, civil society organisations, and donors. This countrywide consultation took place during 2002 at the national and provincial levels. Representatives of many of the institutions involved in the public provision of safety and security were also asked to participate, including the Supreme Court; Attorney General's Office; and the Ministries of Interior, Justice, Commerce and Industry, Mineral Resources and Energy. Provincial governments, municipal councils and assemblies were invited, as were officials from political parties. Interestingly, the Ministry of Planning and Finance was not asked to participate.

As part of the consultative process, police performance surveys were conducted in Mozambique's three main urban centres in August 2002. The objective of the surveys was to solicit the opinions of citizens and have them identify their 'needs and priorities,' thereby encouraging them to take an active role in the provision of their own security.[37]

The strategic plan was a compromise between the wishes of the PRM and those of the other stakeholders who participated in the national dialogue. The plan lays out the country context, the criminal environment, the recent history of the police service and its current state. It then states the PRM's guiding principles and programme. In the context of creating a 'system of public security and order', it describes the necessity of coordination within the wider criminal justice sector and the modernisation of management practices, particularly in the areas of personnel, training, logistics, and social assistance to police personnel.[38] Detailed activities were outlined, together with their corresponding budgets. The plan also addressed operational issues such as police intelligence, improving police capacity for crime prevention, community policing, and women and children's issues.[39]

The other main achievement of *Phase II* was the opening of ACIPOL in October 2000. The academy offered the equivalent of a four-year college degree in police sciences, with cadets receiving an academic education in social sciences and mathematics and specific police training in the subjects of police sciences and technologies and judicial sciences. The intention was to develop a new cadre of police officers with superior education and training to existing personnel. Although the first class was not due to graduate until 2004, plans were developed during *Phase II* for their eventual deployment as so-called model units. While recognizing the educational superiority of the newly trained officers compared to their longer serving colleagues, their lack of operational experience was acknowledged. Consequently, the model unit concept provided for an extended transition period during which the two generations of police would work side by side. The model prescribes a 60:40 ratio of new officers in the new model stations, which were to be opened after 2004. Despite having a majority of new officers, the model unit concept envisaged that stations would be under the overall command of the old generation while the new would take responsibility for patrols, shifts, criminal investigations, coordination with the PPC, and contact with the public.[40] To mollify the older generation of police officers and boost morale, the plan proposed that model stations should have access to equipment normally unavailable in Mozambique, such as radios, computers, patrol cars, and forensic materials. The concept also emphasised the need for the older generation to learn new policing techniques and strategies. [41]

In preparation for *Phase III* and the deployment of the new generation of police officers, 2,136 police personnel attended three-month courses, and 595 police were given classes in specialised police disciplines. Over the first two phases, a total of 9,253 police personnel (approximately 46 per cent of the total police service) were retrained. However, as best practice in organisational behaviour has repeatedly shown, a concentration on outputs rather than outcomes (for example, counting the number of personnel attending classes rather than post-training performance) usually fail to produce sustainable positive results.[42] Consequently, seven years of police reform accomplished little; it failed to alter the patterns of police management, or modernise existing managerial processes and procedures.

Phase III saw the introduction of the model unit concept in a few stations in Maputo. For the older generation of officers, a distance-training programme that includes three months of academy residence has been approved. At the time of writing the programme was awaiting final approval of funding from the Netherlands.[43] Although it is too early to judge whether the model unit concept is succeeding, preliminary indications are positive. As more new generation officers gain day-to-day policing experience, it is expected that they will be transferred to provincial commands to spread the model there. The hope is that the quality of service delivered by the police will improve as more new generation officers graduate from ACIPOL and learn the practicalities of policing.

Judicial Reform

Judicial reform posed a different set of challenges for reformers, in part because of the existence of several overlapping and parallel judicial systems. With respect to the formal institutions of justice, each of the ministries and organizations (the Ministry of Justice, the Supreme Court, the Administrative Court, and the Attorney's Office) had their own reform agenda. Additionally, external actors (in particular UNDP and DANIDA) conducted uncoordinated projects, thus creating further difficulties. There was minimal linkage between judicial and police reform programmes.

The UNDP commissioned an independent consultant who identified significant weaknesses. The key ones were lack of institutional coordination among justice institutions, lack of a sector-wide strategic vision, lack of training, lack of institutional capacity, insufficient political will to tackle the problems of the sector, deficient donor coordination, and corruption. UNDP proposed that the reform priorities were, in descending order: (1) the development of a sector-wide strategic vision, implying also a coordinated action by nationals and bilateral assistance; (2) training; (3) support for the improvement of functioning informal systems of conflict resolution; (4) prison reform; (5) need for greater attention to be paid to gender issues; (6) corruption; and (7) support to the Attorney General's Office.[44] At no time was court administration and management considered a priority.

It proved impossible to coordinate this flurry of judicial initiatives. By 2002 the Supreme Court, the Attorney General's Office, and Justice Ministry had developed their own separate reform agendas and strategic plans. A team of professionals drawn from each of the institutions was therefore formed to integrate and coordinate the plans. The Council for Coordination of Legality and Justice (CCLJ), as the body became known, was supported by UNDP and DANIDA. In 2003 this unified team came up with a comprehensive vision of judicial reform, integrating the plans of the Ministry of Justice, Supreme Court, Administrative Court, and Attorney General's Office for the next five years. Implementation was left up to the officials of each of the institutions.[45] Some of the specific initiatives included access to justice, building a legal library and database, training, and simplifying legal and administrative procedures. However, donor funding to implement this vision was not forthcoming since UNDP and the government have yet to produce a methodology by which judicial reform initiatives are to be achieved. Part of the difficulty appears to be that judicial reform was been considered a 'project' by UNDP, to be executed by a technical assistance unit that (unlike that working with the police) was not integrated into governmental institutions.

In relation to the prison services, the key issues are primarily related to overcrowding, a problem that has been exacerbated by the slow functioning of the formal and informal justice systems. Overcrowding gives rise to numerous problems, from poor living conditions for the prisoners to hygiene and food problems, and the more rapid deterioration of prison infrastructure. The severity of these problems gained public attention in November 2000 when 119 election protesters died from suffocation after being imprisoned in cells with limited capacity.[46]

In 2000 and 2001 the UNDP released a report on the prison system, which led to the creation of a penal policy and implementation programme.[47] In addition to the acknowledged problems, the report also identified a shortage of prison staff and a lack of requisite skills. It also pointed out that Mozambique's body of law was outdated, and that there was a need to increase the work of non-governmental organisations (NGOs) in the prisons and prison reform.[48]

To address the situation, UNDP offered to support the prison system by helping to refurbish facilities, establish alternative ways of dealing with offenders, and, above all, unify the penal system by doing away with the dual systems of incarceration managed by the Ministries of Justice and Interior.[49] Immediate activities that UNDP supported included improving the provision of running water in prisons, renovating prison classrooms and health centres, and providing educational materials. On a long-term basis, UNDP supported the creation of a penal policy team to conduct research on how to implement penal reform and strengthen prison management systems. Additionally, the team was to study staff retention and recruitment policies, having already undertaken a diagnosis of prisons infrastructures and discussed alternative sentencing guidelines in order to relive overcrowding. The fact that penal reform lagged years behind police and judicial programmes is a telling indicator of the importance allocated to it by donors.[50]

EVALUATING UNDP PROGRAMMES

Police Reform

Despite a long list of initiatives, police reform continues to face huge problems according to two external evaluations commissioned by the UNDP and the Swiss government respectively.[51] Part of the problem was that the initial impetus for reform was the wish to accommodate political interests, rather than to address the problem of citizen safety and security, but the greatest challenge concerned management. Studies undertaken by the UN identified the main challenges as corruption, lack of adequate training programmes, legislative gaps, the absence of a long-term planning capacity, the need for legislation regarding police involvement in natural disaster management, and the need for a change of attitude towards domestic violence and HIV-AIDS interventions.[52] Corruption was of prime concern because it undermined public confidence in the police and the potential success of the reforms.[53]

The Swiss government-commissioned assessment noted improvements in the police's protection of human rights but heavily criticised the new four-year police education of ACIPOL and low number of annual graduates (around 40 officers per year). A disproportionate number of the graduating officers are southern Mozambicans, thereby further skewing the national balance within the police between north and south that had occurred when Frelimo soldiers were demobilised and transformed into police personnel. In the opinion of the report, these factors inhibited the pace of reform.[54] The Swiss report also voiced concern that the new officers graduating from ACIPOL would not only enter a service starved of resources but would also face active resistance from the older generation of police. This resistance to change arising from the fear of loss of power and status remains one of the most prominent issues in the PIC.[55]

The UNDP evaluation echoed many of the conclusions in the Swiss study. It analysed the first two phases of the police reform programme and suggested that the lack of equipment for operational units and police stations had created motivational problems for the new graduates.[56] This suggests that the design of the reform process was fundamentally flawed. One key issue, for example, was that funding levels never matched the ambition of the reform programme.[57] For instance, the costs of the police reform in Mozambique were originally estimated at US$50 million, but there was never a prospect of raising even a fraction of that amount.[58] The fact that the international community lacked a reform strategy, with UNDP unable to offer any conceptual or programmatic guidance, only aggravated the situation.[59] In addition, the report highlighted the need for continued improvement of management systems, including internal financial regulations and personnel procedures. Lastly, the report called for the development and incorporation of 'more effective verifiable indicators and monitoring mechanisms'.[60] Nonetheless, it is fair to say that the development of the strategic plan is a major achievement in its own right.

What needs to be kept in mind is that police reform is a long-term process whose success depends in part on changing ingrained cultural patterns and habits. Often this may be possible only through generational change. In the case of Mozambique, since the approach was not to disband the existing police and create a new force afresh, this generational change will necessarily be gradual. It may require at least another decade for investments in police education to take effect. It is also an open question as to whether Mozambique could have successfully integrated substantive managerial change while at the same time transforming the police through the model unit concept; for instance, instilling new managerial techniques may have little effect on the old generation of police. Yet the point remains, that after eight years the reform process is only now beginning to address the issue head-on.

Justice Reform Programme

Evaluations of the judicial reform programme are mixed. Reform is an inherently complicated process, but when each institution in the judicial sector writes its own strategic plan without coordinating with the others, an already difficult project becomes nearly unmanageable. The continued lack of a recognizable national policy remains problematic too, despite the work of the CCLJ.[61] The best that can be said is that each judicial institution claims it is following the guidance of the CCLJ for the design and implementation of their annual plans. Even so, the Ministry of Justice has created its own legal reform commission to work on the revision of judicial legislation, an indication that the authority of the CCLJ is limited.

Despite these problems, the government is optimistic about reforming of the judicial system. According to the President's 2004 report on the State of the Nation, the government claims an annual increase of 30 per cent in the resolution of pending cases.[62] During an address in 2005 to mark the beginning of the judicial year, the President of the Supreme Court, the highest ranking judicial officer in the country, endorsed this finding but acknowledged that the absence of reliable statistics from various districts makes it difficult to verify.

Overall the President of the Supreme Court painted a bleak picture of the justice and rule of law in Mozambique. He mentioned that the courts in 2004 had performed more efficiently and effectively than the year before, but that this progress was virtually obliterated by a rise in the number of cases brought to court. Furthermore, the lack of sufficient numbers of qualified staff, in particular judges and clerks, remains a challenge. Part of the problem could be resolved with more training, but the bigger problems are managerial, such as the lack of knowledge of basic judicial regulations, and unfamiliarity with the basic rules. Supreme Court directive and circulars are frequently ignored by lower courts and administrative staff. In addition, obsolete legal codes, borrowed from the colonial Portuguese system, continue to be crucial obstacles to improvement and reform. [63]

ASSESSING PROGRAMMES

An ideal approach to SSR combines the same standards and principles which apply to the rest of the public sector, adjusted to the sector's unique characteristics. This approach ensures that the reform process is sustainable and addresses real change in the institutions' cultures. UNDP played an important supporting role to the government and the international donor community in Mozambique by facilitating the research and drafting of empirically valid SSR reports and analyses, needs assessments and policy recommendations. It may be argued that UNDP should have taken a more active role in SSR in terms of offering policy guidance and recalibrating SSR priorities to focus more on managerial issues, but the organisation had no expert capacity of its own. It had little choice but to assume a circumscribed role.

Both of UNDP's reform endeavours fell under the rubric of democratic governance. This could have provided an excellent means of drawing together the common threads of the reform process, but UNDP addressed police and judicial reform as if they were separate activities. Despite calls for linking the programmes, little was done to coordinate the work of the projects – and thus make them mutually reinforcing –even though the complementary nature of the strategic planning initiatives could have prompted an early attempt to address the problems in the criminal justice system. For example, although both projects supported strategic planning, synergies between the strategic plans were never maximised. UNDP's secondary role in the formulation of the judicial strategy further complicated the picture. Because of this failure, it is questionable whether the reform process across Mozambique's security and justice institutions is sustainable.

The same lack of coordination was reflected in UNDP's other democratic governance projects. Its parliamentary and media programmes were not linked to its

SSR initiatives, suggesting that the concept of democratic oversight of the sector had not taken root within UNDP. Furthermore, although statements stressing the need for democratic accountability of the sector are regularly issued, none of UNDP's programmes contain any concrete accountability or oversight processes. Since these are difficult areas to tackle, the decision might have been to include accountability issues as part of the general training and retraining of personnel in the sector's various educational institutions. However, accountability also requires designing appropriate institutional mechanisms within the sector's institutions and those of civil society. This does not seem to have been done.

Another disconnect between UNDP's democratic governance discourse and its SSR programme is the designation Justice and 'Law and Order'. The term is potentially at odds with the objective of advancing democracy since in Mozambique it is associated with the actions of the government during authoritarianism. The doctrine of law and order during Mozambique's authoritarian period was based on the heavy hand of the security forces, which operated without regard for human rights or contemporary policing practices. In the authoritarian era, the security forces were more interested in protecting the power prerogatives of the ruling elite than in delivering safety and security – much less accountability – to the citizens of Mozambique. A change in UNDP's terminology would send more appropriate signals.

A final issue deserving of further attention is the short-term cycle of UNDP programmes and its consequent impact on strategic thinking. Implementation of UNDP programming requires the availability of experienced staff, in part because the organisation has no cadre of SSR practitioners. It also depends upon the activities of the government, where resistance to SSR may be strong. Acquiring appropriate local and international staff and wearing away institutional resistance requires extended periods of time, as the long period between UNDP's agreement with the government of Mozambique and the start of work shows. More often than not, reform depends on trust building processes between donor countries, UNDP, and national governments, as well as ready access to funding.

Consequently, UNDP's project cycles need to correspond to the practical realities of SSR reform. There are arguments against extending programme cycles based on the legitimate interests of donor countries, but improvement in the use of performance-based indicators and thorough reviews and evaluations may ease their concerns about programme management. Nevertheless, means must be found to lengthen project and programme cycles in order to meet the needs of all stakeholders.

LESSONS IDENTIFIED

Although much has been written in the SSR literature about the need for a holistic approach embracing both security and justice institutions, Mozambique's reform programmes were fragmented. The UNDP, for example, supported a wide range of reforms, but it did not address the crucial linkages within and between these institutions in Mozambique. If the linkages between military reform, demobilisation, and police reforms had been recognized, some of the limitations in the SSR process could have been anticipated. Similarly, reform's unexpected or unintended consequences could have been foreseen. As it was, the initial lack of attention paid to the judicial sector allowed corruption to establish itself as the institutional norm. Finally, the original Mozambican vision of policing embracing a militarised policing model is arguably changing as issues of crime prevention become more important. These problems suggest that a linear approach to strategic planning and implementation needs to incorporate flexibility mechanisms.

A holistic approach need not mean a single implementation plan. Rather, it implies an overall methodology that selects entry points on an institution-by-institution basis, and analyses the effect of those entry points on other institutions in the sector. It also suggests that, across the sector as a whole, these entry points should complement and reinforce each other. The fact that at the strategic level a reform programme involves all the institutions in the sector does not mean that an agency such as UNDP should necessarily include all of them into its programming. Rather, it implies that programme design must begin with an awareness of other SSR initiatives and the possibility that programming in one SSR area will affect the others.

The UNDP in Mozambique has learned many lessons since 1997, but it remains unclear as to how well those lessons have been distilled and disseminated throughout the organisation; experience suggests that few have been fully absorbed, particularly with regard to the central role of management in SSR.

Most donors and multilateral cooperation agencies now accept the need for an integrated approach to SSR, yet despite UNDP's involvement, Mozambique's SSR programme still lacks an integrated and effective implementation plan capable of coordinating the activities of different government bodies and international donors. There is no clear focus and sub-optimal use of scarce financial resources; projects do not achieve their objectives because expectations have been raised beyond the capacity of the donor community and the national government to provide the financing and skilled personnel required to sustain them. All too often, managerial reform is omitted, and training programmes are merely an accounting exercise that registers outputs without affecting the actual performance of the sector. UNDP continues to struggle to bridge its police and justice reform initiatives, and connect them to other democratic governance initiatives. Even so, it is essential that UNDP succeed in its mission to promote greater accountability and improved oversight of the police, for these are key steps in the transition to democratic rule in Mozambique.

NOTES

1. Laudemiro Francisco interview with Henny Matos, Assistant Resident Representative, Governance and Environment Unit, UNDP (Maputo, 28 Jan. 2005). See also UNDP/UNOPS, Moz/95/015, 'Support to the Mozambican Police Force', *Restructuring the Mozambican Police: A Mid-Term Evaluation* (Maputo 1999) p.26.
2. The UNDP has not participated in any defence projects mainly because military reform is considered outside the organisation's mandate. This reluctance flies in the face of the organisation's own recommendations to engage in military reform; see Valter Fainda, 'Security/Police/Drugs' in UNDP.

Democratic Governance in Mozambique: Priorities for the Second Generation 2002–2006 (Maputo: UNDP 2000) p.27. The Mozambican military is one of the national institutions that have successfully achieved national reconciliation but its capabilities remain limited.

3. Albie Sachs and Gita Honwana Welch, *Liberating the Law: Creating Popular Justice in Mozambique* (London: Zed Books 1990).

4. On the causes and incidences of the civil war see João Cabrita, *Mozambique: the Tortuous Road to Democracy* (Basingstoke: Palgrave 2001); Christian Geffray, *The Cause of the Arms: Social Anthropology of the Contemporary War in Mozambique* (Porto: Edições Afrontamento 1991); Jeremy Weinstein and Laudemiro Francisco, 'The Civil War in Mozambique: The Balance between Internal & External Influences' in Nicholas Sambanis and Paul Collier (ed.), *Understanding Civil Wars: Evidence and Analysis*,Vols. I and II (Washington DC: World Bank 2005).

5. UNOMOZ (United Nations Operation in Mozambique) was established under the United Nations Security Council Res.797 (1992), 16 Dec. 1992. See also *General Peace Agreement of Mozambique, 1992* (Maputo: AWEPAA/African-European Institute 1993). On the role of UNOMOZ in demobilisation see Sam Barnes, *Reintegration Programmes for Demobilized Soldiers in Mozambique* (Maputo: UNDP 1997).

6. The Law No. 19/92, *Creation of the Police of the Republic of Mozambique*, Boletim da Republica 53, Ia Serie. 3° Suplemento (1992) created the Police of the Republic of Mozambique (PRM) to replace the People's Police of Mozambique (PPM) created by the Law No. 5/79, *Creation of the People's Police of Mozambique*, Boletim da Republica 60, Ia Serie (1979). Contrary to other post-conflict situations, the police in Mozambique were not subject to the core provisions discharged under the GPA. This fuelled suspicions within Renamo that the police were the de facto security force of Frelimo. In response, the government claimed that it needed to contain Renamo leaders' threats to use force to gain power. See Martinho Chachiua, 'Internal Security in Mozambique: Concerns versus Policies', *African Security Review* 9/1 (2000) < www.iss.co.za/Pubs/ASR/9No1/%20SecurityMozambique.html > .

7. UNDP/UNOPS, Moz/95/015 (note 1) p.7.

8. *Defense and Security Law*, 17/97 of 07/10, Boletim da Republica 40, Ia Serie. 3° Suplemento (1997).

9. This gives a ratio of 1:1,089 officers to citizens, which is below the preferred international standard of 1:350–450. See Government of Mozambique, *Plano Estratégico da Polícia da Replica de Moçambique* (PEPRM), 2003–2012 (2003) p.34.

10. Attorney General's Annual Report to the Parliament (Maputo 2003) < www.govmoz.gov.mz/ > (accessed 24 Nov. 2004).

11. The judicial police are to be run by a deputy attorney general assisted by a police representative. See UNDP/UNOPS, 'Report for the Mid-term Project Evaluation Moz/00/007, 'Support to the Police of the Republic of Mozambique (Phase II)'(Maputo, 30 Sept. to 18 Oct. 2002) p.6.

12. There are two prison systems in Mozambique; a pre-trial and maximum-security system is managed by the Ministry of Interior, while the prisons for convicted persons overseen by the Ministry of Justice.

13. Luis de Brito, *The Condemned of Maputo* (Maputo: UNDP 2002). See also UNDP, *The Prison System in Mozambique* (Maputo: UNDP 2000) pp.30, 58.

14. Ibid.

15. Authors' interview with Emilio Valverde, UNDP Chief Technical Adviser to the Police Reform Project and former UNOPS programme manager for Mozambique (Maputo, 25 Jan. 2005).

16. See UNDP Moz/95/015/F/01/31, 'Support to the Police of the Republic of Mozambique (PRM) – Phase I', *Project Document* (Maputo 1997).

17. Ibid.

18. Switzerland played a crucial role in the establishment of ACIPOL. See UNDP Project Moz/98/006/A/01/99, 'Support to the Police of the Republic of Mozambique', which was signed by Mozambique and the UNDP in April 1999. Contrary to UNDP Moz/95/015/F/01/31, which it was intended to complement, the Swiss initiative was a nationally executed project. The United States committed some $200,000 for training and equipment.

19. UNDP/UNOPS, Moz/95/015, 'Support to the Police of the Republic of Mozambique', *Terminal Report* (1999) pp.13–17.

20. Phase II is laid out in the Programme Moz/00/007, 'Support to the Police of the Republic of Mozambique (PRM) – Phase II', which was signed by Mozambique and UNDP in July 2000.

21. See UNDP/UNOPS, 'Report for the Mid-term Project Evaluation Moz/00/007, 'Support to the Police of the Republic of Mozambique (Phase II)' (Maputo 2002) p.3.

22. Interviews with a senior member of the Technical Unit for the Implementation of the Reform Programme for the Police of the Republic of Mozambique (Maputo, 21, 26 Jan. 2005), and with the Unit's Financial Manager (Maputo, 25 Jan. 2005). The unit is in charge of implementing the strategic plan for the police.
23. Project ID 360334, 'Support to the Police of the Republic of Mozambique, Phase III' (Maputo 2004) pp.5–6. See also Government of Mozambique (note 9) p.12. The first discussions concerning integration and coordination were broached in May 2003, with project work expected to begin in Jan. 2004. Unfortunately, the agreement was not signed until May 2004 (MOZ/001/03), and as of Jan. 2005 work still had not begun.
24. This was project UNDP/Moz/98/003, 'Support to the Justice Sector', *Programme Support Document*. Interview with senior member from the Justice Project Implementation Unit (Maputo, 20 Jan. 2005).
25. In 2002 UNDP published an internal 'lessons learned' study of its security sector activities around the world but it was never widely circulated within the organisation.
26. UNDP/BCPR, *Justice and Security Sector Reform: BCPR'S Programmatic Approach* (NY: UNDP 2002). The BCPR document uses the term Justice and Security Sector Reform (JSSR). As of early 2005, this document remains the only official UNDP paper on SSR.
27. UNDP, 'Coherence, Cooperation and Comparative Strengths', conference report from *Justice and Security Sector Reform*, Oslo, 10–11 April 2003 < http://www.undp.org/oslocentre/docsjuly03/ JSSR%20Conference%20Report-Final%2026%20June.pdf#search = 'OSLO%20conference %202003%20JSSR' > .
28. Interview with Henny Matos, Assistant Resident Representative, Governance and Environment Unit, UNDP (Maputo, 28 Jan. 2005).
29. Authors' interview with senior PRM staff member (Maputo, 20 Jan. 2005). The issue of resistance was noted by the Spanish *Guardia Civil* Study and the Project Document. See Moz/95/015, *Project Document* (note 16) p.7.
30. E-mail interview with Moisés Venâncio, UNDP, New York Office, 19 Jan. 2005.
31. Interview with a high-ranking police officer. Maputo, Jan. 2005. See also Martinho Chachiua, 'Internal Security in Mozambique: Concerns versus Policies', *African Security Review* 9 (2000) <www.iss.co.za/Pubs/ASR/9No1/%20SecurityMozambique.html> .
32. The Law establishing the PRM defines it as a 'paramilitary force,' explaining the government's preferences for a model like the Spanish *Guardia Civil* (SGC). The Law 19/92 (1992) created the Police of the Republic of Mozambique (PRM) to replace the People's Police of Mozambique (PPM), which had been created by Law 5/79 (1979).
33. Martinho Chachiua, 'Internal Security in Mozambique: Concerns versus Policies', *African Security Review* 9 (2000) <www.iss.co.za/Pubs/ASR/9No1/%20SecurityMozambique.html> .
34. Fainda (note 2) p.23.
35. Elwood Holton and Timothy Baldwin (eds.), *Improving Learning Transfer in Organizations* (NY: Jossey-Bass 2003).
36. Ministerial Decree 01/GMI/02 (2002).
37. The survey was carried out by the United Nations Interregional Crime and Justice Research Institute (UNICRI) in Maputo, Beira and Nampula using the International Crime Victim Survey (ICVS) framework. See UNICRI, *Strategic Plan of the Police of the Republic of Mozambique: Results of Surveys on Victimization and Police Performance* (Turin, Italy: UNICRI 2003) p.1. Citizens of the capital were least satisfied with police performance compared to the other two major cities. The survey found that 96 per cent of police officers were satisfied with their own performance. See UNICRI, pp.21–2. See also Ética Moçambique, *Estudo Sobre Corrupção em Moçambique 2001* (Maputo 2001) p.86; CEP-UEM, *Inquérito Nacional de Opinião Pública* (Maputo 2001).
38. See Project ID 360334, 'Support to the Police of the Republic of Mozambique, Phase III' (Maputo, Nov. 2004) pp.5–6. See also Government of Mozambique (note 9) p.12. Authors' interview with Mr Emilio Valverde (note 15).
39. Government of Mozambique (note 9).
40. Authors' interview with Mr Emilio Valverde (note 15).
41. Ibid.
42. It should be noted that the recruitment and training of rank and file police personnel is ongoing at the Matalane facility. During Phase II, two eight-month courses with 1,433 new recruits were completed.
43. Author's interview with senior staff member, Academy of Police Sciences (ACIPOL) (Maputo, 20 Jan. 2005).
44. Samuel Levy, 'Legal/Justice Sector,' in UNDP (note 2) p.20.

45. The Ministry of Interior is not part of the Council. It is expected that the Ministry may be invited when the issues at stake are relevant to the police. Author's interview with senior staff member of the Conselho da Coordenação da Legalidade da Justiça (CCLJ) (Maputo, 24 Jan. 2005). See also *Attorney General's Annual Report to the Parliament* (Maputo 2003) <www.govmoz.gov.mz/ > (accessed 24 Nov. 2004).
46. 'MOZAMBIQUE: Commission investigates prison deaths', IRIN, 8 Jan. 2001.
47. Government of Mozambique, 'Prison Policy and Strategy for Implementation,' Resolution 65/2002. approved by the Council of Ministers, 27 Aug. 2002. Boletim da Republica 34, Ia Serie. 2° Suplemento (2002).
48. UN System, *Mozambique Common Country Assessment* (UN System 2000) p.96.
49. UNDP, *The Prison System in Mozambique* (Maputo: UNDP 2000); UNDP, *Open Prison Centers in Mozambique* (Maputo: UNDP 2001).
50. Author's interview with staff member, Unidade Técnica de Unificação do Sector Prisional (UTUSP) (Maputo, 27 May 2005).
51. See Dominique Wisler, Markus Mohler and Martins Kumanga, 'Support to the Police Reform' in Mozambique: *Final Report of the Evaluation of the Swiss Development and Cooperation Agency Project* (Maputo, 30 Aug. 2001); UNDP/UNOPS, PRODOC MOZ/00/007 Phase II, 'Support to the Mozambican Police Force', Terminal Report (Maputo 2003).
52. UN System (note 48)) p.98. Interview Mr Emilio Valverde (note 15).
53. Although there were no studies on police performance, the general perception was that it was very weak. A survey on corruption carried in three provinces in 2001, including the country's three major urban centres (financed by the United States Agency for International Development (USAID) confirms this: more than 70 per cent perceived the police as very corrupt; 58.8 per cent and 58.1 per cent thought the same about the government and the courts respectively. See Ética Moçambique, *Estudo Sobre Corrupção em Moçambique 2001* (Maputo 2001) p.71. Furthermore, 76.2 per cent of people interviewed do not contact the police to ask for help in dealing with local problems. See CEP-UEM, *Inquérito Nacional de Opinião Pública 2001* (Maputo 2002) Table 12, p.10.
54. Wisler *et al.* (note 51).
55. Anicia Lalá and Andrea Ostheimer, *How to Remove the Stains on Mozambique's Democratic Track Record: Challenges for the Democratisation Process between 1990 and 2003* (Maputo: Konrad Adenauer Foundation 2003). There are also allegations that some members of the PIC are linked to organized crime and have blocked initiatives that threaten their self-interests.
56. See UNDP/UNOPS, PRODOC MOZ/00/007 Phase II, 'Support to the Mozambican Police Force', Terminal Report (Maputo 2003).
57. Even when adequate cost analyses of the reform programme were conducted, they were highly vulnerable to external factors, such as the devaluation of the currency. These factors were not included in the original estimates.
58. See Pamela Rebela *et al.*, *Support to the Police of the Republic of Mozambique, Phase II, Formulation Mission: Final Report* (Maputo 1999) p.1, quoted in Wisler (note 51) p.5.
59. Ibid.
60. UNDP/UNOPS 'Support to the Mozambican Police Force,' Terminal Report pp.6–7, 10.
61. UNDP, Moz/98/003, 'Support to the Justice Sector in Mozambique', *Annual Programme Report* (July to Dec. 2000).
62. GoM, 'Pela Redução da Pobreza Absoluta, Rumo ao Desenvolvimento Sustentável', Informação Anual de Sua Excelência Joaquim Chissano, President da República de Moçambique, à Assembleia da República sobre a Situação Geral da Nação (Maputo, 29 April 2004).
63. AIM (Agência de Informação de Moçambique), 'Huge Backlog of Cases in Mozambican Courts', (Maputo), 1 March 2005 <http://allafrica.com/stories/200503010575.html> (accessed 2 March 2005).

Police Reform Amid Transition in Serbia: The Organization for Security and Cooperation in Europe

MARK DOWNES AND RORY KEANE[1]

Much has been written about the structure, mandate and approach of the Organization for Security and Cooperation in Europe (OSCE).[2] Rather less, however, has been written about the effectiveness of the OSCE's programming and, in particular, its activities in the field of security sector reform (SSR). This article examines the OSCE's groundbreaking engagement in police reform in Serbia from the end of 2000 to the end of 2004. The depth and extent of Serbian political instability during this four-year period cannot be under-estimated: a dictator, Slobodan Milošević, was removed from power and transferred to stand trial for war crimes;[3] conflict flared in the south of the country, resulting in a fledgling peace process; the existing country, the Federal Republic of Yugoslavia, of which Serbia was an integral part, was dissolved and a new country, the State Union of Serbia and Montenegro, formed; a reformist prime minister, Zoran Djindjić, was democratically elected and assassinated, reputedly by individuals belonging to an elite police unit; a coalition government collapsed and an electoral minority prime minister, Vojislav Kostunica, chosen; public participation in three elections for the presidency of Serbia failed to reach the threshold thought necessary for legitimate appointment; and in June 2004 an reformist candidate, Boris Tadic, was elected president.

In this article the OSCE's experience in Serbia is used to highlight the key ingredients of a police reform process, and the main issues that should be taken into consideration when planning for the next generation of missions in transitional situations.[4] It underlines the structural and endemic problems faced by the OSCE – symbolised by the lack of an overarching strategy or institutional approach to police reform – which hampers and limits the organization's potential engagement in SSR.

SECURITY UNDER MILOŠEVIĆ

The expected post-Cold War peace dividend never occurred in the western Balkans. Rather, the region experienced conflict and subsequently a slow and painful democratic transition process. Former President Milošević's approach to the security sector involved a highly politicised, militarised, and centralised police force, a secret police and intelligence service; a relatively weak and compliant armed forces under his directorship; and a judicial branch that lacked independence and objectivity. In practice, Milošević used the police as an extension of his personalised political rule; they were designed to control and eliminate opposition and civil liberties, rather than uphold the rule of law.[5] Equally important, 'the police – more than any other state structure – became implicated in organized crime to the extent that organized crime was one of the "pillars" of the Milošević regime'.[6]

It should not, therefore, be surprising that in the aftermath of Milošević's removal from power in October 2000, the security sector found itself estranged from the public. Ten years of international isolation and economic sanctions compounded the sector's dysfunctional ethics, structures and strategies, while the equipment that survived NATO's Kosovo campaign had become obsolete. These factors, which were exacerbated by widespread corruption, high unemployment, and an ingrained culture of organised crime that affected not just the security sector but also politics and business, ensured that implementing meaningful SSR was a colossal challenge.

OSCE's ROLE IN SSR

The first OSCE mission (to Kosovo, Sandzak and Vojvodina in 1998), was a monitoring assignment that lasted a year – Milošević refused to renew its mandate. It was followed by the mission that is the subject of this article, which was established following the admission in November 2000 of the Federal Republic of Yugoslavia to the OSCE as the 55th participating state.[7] In preparation for the deployment of the new mission, an OSCE Rapporteur mission visited the Republic in December 2000, and determined that police reform would need to focus on decriminalising and depoliticising the police, recreating public trust and confidence in the police, and tackling organised crime. It would be some years, however, before the OSCE mission actually addressed these issues, as the initial focus was on large scale retraining. This was in part because few of the personnel in the OSCE's Law Enforcement Department (LED) were even aware of the Rapporteur's report. This indicates the gap that existed between the field mission and headquarters in Vienna.

An outbreak of political violence in southern Serbia in December 2000 focused political attention on the crucial role (positive and negative) that the security services played in the democratic transition of Serbia. The violence (between an Albanian rebel group and the Serbian authorities) was in many ways a spillover from Kosovo, which, with its ethnic tensions, underdevelopment, high unemployment and institutional neglect, provided fertile ground for conflict. Significantly, the prime target of the insurgency (for the violence was nothing less) was the Serbian police.[8] In trying to combat the attacks, the police were gravely hampered by their own reputation, for policing was a central element of Albanian grievance in the region.

Police reform was also a fundamental part of a peace plan put forward to end the conflict. The plan, tabled by the then Serbian deputy prime minister, Nebojsa Covic, envisaged boosting the number of Albanians in state institutions, including the police, and creating a multi-ethnic police element (MEPE) for the region. The OSCE was tasked with overseeing its implementation, which represented the main entry point for the OSCE's role in its subsequent SSR endeavours. The OSCE's initial role can thus be best described as crisis stabilisation and management. The immediate need was to integrate ethnic Albanians into Serbian police structures and establish joint Albanian/Serbian patrols in towns and villages that were openly hostile to a mono-ethnic police presence. This emergency priority led to the OSCE undertaking the large-scale basic training of the MEPE in a short time period.[9]

While a later evaluation found that the MEPE did not have the necessary skills to ensure the delivery of police services,[10] its performance and role as a confidence-building measure cannot and should not to be underestimated. It is safe to say that the MEPE played a significant role in averting serious conflict; it alleviated ethnic and social tensions. In this sense, the MEPE was highly successful. Further, its success highlighted the need for focused, circumscribed approaches and entry points that correlate to the political realities of post-conflict environments. The underlying issue, however, was how and when to instigate transition from one phase of SSR to another; there was no overall framework capable of defining either end goals or the principles needed to guide engagement.

In tandem with training the MEPE, an OSCE police consultant was appointed to undertake a comprehensive study of policing in Serbia and to recommend what changes were necessary in order to modernise the service along contemporary Western principles. The resultant 'Study on Policing in the Federal Republic of Yugoslavia' – hereafter the Monk Report, after its author, Richard Monk, the senior police adviser to the OSCE secretary-general in Vienna and head of the OSCE's Strategic Police Matters Unit – concentrated on the need to initiate cultural, procedural and training changes so as to reform the police in line with European norms and standards. The publication of the Monk Report provided the OSCE with both expert guidance and a sense of direction. It also led in December 2001 to the OSCE being assigned the role of 'coordinator of the international community' by the Ministry of the Interior.

The task of translating the report's findings into concrete reform activities was given to a small group of OSCE personnel, who, along with staff from the Serbian Ministry of Interior, developed a police reform programme with six priority areas: (1) police training and education, (2) organised crime, (3) border policing, (4) police accountability (including external oversight), (5) community policing and (6) crime scene management. These areas became the focus of OSCE's reform efforts.

It should also be noted that the OSCE was not alone in assisting the ministry in police reform. Along with its bilateral activities, a local non-governmental organization (NGO), the League of Experts-LEX, began collaboration with the Danish Institute for Human Rights, which in March 2002 resulted in the ministry publishing its vision of police reform. This provided detailed three-year, five-year, and long-term action plans required for establishing a modern, representative and democratic police service. The essence of these plans correlated well with the OSCE advice.[11]

COSTS AND OUTCOMES

It is now more than five years since the publication of the Monk Report, which in many ways marked the beginning of the second stage of reform within the Serbian police. Although today's police are distinctly different from the politicised service that was used as a tool of oppression during the Milošević administration, 'fundamental structural and operational changes that would create the conditions for modern policing have not yet taken place'.[12] It might be argued that given Serbia's political instability and the need to overhaul the police service's structure, legal foundations, management practices, and work culture, five years is too short a time in which to evaluate the success or failure of the SSR programme.[13]

Furthermore, the goals that the ministry set itself in 2001 and 2002 were overly ambitious and unrealistic. They were not translated into a strategic plan with defined timelines, goals, objectives and activities either. Even so, the first years of a reform process should indicate whether or not a given SSR programme is moving in a productive direction. The OSCE's experience therefore raises interesting questions regarding the criteria and standards that should be used to evaluate programmes, and how such measurement indicators can be utilised in programme design.

Since the Monk Report, the Ministry of the Interior has embarked on a wide reform programme, much of it following from the report's recommendations, including a re-alignment of education curricula and priorities, and the introduction of demographically representative personnel.[14] This was achieved through the recruitment of more female police officers and the establishment and subsequent integration of the MEPE in southern Serbia. The ministry also made extensive strides in opening its activities to public scrutiny, making its operations more transparent; senior officials held regular press conferences, biannual police progress reports with detailed crime statistics were published, and notices concerning the disciplinary procedures against police were issued.

Meanwhile, within the service the need for a philosophical shift in the manner of policing was recognised, and efforts were made to institute community-based policing principles in pilot sites throughout Serbia. The recognition may be partly attributed to the community-based policing initiatives launched with OSCE assistance, which integrated public opinion surveys with the establishment of municipal-level security committees. Together, these achievements contributed to a gradual changing of the attitudes of the Serbian public towards their police.[15]

On a more structural and organizational level, a division was effected between state and public security sectors (i.e. between the intelligence and police services). An Office of the Inspector General was established in mid-2002, though it was not fully staffed until one year later, and questions remain about its work being politically motivated. At about the same time (April 2003) the ministry introduced a new code of ethics. It also presented a new law on policing and on police education to the National Assembly, both of which were critical for restructuring the police. Unfortunately, due to the lack of political will, neither law has yet passed into legislation. The same can be said about the overall accountability and oversight architecture, even though the OSCE proposed a model in winter 2002–3.[16]

Concerning the reform of police personnel, the task is both intricate and problematic. Indeed, the extent of the reform required is overwhelming. According to a Serbian NGO, up to 70 per cent of all police officers (approximately 20,000 people) would have had to be dismissed if disciplining and vetting were to be thorough with respect to corruption and the other compromises made by the police under Milošević's regime.[17] Of course, 'cleansing' a police of the majority of its personnel is not only impossible to achieve, but also counterproductive in the short term. New disciplinary systems have therefore been put in place, and allegedly corrupt or compromised police officers gradually dismissed. However, 'no comprehensive transparent human resource policies, particularly at the higher professional levels' exist.[18] Consequently, some dismissals have probably perpetuated the politicalisation of the police (one of the principal areas in need of reform) because on assuming power each political party installs its adherents and punishes its adversaries without regard to professional competence.[19]

It is difficult to evaluate the financial cost of the OSCE's contribution to reform. The annual budget of the OSCE Mission in Serbia and Montenegro is approximately €9.8 million.[20] Of that around €1.5 million goes towards the functioning of the Law Enforcement Department (LED), while a similar amount goes into the Rule of Law Department. The LED funds are used to provide expertise in areas including organised crime, crime scene management, internal affairs, community policing, strategic management, border policing, and police training and education.[21] The core budget is also used to operate three police training centres, two in Serbia and one in Montenegro.

The costs of specific programmes are financed through voluntary contributions from OSCE member states, which have over the past few years amounted to €2.5 million. These funds are used to provide technical equipment, specialist training and capacity development. In addition, bilateral donors have undertaken specific programmes outside the auspices of the OSCE. The major bilateral donors include the UK through its access to justice programme and support to the border-policing unit; Norway through police assistance in the Vojvodina region of northern Serbia; and Switzerland through its participation in the development of community policing pilot sites. Bilateral contributions to police reform easily equalled the amount received by the OSCE in voluntary contributions.

The OSCE's role of coordinating police reform on behalf of the international community was one of the most difficult tasks it confronted. It also provides a good example of the difficulties of coordinating multi-donor engagement in politically sensitive programmes. The fact that the OSCE was the coordinator of other programmes and an implementing agent made its coordinating function all the more arduous, while national self-interest continually undermined its efforts at coordinating bilateral donors. The result was that the Ministry of the Interior was able to shop among donors for the best equipment 'deals'. Numerous bilateral donors were willing to engage in the more visible reform areas such as community based policing, but the long-term institutional areas, such as financial and human resource management, were largely neglected.

OSCE DOCTRINE

One of the OSCE's greatest strengths is the degree of field-level autonomy given to its missions. This provides field missions with the latitude to develop policies that are specific to their operations and political contexts. It also permits greater flexibility in policy formulation, and the development of narrowly focused country specific programmes, which encourage local buy-in. The OSCE's greatest strength, however, may also be its greatest weakness, as the high degree of field level autonomy seems to inhibit the organization from developing 'best practices'. In the case of SSR, this means the lack of an agreed strategic framework for reform that field missions could use to focus resources and tailor programmes to their specific country's circumstances. For this reason OSCE doctrine on SSR remains a work in progress. Lessons learned between the policing components of various missions are being exchanged through word of mouth rather than systematically mapped out with suggested entry points, approaches, and guidance notes.

Given the absence of a comprehensive SSR framework, the OSCE's reform efforts appear to occur in a haphazard manner, remaining more dependent on personalities in the field missions than on corporate policies. Further, although the OSCE has the available expertise, it may not possess the institutional structure to overcome this dilemma. The OSCE secretariat in Vienna is divided between the main policy body, the Conflict Prevention Centre (CPC) and thematic units such as the Strategic Police Matters Unit (SPMU), the Anti-Terrorist Unit, and the Anti-Trafficking Unit. Ideally, these units should develop policy guidance and an operational framework for field missions, but because of the disparate structure this has not happened.

Field missions – and this was apparent in Serbia and Montenegro – often expend a significant amount of their limited resources on reacting to political developments, rather than adopting a long-term approach to reform. In particular, the role of the SPMU needs to be re-evaluated. The SPMU is in a unique position to gather best practice from field missions and to develop an OSCE approach to SSR, thus ensuring organizational policy coherence. Due to a lack of vision and the dilution of its core purpose, neither the OSCE nor the SMPU have been effective in this regard.[22]

Additionally, the SPMU should be used as a clearing house for OSCE field missions, offering advice on how to engage country counterparts, as well as independent evaluators of reform programmes. The failure to develop credible indicators with which to measure the 'success' of its engagement in SSR has meant that, all too often, the effectiveness of OSCE programmes has been limited. In the Serbian case, for instance, while the Monk Report established a baseline, and an OSCE review was subsequently conducted in 2004, individual projects within the programme (such as the training curriculum used by the OSCE) were not assessed for effectiveness. The overarching strategic approach adopted by the OSCE was not evaluated either.

ANALYSIS OF ACTIVITIES

Planning and Internal Management

Given the absence of a corporate OSCE approach to police reform, and the organization's dependence on the personalities employed in the field mission, the planning of OSCE engagement in Serbia was fluid at best and at worst ad hoc.[23] Based upon its initial focus in southern Serbia, the OSCE undertook a broader training programme for the Serbian police, all the while keeping to the rubric that training was the keystone to police reform.[24] This emphasis on training defined the OSCE's engagement for the first two years following the fall of Milošević.

Early 2003 saw a radical strategic shift in OSCE's police reform activities with the adoption of a longer term, more strategic approach. While the need for this strategic shift had been highlighted in the Monk Report of 2001, it was not until two years later that the LED had the requisite leadership in place to implement the report's recommendations. The two-year delay in reorienting the OSCE programme may have had something to do with the senior mission staff being primarily concerned with generating 'outputs,' (i.e., number of police officers trained, number of different training courses offered, etc.), rather than in 'tangible outcomes' (i.e., the creation of an effective, rights-respecting police service).[25] The two-year delay also suggests that introducing a rigorous evaluation process at the beginning of the SSR process might have minimised the loss of time; such an assessment would have emphasised concrete results instead of the perpetuation of a relatively mindless and ineffectual numbers game.

A strategic shift from police training to police reform was essential if the OSCE's involvement in Serbia was to have a long-term, sustainable effect on Serbia's police. This shift called for a fundamental change in the type of personnel required by the mission and a new LED organizational structure. In other words, before reaching out to engage in SSR activities with the police, the OSCE had to reform its own organization.[26] The new structure created operationally focused police reform units, each tasked with one of the thematic areas laid out by the Monk Report and endorsed by the Serbian Ministry of Interior. Additionally, a Strategic Development Unit (SDU) was formed, whose responsibility was, first, to concentrate on the development of medium to long-term strategic plans across thematic areas; second, to evaluate OSCE projects; and third, to assist the Ministry of Interior in strengthening its strategic management capacity. With this revised internal structure (a process that took approximately four months), the OSCE was finally in a position to re-engage and offer a sustainable and coherent SSR programme.[27]

The organizational change within the OSCE's field mission, however, had to be matched by a comparable change in personnel. The majority of police trainer positions were to be phased out and police officers with operational expertise employed.[28] Furthermore, it was recognised that reforming an institution such as the police is an inherently political and public administration activity, and that the LED needed to have such expertise within its own ranks. This meant hiring civilian personnel, a problematic endeavour within the OSCE in that the organization's personnel policies militate against hiring non-police personnel into the police components of its field missions, as does, for instance, the UN's Department of Peacekeeping Operations.

The issue that the Serbia programme had to reflect on regarding staffing was that SSR is not only about the capacity or integrity of individual police officers, judges, or prison guards. It is about building effective, rights respecting, accountable institutions in which skilled, trained individuals perform a public service – one that must, moreover, change over time to meet the evolving needs of the populace employing it. Restructuring, reforming, building institutions (logistics, procurement, communications, budgeting, cost accounting, human resource management, auditing and oversight mechanisms) cannot be carried out solely by sworn police personnel.[29]

In fact, these activities, whether in a recipient police service or a donor SSR organization, should not be performed by sworn police personnel because such personnel are prohibitively costly and, in these functions, highly inefficient. The same holds true for oversight and accountability by the executive branch of government, as these are issues of governance, public administration, and public service reform.[30] Consequently, the LED needed a mixed staff of operational police personnel to work in the six areas suggested by the Monk Report alongside staff who possessed an entirely different set of skills, talents, and experience. The latter enabled the LED to work with the Security and Defence Committee in the Serbian parliament in order to advance a comprehensive approach to police accountability and oversight.

Renewed Engagement

The impact of this strategic shift is best illustrated by the OSCE's engagement in southern Serbia. With the OSCE's success in establishing the Multi-Ethnic Police

Element – thereby managing the crises of the immediate post-conflict period – it was anticipated that the OSCE would scale back its southern Serbian activities in 2003. Following a review of the security situation in southern Serbia, however, it became clear that the OSCE's MEPE project was only the first phase of a longer reform process.[31] The review of the situation in south Serbia noted that, although symbolically important for grounding the peace process, the MEPE was not capable of carrying out routine policing tasks. Because of the short programme, MEPE officers had little practical experience or skills in investigating crime, which was one of the reasons why the MEPE was operationally ineffective.[32] Another reason was that its personnel were assigned to remote stations and kept segregated from 'normal' police officers.[33] This led, in part, to the public belief that there was a cleavage between the Serbian police and the MEPE, further disgruntling individual MEPE officers because they saw limited potential for career advancement.

Recognising the situation for what it was, the OSCE pushed for the greater integration of the MEPE into the Serbian police and engaged in a deeper, longer term SSR programme, rather than pull out of southern Serbia. The result was a strategic shift with a focus on operational policing and the implementation of community policing, the provision of technical advice in reorganising the MEPE into the regular police, and assistance in developing accountability mechanisms.

Ownership/Civil Society

As a matter of policy, the OSCE focused its engagement only on programmes that originated from the senior levels of the police management, and which had the explicit support of the political leadership within the Ministry of the Interior. The mission developed a public image of 'assisting the reform process', while in reality it was often the driver of the process. In practice, it meant working closely with the middle management of the Ministry and, in most cases it was the middle management level that was the main engine of the reform process. Given that long-term police reform is institutional in nature, this may be not only inevitable in terms of operational activities, but also prudent because of middle management's centrality in determining the cultural norms of an institution.

It was here that resistance to reform was generated. While political pressure from international organizations may persuade and/or pressure senior management to sign off on a reform programme, concrete reform takes place during implementation and that, invariably, is the prerogative of middle management, whose ability – actively, passively, and/or informally – to impede reform is unparalleled. Although it is difficult to disentangle the resistance of middle management from Serbia's overall political instability, bureaucratic resistance to reform derived from managers dragging their feet and refusing to give priority to reform endeavours. For example, although the Law on Police Education was drafted and officially proposed, with the ostensible political support of senior police management, it remains in draft form. The same held true of the OSCE's inability to obtain assurances that the Serbian personnel who were given 'training' in order to become 'police trainers' would, in fact, be assigned as police trainers. Verbal assurances were never translated into the bureaucratic changes that signify sustainable reform.

Effectiveness of Reforms

As suggested above, while the MEPE programme was highly successful, and some progress occurred in institutional reform, significant challenges remained. The government of Serbia, the Ministry of Interior, Serbia's police officers and the reform process itself may be at a critical point, in part because Serbia's political instability has stymied long-term police reform and a sustainable reform process has not yet been launched. Meanwhile, police reform requires a reorganization of the ministry, the restructuring of police operations and education, and a streamlining and modernisation of the burgeoning administration.

The entire organization, structure, and culture of the police remains highly centralised, and committed to outdated management techniques.[34] At present the Ministry of the Interior and the Serbian police are inseparably integrated and highly politicised with little distinction between control and accountability. The establishment of the Office of the Inspector General in 2002 has been less than successful. The structure exists, but not the substance. The politicisation of the office by the Kostunica government has done little to enhance either its legitimacy or effectiveness – which emphasises the need to disentangle control and accountability, and decentralise the operations and activities of the ministry and police. A suggestion by the Serbian Minister of Interior, Dragan Jočić, that he was considering abolishing the Office of the Inspector General was worrying,[35] not least because it underlined the political reality that the Serbian government appears to be little interest in consolidating the democratic oversight and accountability of its security services.

The ministry also lacks transparent budgetary procedures, cost accounting, human resources planning and management, and career development. It is alleged the police have their own, extra-budgetary sources of income 'that are not subject to parliamentary approval and some of which may be illegal'.[36] What is certain is that authority is rarely delegated from senior management within the ministry to district commanders, let alone local station chiefs, with the result that even the most basic decisions go to the minister.[37] This top-down approach not only perpetuates the legacy of the Milošević regime, but also demoralises police personnel, stifling the belief that serving in the police is a viable career option for talented recruits. Finally, the police still need to undergo a comprehensive weeding and vetting process, not merely for war crimes, but also for alleged corruption.[38]

That said, the OSCE's concentration on circumscribed professional and operational issues (border security, crime scene management, community policing, police education, and organised crime) might have been appropriate, offering entry points on which long-term reform could be grounded. Without a reliable partner with whom to collaborate, the OSCE may have had little choice but to tone down its reform ambitions. Seen in this light, the assassination of Prime Minister Djindjić in

March 2003 illustrates not only what reforms were still required, but also why the OSCE strategy was politically realistic.

Djindjić's assassination signalled the active resistance to reform by organised crime syndicates (inside and outside the police), private business, residual elements of the former regime, and nationalist anti-democratic forces, many of whom also existed within the police and other security services.[39] During the years of sanctions, the Serbian state, with police acquiescence, organised smuggling activities, parcelling out lucrative 'franchises' in exchange for loyalty.[40] Many of these same intertwined business-police-political groupings are also deeply implicated in war crimes in Bosnia-Herzegovina, Croatia, and Kosovo. When Djindjic, under pressure from the West, began to pry into this unholy trinity through extraditions to The Hague War Crime Tribunal and organised crime investigations, he was assassinated by members of an elite Serbian police unit (Unit for Special Operations – JSO). Under the six-week state of emergency that followed his assassination, the government arrested thousands alleged to be involved in organised crime. Over 11,000 suspects were interrogated during Operation 'Sablja' 2,700 reputed criminals were detained,[41] while charges were lodged against almost 4,000 persons.

On the surface it appeared that the government was serious about eradicating organised crime within governmental structures, including the police. The 'outputs' were impressive, as police identified their own colleagues as the perpetrators of the murder and brought them before a court of law. However, many questioned the government's sincerity. The International Crisis Group, for example, claimed that Operation 'Sablja' failed to root out the financial underpinnings of the numerous criminal organizations, because the government was unable or unwilling to overcome strong obstructionist resistance within the armed forces, intelligence services, and police, not to mention its own political party ranks.[42] More pointedly, others argued that significant elements within the security sector not only resisted Operation 'Sablja' but were also actively engaged in organised crime in association with political and business interests.[43]

Given this, it is unrealistic to believe that the OSCE had an opportunity to conduct sustainable long-term institutional police reform. The combined powers of the various political, criminal, and business elements were fundamentally opposed to lasting reform; the fact that they not only 'negotiated' the transition from the Milošević regime, but also assassinated a prime minister and thwarted the subsequent investigation in defence of their self-interests is proof of this.

Operation 'Sablja' also underlined the deficiencies within the Serbian police. It was reported that their criminal investigation techniques were shoddy at best, relying on confessions instead of investigative expertise and the patient accumulation of forensic evidence because such skills did not exist in sufficient depth within the police.[44] If this is the case, then the OSCE's choice of short to medium term entry points that were technical and operational in nature (crime scene management and criminal investigation, for instance) must be questioned. Even so, the OSCE's role was arguably correct. For example, it played an instrumental role in developing legislation allowing the use of video footage as evidence in criminal prosecutions. Although this may appear to be a minor matter, it was a major step forward in reform because it strengthening the investigative capacities of the Serbian police. Furthermore, given the police deficiencies evident during Operation 'Sablja', the OSCE's focus on reforming police education showed foresight; training institutions were amalgamated, the police curriculum was revised, and in-service courses were developed. Consequently, the OSCE's intention of improving the professional skills of the police in selected technical areas may have been the only realistic reform option. Additionally, it opened up a broader dialogue within the police on the future direction that the reforms/modernisation process might take. However, structural reform and cultural change are long term objectives, so perhaps the OSCE could have done more to ensure that its engagement (especially in the education sphere) had long term impact. It could, for example, have ensured that the training packages and modern practices were implemented system wide, rather than on an ad hoc basis.

Measurement

The Monk Report represents the baseline study from which all future progress can be measured, while the 2004 report details the progress that had been made since the OSCE first engaged in police reform activities.[45] In fact, much of the progress made in recent years has been about sowing seeds of reform that will take years to bear fruit. The revision of training curricula in line with international standards, for example, and the recruitment of more female officers and officers from ethnic minorities are part of reforms that may have a long-term impact. Similarly, the introduction of community policing programmes throughout the country and the modernisation of policing procedures and equipment provided senior managers with a means to challenge and change the ethos and philosophy of the service.

No project specific evaluations have been carried out by the OSCE so it is impossible to assert whether OSCE's strategy and efforts were successful or not. Although it is necessary for the OSCE to assess the quality and impact of its training curricula and the content of its programmes so as to ensure that lessons are learned and mistakes are not perpetuated, this has not been done. A detailed evaluation of specific reform areas would enable the OSCE to identify where its programming could be improved and what the obstacles to change have been. Such analysis/evaluation is essential not only for the OSCE engagement in Serbia to be effective, but also for lessons to be learned at an institutional level. Such analysis would feed into the institutional understanding of reform within the security sector, assist the development of police reform, and facilitate the development of the next generation of OSCE policing missions.

Lessons

The need to establish best practice is crucial for all development actors engaged in SSR. Lessons learned are the building blocks for strategic planning in future programmes, guiding the development and resourcing of activities that can be undertaken as part of the SSR process. Further, the development of operational frameworks based on lessons learned (including comprehensive indicators) could help to frame reforms and provide a means of evaluating progress.

A consideration of the OSCE's programme in Serbia is instructive in several ways. Because of budgeting cycles, personnel policies, and political imperatives, international organizations, including the OSCE, have historically focused on short-term SSR programming, which usually concentrates on training initiatives. Such programmes have a limited effect on the long-term reform of the security sector because they rarely modify the work, culture and values of the police, let alone affect the institutional core of the organization. Nevertheless, a distinction has to be made between securing the peace and creating a long-term stable and viable security system. The MEPE experience offers a good example of a well-conceived, short-term SSR crisis management solution that focused on a training regime revolving around ethnic integration and joint patrolling.

Once a degree of confidence building was attained, the OSCE needed to overhaul its own structure and programming in order to meet political realities and operational exigencies, and engage in the longer-term process of building a viable and accountable security apparatus. This called for personnel capable of rebuilding an organization, a class of individuals with skills that are more readily obtainable outside the ranks of police personnel and, in the case of the OSCE, outside its customary pool of staff seconded from national police services.

Additionally, transitions from one type of SSR programme to another highlight the need for international organizations and implementing agencies to be highly flexible, and able to take advantage of changing political realities within recipient countries. Structures and personnel that may have been advantageous during one period of time may prove debilitating in another. In this sense, it behoves organizations such as the OSCE and UN Peacekeeping to work primarily on a project basis. It may be more productive if personnel seconded to the OSCE, for instance, are contracted for particular projects over a definitive time, rather than for the ubiquitous, extendable six-month 'tour of duty'. This is particularly important for the OSCE, given that the organization has not formulated a corporate SSR strategy.

Because of Serbia's level of political flux, the process of police reform was never certain. Although the OSCE and some elements within government were committed to the process, the level of instability made long-term SSR initiatives difficult to plan and implement. The OSCE's experience thus highlights the need for donor institutions to understand the inherently political nature of SSR and to tailor reform efforts to coincide with the relationship between the political drivers of change, resistance to change, and the role of potential entry points in unstable environments. As illustrated here, short-term, surface-level SSR (e.g., police training) has little productive utility unless connected to longer-term structural, organizational, and managerial reforms, although such holistic and comprehensive processes may not always be straightforward, or even possible under conditions of severe political instability.

The need to understand the different phases of post-conflict transition is clear from the OSCE's experience in Serbia. Securing peace and ensuring long-term stability, requires different objectives, activities and personnel. While early attempts by the OSCE to encourage deep institutional reform may have been difficult, the lack of a fully fledged OSCE strategy on SSR, or a holistic understanding of the post-conflict dynamic, meant that opportunities to widen reforms were missed.

NOTES

1. Dr Rory Keane was previously spokesperson of the OSCE Mission to Serbia and Montenegro, and now works on post-conflict peace-building policy. Dr Mark Downes currently works as the administrator of the OECD Development Assistance Committee Network on Conflict Peace and Development Cooperation. He was previously the head of the Strategic Development Unit of the Law Enforcement Department of the OSCE Mission to Serbia and Montenegro. The opinions expressed and arguments employed in this article are the sole responsibility of the authors and do not necessarily reflect the official views of the OECD, or the governments of any OECD member countries.
2. See Maria Raquel Freire, *Conflict and Security in the Former Soviet Union: The Role of the OSCE*, (Aldershot: Ashgate 2003).
3. Milošević's removal from office may best be described as a negotiated transition arranged after an election that he and his party lost, for many of his entourage and supporters switched allegiances in order to maintain their personal prerogatives. The assassination in 2003 of his successor, Zoran Djindjić, underlines the negotiated nature of the transition from Milošević, for Djindjić's own elite police (a unit that supported his assumption of power) was identified as responsible for his murder.
4. This article concentrates exclusively on the larger Serbia part of the OSCE's work although work was ongoing in Montenegro also.
5. During the Kosovo war, the Serbian police were provided with helicopters, armoured personnel carriers, and heavy weaponry that police do not customarily possess. One of the reasons for equipping them in a military fashion was that Milošević deemed the police politically more reliable than the military.
6. Marijana Trivunović, 'Status of Police Reform after Four Years of Democratic Transition in Serbia', *Helsinki Monitor* 3 (2004) p.172.
7. The mandate of the new mission, which was established in Jan. 2001, included a focus on the rule of law, democratisation, media development and law enforcement.
8. 'Of the 386 attacks logged [between May 1999 and Dec. 2000], more than three quarters were directed against the police'. Gordon Peake *Policing the Peace: Police Reform Experiences in Kosovo, Southern Serbia and Macedonia* (London: Saferworld 2004) p.29.
9. A total 406 MEPE officers were trained as part of the three month programme. This period of training was supplemented by 15 weeks of 'on-the-job' training (commonly referred to as field training) and a supplementary 24 weeks probationary period. Officers already serving in southern Serbia (non-MEPE officers) received additional training on issues such as human rights, police ethics and guidelines for operating in a multi-ethnic environment.
10. See Mark Downes, 'South Serbia' in Law Enforcement Department of the OSCE mission to Serbia and Montenegro, *Police Reform in Serbia; towards the creation of a modern and accountable police service* (OSCE 2004).
11. See Danish Institute of Human Rights,'Vision Process for the Reform of the Ministry of Interior of Serbia', <www.humanrights.dk/departments/international/partnercountries/thebalkans/balkanother/Serbia_DIHR/> (accessed Nov. 2005).
12. Trivunovic (note 6) p.175.
13. See OSCE (note 10).
14. The Ministry also disbanded the Special Forces Units operating in southern Serbia. These were integrated into a new force (the gendarmerie) in 2001.
15. This was evident from public perception surveys carried out by the OSCE and the Ministry of the Interior as part of the introduction of community based policing.
16. Developed by the Accountability and Community Policing Unit within the Law Enforcement Department.

17. Helsinki Committee for Human Rights in Serbia, *Human Rights and Accountability: Serbia 2003I8* (Belgrade: Helsinki Committee for Human Rights in Serbia 2004) p.94.
18. Trivunovic (note 6) p.180.
19. For a discussion of the continued politicalisation of the police, see 'Police Torture Case Divides Serbia', <http://amisnet.org/en/2876> (accessed Nov. 2005).
20. See the OSCE Unified Budget for 2004, adopted at the 489th Plenary Meeting of the Permanent Council on 24 Dec. 2003, PC.DEC/590.
21. OSCE Law Enforcement includes 24 international staff (12 trainers and 12 specialist staff) and 30 national staff.
22. The final report from the Panel of Eminent Persons 'Common Purpose: Towards a More Effective OSCE' (OSCE, June 2005) highlights that the CSCE/OSCE quickly recognised the need for a comprehensive approach to security issues. The panel's report sought to re-align OSCE activities with this original goal.
23. Written response by a former OSCE LED staff member to questions posed through email correspondence, March 2005.
24. Most OSCE LED staff prior to 2003 were police trainers without extensive experience in police reform projects, and hence unsuitable to manage a strategic reform programme. The lack of a strategic approach to reform meant that as of Sept. 2002, the LED had no cogent plans for its 2003 activities.
25. Written response by a former OSCE LED staff member, March 2005.
26. Ibid.
27. Ibid.
28. The personnel situation within the OSCE is problematic given the organization's dependence on staff seconded from national administrations, the limited number of national staff participating states have available for secondment, and the limited durations seconded staff are permitted to spend in any one field mission. This, coupled with the limit placed by many countries on the amount of total time their personnel can spend on international duty, means that key personnel may have a limited effect on the reform process.
29. The prevalence of non-sworn personnel in the police is increasing throughout the Western world, so it is safe to presume that the same logic would apply to SSR programmes in post-conflict countries as well.
30. Currently neither the structural make-up of OSCE field missions nor its budgetary compartmentalisation enables a comprehensive SSR response that takes into account all these skill sets. For example, OSCE parliamentary oversight work falls within the mandate of the democratisation department and budget, while accountability straddles both the rule of law and law enforcement departments and budgets. Creating a synergetic and holistic SSR programme in such fragmented circumstances is exceedingly difficult. Seconded personnel typically work a six-month rotation, which may be renewable. Fieldwork, however, requires a minimum of six months before an individual can work to his/her productive capacity; it requires that length of time to become sufficiently versed in the work of the mission, and the dynamics of the national situation.
31. Undertaken as part of the research for OSCE (note 10).
32. Mark Downes, 'From Securing the Peace to Ensuring Stability', paper presented at conference on 'Community Based Policing', IPA, New York, 22 March 2004.
33. The term 'stations' is used loosely. MEPE officers were stationed in 'containers' for between 4 and 15 days, many of which were in remote locations. For an overview of the reform of the MEPE see OSCE (note 10).
34. Ibid.
35. See *Danas*, 29 March 2005, p.1.
36. International Crisis Group (ICG), *Serbia: Spinning its Wheels,* Europe Briefing No.39, (Belgrade/Brussels 23 May 2005) p.7.
37. See 'Organizational structure and strategic planning' and 'Administrative reform, human resources and career development' in OSCE (note 10).
38. With regard to alleged war crimes, 'the Serbian war crimes prosecutor, Vladimir Vukćević, has stated that the 'police take no initiative to detect crimes on their own', and 'there is resistance in the Ministry of Internal Affairs to policemen going out on their own and finding perpetrators'. ICG (note 36) p.6.
39. This was clearly illustrated in the report produced by the commission headed by vice-premier Zarko Korać that was tasked with probing Djindjić's security arrangements following his assassination. The report (published in Aug. 2003) highlighted the insidious influence of the JSO Special Operations

Unit, describing its existence as 'a negative factor in the functioning of the entire security system in the Republic of Serbia' and as a 'cancer on the body of the security structures'. See 'A report on the establishment, organizations and operation of the security system of the Prime Minister of the Government of the Republic of Serbia Dr. Zoran Djindić, with measures proposed' (Belgrade Aug. 2003).
40. Trivunović (note 6) p.172.
41. Vladimir Matić, *Serbia after Djindjić: Can Invigorated Reforms be Sustained?* (Boston: Public Int. Law and Policy Group 2003).
42. See Marina Caparini, 'Serbia and Montenegro' in *Stockholm International Peace Research Institute Yearbook 2004* (Stockholm: SIPRI/OUP) p.273.
43. Trivunović (note 6) p.184.
44. Ibid.
45. OSCE (note 10).

Neighbourhood Peacekeeping: The Inter-American Development Bank's Violence Reduction Programs in Colombia and Uruguay

ERIK ALDA, MAYRA BUVINIĆ AND JORGE LAMAS[1]

Although crime and violence is a significant hindrance to development, development banks have often shied from working directly on the issue.[2] One lender stands out from this trend: since the mid-1990s the Inter-American Development Bank (IDB) has explicitly directed loans to violence reduction efforts on the basis that the everyday violence and insecurity which afflicts much of Latin America hinders economic and social development in the region.[3]

The IDB adopts a broad policy approach and programming focus, holding that the many causes of violence require multiple solutions to address the social, political, economic and cultural contexts in which violence occurs. Funded programs include efforts to strengthen criminal justice institutions, reform aspects of the police, improve the treatment of domestic violence victims, reduce the potential for youth to become involved in crime, strengthen civil society organizations and raise social awareness. This article examines the IDB approach using project reports, evaluation data, and staff interviews to describe and reflect on programming in Colombia and Uruguay, where the first 'stand alone' loan projects intended to prevent violence and crime have been undertaken.

LATIN AMERICA'S VIOLENCE PROBLEM

Latin America, mirroring a depressing worldwide trend, has become a significantly more violent place over the last 20 years. For example, between the mid-1980s and the mid-1990s, average homicide rates in the region rose by more than 80 percent.[4] Some widespread types of violence are largely unseen and typically go under-reported, particularly violence in the home. Some 20 to 30 percent of adult women with partners report physical abuse at some point in a relationship, and more than half of all women with partners report experiencing sexual, psychological or physical abuse at some point.[5] Studies have suggested that violence against children is also pervasive.[6] Violence regularly polls as the fourth or fifth main concern of citizens, but in 2005 it jumped to second most important area of concern in the region (see Table 1).

A single, coherent, empirically supported explanation of the sharp increase in violence in Latin America has yet to emerge. The most compelling data at the macro-level links rising violence to the growing demographic shares of the population in younger age classes, which statistically are more prone to aggression. There also is a significant relationship between violence and high (and increasing) income inequality in the region.[7] In some parts of Latin America, for example, 'the income of the wealthiest fifth of households is 30 times greater than that of the poorest fifth'.[8] Social exclusion of groups by ethnicity and/or race, closely linked to inequality, may also fuel violence. Another likely contributing factor is the rapidly growing trade in weapons and drugs linked to globalization, organized crime and the fallout from the civil conflicts of the 1980s. Finally, there is evidence that inertia is at play at the societal level, and that violence begets more violence.[9]

In addition to these macro level variables, several specific institutional, community, household and individual level factors help explain Latin America's comparatively high levels of violence. Criminal justice systems lack institutional capacity to address rates of violence, while conditions in poor urban slums with deteriorated infrastructure can act as triggers of violence. An authoritarian culture that condones male violence against women and children, high rates of unemployment among youth, and a tradition of heavy drinking among males also serve as contributory factors.[10] Although poverty has not been directly linked to the rise in violence, it can aggravate its consequences, as the poor lack the resources needed to minimize the impact of violence on themselves and their families.[11]

Multiple Costs of Violence

The pervasiveness of violence is a major obstacle to the region's economic and social development. Violence hinders growth, exacerbates poverty, generates a climate of fear among citizens and presents difficult challenges for democratic

TABLE 1

RANKING OF CITIZEN CONCERNS IN LATIN AMERICA (2000–2005)[i]

2000		2001		2002		2003		2004		2005	
Problem	%	Problem	%	Problem	%	Problem	%	Problem	%	Problem	%
Unemployment	21.28	Unemployment	22.42	Unemployment	25.25	Unemployment	28.37	Unemployment	29.04	Unemployment	29.91
Education	21.18	Corruption	10.12	Low Salaries	11.78	Low Salaries	10.73	Inflation/ Economic Crises	14.66	Crime and Violence	14.01
Corruption	9.1	Poverty	9.39	Corruption	11.37	Corruption	10.45	Poverty	10.74	Political Problems	8.76
Crime and Violence	7.96	Crime and Violence	8.97	Poverty	10.34	Poverty	9.74	Crime and Violence	9.39	Inflation/ Price increase	8.71
Poverty	7.18	Unemployment Instability	8.92	Crime and Violence	7.41	Crime and Violence	8.29	Corruption	7.99	Poverty	6.53
Low Salaries	6.97	Low Salaries	8.5	Unemployment Instability	6.31	Unemployment Instability	5.54	Other	4.67	Corruption	6.12

i Authors calculations based on data from the Latinobarometer. Latinobarómetro is an annual public opinion survey of approximately 19.000 interviews in 18 countries in Latin America representing more than 400 million inhabitants. Available at http://www.latinobarometro.org/index.php?id = 150 (accessed February 2006) governance and peaceful coexistence. Attempts to arrest violence stretch government resources and redirect them from more economically productive purposes. It aggravates economic uncertainty, thereby undermining development processes. Violence in Latin America imposes estimated annual economic costs of US$15 billion in lost wealth and income, costing countries anywhere between 5 and 25 percent or more of their gross domestic product (GDP) in particular years. Specific forms of violence, such as violence against women, can cost countries up to two percent of GDP.[12] These numbers are especially telling in a region where average per capita GDP growth over the past decade was either negative or stagnant.

The IDB funded and conducted research that sought to break down and quantify the economic costs of violence in four categories: direct costs, indirect or non-monetary costs, and economic and social multiplier effects.[13] Direct costs of violence measure the value of resources spent in goods and services to prevent violence and attend to victims, and the expenditures made on public security and criminal justice system to apprehend and/or prosecute perpetrators of violence. This is measured by health impacts (health expenditures due to criminal violence), public costs (public and private expenditures on police, security, judiciary), transfers (value of asset transfers, ransoms and bribes), and intangibles (amount civilians would be willing to pay to live without violence) (Table 2).[14]

'Indirect costs' include measures of the non-monetary effects on victims of violence, such as increases in morbidity and mortality due to homicides and suicides, substance abuse, and depression. The non-monetary effects of violence are tabulated using a health measure, the disability adjusted life year (DALY), which quantifies the years of healthy life lost to violence-related mortality and morbidity.[15] In Latin America, violence ranks as the most important cause of DALYs lost for men in the ages 15 to 44. Men lose more DALYs from violence in Latin America than in any other region of the world.[16] Between 18 and 27 percent of disability adjusted life years lost in Colombia during 1989–95 were attributable to homicide.[17]

The third measure of violence – the economic multiplier effect – records the impact that crime and violence exert on the overall economy. Violence generates

TABLE 2
ECONOMIC COSTS OF VIOLENCE IN LATIN AMERICA AS A PERCENTAGE OF GDP[i]

	El Salvador	Colombia	Venezuela	Brazil	Peru	Mexico
Direct Costs	9.2	11.4	6.9	3.3	2.9	4.9
Health Losses	4.3	5	0.3	1.9	1.5	1.3
Material Losses	4.9	6.4	6.6	1.4	1.4	3.6
Indirect Costs	11.7	8.9	4.6	5.6	1.6	4.6
Investment and Productivity	0.2	2	2.4	2.2	0.6	1.3
Labor and Consumption	11.5	6.9	2.2	3.4	1	3.3
Transfers	4	4.4	0.3	1.6	0.6	2.8
Total	24.9	24.7	11.8	10.5	5.1	12.3

Source: Londõno and Guerrero, 1999.

significant multiplier effects such as lower accumulation of human capital, decreased participation in the labour market, lower on-the-job productivity, higher rates of absenteeism, and lower incomes. Uncertainty generated by violence has led to lower rates of savings, investment and production; a failure to implement economically efficient programs; less effective economic policies; higher formal and informal unemployment rates; and higher poverty levels.[18]

The final measure of the costs of violence is the social multiplier effect, which records the intergenerational transmission of violence, erosion of social capital, reduction in quality of life, and decline in participation in democratic processes. Although the empirical evidence needed to document these social multiplier effects is the most difficult to gather, their impact on development may be the most lasting. For instance, violent homes in Latin America have been shown to be more likely to produce violent children than non-violent ones.[19] Moreover, children raised in violent homes are more likely to show behavioural problems in school, repeat grades and drop out of school.[20]

ECONOMIC REASONING FOR SUPPORTING ANTI-VIOLENCE INITIATIVES

In 1996 the IDB was the first development bank to lend money to its member countries for the explicit purpose of addressing insecurity. This was not entirely new ground, for it had been observed that existing lending areas affected levels of violence. Two areas of lending in particular (aspects of which can be seen in the Colombia and Uruguay projects) exemplify this.

The first is investments in the area of social prevention, namely actions taken to decrease the likelihood that individuals in high-risk groups become either victims or perpetrators of violence. Such programmes include pre- and postnatal care of at risk or low-income mothers; early childhood development programmes; incentives for disadvantaged youth to complete high school education; and courses in peaceful conflict resolution for high-risk groups.[21]

The second area of lending is 'situational prevention', or activities that focus on protecting citizens from potential victimization.[22] These actions include erecting physical obstacles and mounting surveillance systems to inhibit criminal acts in specific places such as residences, businesses and public spaces. Some programmes try to design out crime by improving the security of housing, vehicles, and other property, often through door-to-door visits advising residents about ways to improve security. Police and security experts have worked with urban planners and designers to incorporate safety issues into municipal and private developments. Some programs claim 70 per cent reductions in burglary rates as a result.[23]

Taken together, evaluation results from this area of lending suggested that further benefits could accrue from even more targeted work on violence reduction. In that spirit, IDB President Enrique V. Iglesias launched the IDB's direct work on violence reduction in 1996. Despite broad political support among the countries of the region for collaboration between multilateral development banks and national institutions to reduce and prevent violence, considerable risks accompanied this new area of lending. Underwriting the work required bold leadership, sound justification and guidance. There was also resistance and scepticism to overcome. At the outset, the IDB Board had to be convinced of the merits of what was potentially a politically risky course of action. The Board believed that the Bank should have been reducing, rather than expanding, the already wide spectrum of its activities. Another difficulty was squaring this new line of lending with clauses in the IDB charter, which restricts work with certain actors such as the police, and stipulates that the IDB should not interfere directly in the political affairs of member countries.[24]

Ultimately, development arguments won over the sceptics. The research commissioned and carried out by IDB staff stressed the developmental benefits that could accrue from investing in violence reduction. Therefore, the proposed new line of programmes would meet the 'economic justification' test required by the IDB's Charter, which asks whether programming choices can be justified solely on economic grounds.[25] Guiding, evaluating and formulating programming choices through rigorous economic research and data would become a hallmark of the IDB's approach.

Another distinct feature of the IDB policy approach is an emphasis on prevention. Again, the rationale is economic, grounded in research that shows its greater cost-effectiveness when compared with control interventions.[26] In addition, prevention fits well with the conceptual paradigm that links domestic and social violence and the IDB's strong tradition of social sector lending. Emphasizing prevention would also help define and delimit actions in certain projects to avoid contradicting basic principles established in the IDB's charter.

To help IDB staff respond to government requests in potentially proscribed areas, detailed guidelines for the design of violence reduction projects were prepared.[27] These guidelines delineate the overall preventive approach for IDB interventions, give examples of proscribed activities, and provide a general framework of the areas in which the bank can and cannot lend. When identifying areas of lending, IDB staff and consultants hired to work on projects refer to these guidelines to ensure that final projects conform to bank policy.

The design of violence prevention and citizen security projects are based on analyses carried out by IDB staff and consultants on the main challenges faced in a specific country. A thorough baseline profile is compiled to identify specific needs that require attention, and project design tailored accordingly. The IDB designs and funds projects, but it does not directly execute them. Actual implementation is the responsibility of national and local governments. Due to the complex and multi-faceted nature of citizen security projects, project management usually involves a lead executing agency that coordinates the actions of several ministries (e.g. education, health, community development) as well as of non-governmental actors. In the projects in Colombia and Uruguay, the Ministry of Interior coordinated the IDB intervention.

Measuring Impact

As in any IDB-financed operation, monitoring and evaluation of project impacts were important features of project design, even more so to observe whether this new line of lending activity was having the desired effects. In particular, it was important to show that the projects themselves were beneficial in terms of reduced violence in order to justify this new area of lending. The selection of indicators to monitor and evaluate this new form of lending projects presented something of a conundrum. Project performance is normally measured in comparison to other projects, but since most violence reduction interventions were being tried for the first time there was no past performance record and little operational experience to draw from. Therefore, the project's information requirements incorporated a wide variety of sources, including literature evaluating the impact of violence prevention programs in developed countries.

The IDB has now developed a body of information on its work. To ensure proper impact evaluations, project preparation involves the use of victimisation surveys and other tools. This creates baseline data that allow a comparison of pre- and post-intervention situations, and the measurement of results. The IDB collects two main types of data to assess program effects: macro evaluations that attempt to determine whether a programme as a whole has lowered violence levels, and micro evaluations that determine whether beneficiaries of specific interventions (e.g. an after-school sports programme) experience lower levels of violent behaviour than equivalent non-beneficiaries. This second type of evaluation is methodologically straight-forward and particularly helpful in compiling a list of approaches determined to be effective. As the IDB accumulates experience in this area, the data collected provides a basis for comparison with ongoing projects and serves as an information source from which to incorporate best practices and lessons learned.

OPERATIONS IN COLOMBIA AND URUGUAY

Since 1998 the IDB has approved US$130 million for six stand-alone violence reduction projects in Latin America.[28] The Uruguay project ran from 1998 to 2002 ($ 17.5 million loan), and is now fully completed. As of 2006, the Colombia project ($ 57 million) was fully executed in the capital city, Bogotá, while evaluations are underway in the cities of Cali and Medellin. The IDB's violence reduction projects have been wide-ranging and multifaceted in both countries, incorporating activities in the following six areas: institutional strengthening; preventive policing; work with victims of domestic violence, helping at-risk youth, civil society initiatives and raising social awareness. The following sub-sections reflect on the management of each programming area and evaluate the results that have emerged.

Strengthening Criminal Justice

Given their ineffectiveness, the high levels of public distrust in both the Colombian and Uruguayan criminal justice institutions are understandable.[29] These institutions lack the capacity to either craft or enforce appropriate crime prevention policies. Management is weak, and the institutions do not have the necessary human resources with the capacity to collect, analyze and interpret data on crime and evaluate results. There is little tradition of working with other government sectors either to collect reliable information on crime and violence or to coordinate interventions. Access to the justice system is very limited for many Colombians and Uruguayans; the high cost of presenting a case before the courts limits low-income citizens' access to legal services. Taken together, these factors have undermined the credibility of the judicial system, which has led to the rise of providers of private justice offering conflict resolution services outside the law, generally through violence

To respond to these problems, the IDB prioritized institutional strengthening actions in its lending operations, allotting $4.1 million in Colombia and $1.1 million in Uruguay.[30] Information management systems were provided to the ministries of interior in both countries so as to monitor and evaluate crime data in order to identify problems, track progress and develop appropriate responses. The basic hardware needed to run these systems (computers and printers, for examples) did not exist in sufficient quantities, and so were supplied as part of the project's start-up. An issue that quickly emerged was the lack of capacity among recipient agencies to design and manage some of the projects and systems being proposed. Thus, the lending portfolio included training of personnel in strategic planning, monitoring and evaluation, client orientation and public communication, as well as in technical areas.

Evaluations recorded positive results. In Bogotá, additional IDB funding combined with the municipal administration's own commitment to develop policies and programs for citizen security resulted in the creation of effective new institutions, including an office for citizen security and a city-wide 'violence observatory', which gathered detailed information on crime and violence. The information was then used as the basis for policy formulation. For example, access to information led to the adoption of effective policies to combat crime, including the control of firearms and restrictions in the sale of alcohol. The changes are reflected in drastically improved crime statistics. Murders in Bogotá dropped by 65 percent between 1994 and 2003.

In Uruguay, institutional strengthening activities helped usher change in the organizational culture of the Interior Ministry. Previously, the emphasis had been on controlling violence after it occurred, but the IDB intervention prompted a shift toward prevention. The ministry's development of violence prevention policies and an action agenda is one indicator of that shift. Renovations of basic equipment for data collection and staff training in the ministry have also proved valuable. The funding of a unified geo-referenced system that maps crime reports against other social data proved particularly beneficial, helping identify crime hot spots and encouraging inter-agency cooperation on crime and violence reduction.

Police Reform

The poor performance of the police is at the core of Latin America's citizen security problem. Common problems afflicting the region's police include a tendency to over-extend their responsibilities, low capacity in intra- and inter-agency coordination and cooperation, deficient internal and external control, excessive bureaucracy and centralized decision-making.[31] Practicing a style of policing that is reactive rather than proactive, the police are cited frequently for recurring illegal practices, abuse of power, corruption and excessive use of force.[32] Officers tend, in the main, to be poorly educated, poorly trained and poorly paid.[33]

Although demand for financing police reform has been high, the IDB has had to tread carefully in order to finance interventions that did not contravene the restrictions in its charter, interfere in national political matters and/or violate human rights standards. The Bank's *Guidelines for the Design of Violence Reduction Projects* stress that 'in all their work with police forces, IDB teams should emphasize the strengthening of the preventive functions of the civilian police force'.[34] The IDB also does not fund the acquisition of lethal or potentially lethal equipment (e.g., weapons, ammunition). Thus, IDB loans have emphasized certain aspects of police reform such as professional police training and preventive and community policing.[35] To date, these limitations in scope have precluded the IDB from financing more comprehensive police restructuring and reform in such areas as salary and incentive structures, decision-making, and internal and external accountability.[36]

In both the Colombia and Uruguay programs, the IDB has made funds available for efforts to improve information management and strengthen police planning capacity. In Colombia, the IDB funded a review and modification of the police-training curriculum and the provision of training courses in human rights, while in Uruguay projects focused on preventive and community policing and training the police in how to deal with high-risk groups, such as women and youth.[37]

Despite the constraints imposed by lending guidelines, these measures appear to have had a positive impact. For instance, in Bogotá police captures increased by 400 percent between 1994 and 2002, and the number of firearms handed over to the police tripled between 1995 and 2003.[38] The installation of new information management systems enabled the police to improve their response time and effectiveness. The strengthening of police planning capacity and use of information management in Bogotá allowed the introduction of results-oriented management that rewards police according to trends in crime indicators; this is modelled on the COMPSTAT system developed in New York City.[39] Police departments in Colombia underwent yearly evaluations that examined performance on crime reduction, capture of criminals, and recovery of guns and stolen property. The success of such programs is linked directly to other unique features of Bogotá's experience. In particular, the sustained commitment of different administrations has translated into a prioritization of violence reduction actions and a roughly tripled police budget.

Although police reform in Uruguay did not enjoy a similar level of political support, evaluations indicate a change in orientation among officers trained in the philosophies and methodologies of community policing and community relations. In addition, 585 police received training on the use of more sensitive methods in treating victims of domestic violence. New courses on preventive policing were introduced as a requirement for promotion, and certain positions now require higher levels of education. Polling surveys suggest the positive effects of these reforms, indicating a 25 percent increase in the number of citizens that express confidence in police performance.[40]

Work with Victims of Domestic Violence

Domestic violence is a major problem in the region.[41] In response, the IDB concentrates its lending activities on tackling both domestic and social violence risk factors, principally through social prevention. In addition to strong moral arguments for this policy, there is also a sound development rationale. Domestic violence reduces women's earnings, and research has shown the intrinsic as well as the instrumental value of mainstreaming attention to the issue.[42] Violence is mostly a learned behaviour and, as one of the earliest opportunities for learning violence is in the home, early prevention of domestic violence helps avoid transmission to future generations.

Studies on domestic violence and early intervention show that violence can be unlearnt, thereby reducing the likelihood that children growing up in a potentially violent household will become offenders when they reach adulthood.[43] This dynamic also re-emphasizes a sound cost justification: preventing children from developing into abusers is far more cost-effective in the long-term than having to pay for incarceration.[44]

In Colombia, a major element of the project's focus was improving the interface between the police and victims of abuse. This included training in appropriate handling of domestic violence as well as an institutional innovation called 'family police stations' in Bogotá. As well as regular police services, these multi-service centres were staffed with a range of specialists able to provide multiple services to victims of domestic violence, including medical screening, psychological counselling and legal aid. Most families afflicted by domestic violence relied on these services relating to children such as food allowances, custodial and spousal visits.[45] The stations also served to decongest the increasingly high number of cases in the courts. Evaluation data indicates that victims rated them as the most helpful public sector institution in addressing issues of domestic violence.[46]

Evaluations show room for improvement that could be incorporated in future project design. Although these stations were effective in providing protection to victims, they were less adept at mediating cases of physical aggression against women, which constitute about 40 percent of their caseload. Many of the mediated conciliation agreements lacked an enforcement component, and often failed to prevent further, frequently more intense, aggression.[47]

In the Uruguay project, activities included campaigns to increase public awareness of the scale of the issue, and training for public officials in appropriate responses to victims of domestic violence.[48] The bulk of the $1.1 million dollars allocated to preventing domestic violence went to improved assistance and rehabilitation services for victims of domestic violence through counselling and psychological treatment.[49] The project produced positive results: a decrease in the number of households reporting domestic violence incidents was associated with nine projects designed to improve services for victims in areas where access to such services previously had been sparse. Research data showed a decline in psychological abuse from 46 percent in 1997 to 33 percent.[50] Also, parallel work with the police may have contributed to the reduction of domestic violence against women. In each police district, for instance, officers received sensitivity training to better respond to victims of abuse, and an 'action guide' for dealing with domestic violence cases was developed and distributed to police stations across the country. These initiatives (combined with an increased public confidence in the police) helped increase the number of charges filed by more than 200 percent between 1997 and 2000.[51]

The loan also generated additional follow-on benefits as it encouraged the Uruguayan government to begin its own work on domestic violence. This has led to three significant outcomes: training for 600 staff in the health, education and justice ministries to identify and provide better services to victims; the development, under the Ministry of Education and Culture, of a national plan to fight domestic violence; and a new law intended to prevent domestic violence that received legislative approval in 2003.[52]

Work with At-Risk Youths

Levels of youth crime and violence have experienced exponential growth in recent years. In Colombia, for example, 15 to 34-year-olds accounted for 60 percent of homicides in the late 1990s. Governments request the IDB to finance efforts to reduce levels of youth violence, and address risk factors such as association with gangs or other high-risk peer groups, and alcohol and substance abuse.[53] The Colombia and Uruguay loans include funding for activities such as skills training and income generation programs to facilitate youths' entry into the labour market; remedial training to facilitate re-entry into the school system; development of training curricula in conflict resolution, mediation skills and coexistence; and recreational activities to promote constructive use of leisure time after school and during weekends.[54]

Although there is no evaluation data that directly correlates these interventions with reductions in violent behaviour, the results do suggest moderate success in interventions that sought to place youth in the labour market and schooling, as well as changes in aggressive attitudes. Course attendees have also shown improvement in how they handle conflict in the school and at home. As with initiatives in the field of domestic violence, the IDB's funding of initial programs has led to follow-up programming by the Uruguayan government. For example, the country's National Administration for Public Education is committed to continuing school-based violence prevention activities.[55]

Funding for after-school and recreational activities in Bogotá also appears to have had an impact. Participants in these programs expressed interest in creative and artistic activities and showed significant changes in their perception of violence.[56] Evaluations suggest that these programs reinforced the development of values and promoted peaceful coexistence.[57] In addition, the programs provided alternative ways to occupy youths' free time, and promoted their role as social agents in their communities. Many program participants became positive mentors to other youths in the community.

Particularly positive results were recorded in the area of schooling. Despite limited resources directed at the problem of school desertion, the majority of youths who attended school training were able to go back to the formal education system.[58] However, programs to enhance access to employment opportunities were less successful. While training programs provided beneficiaries with basic business and technical skills, they did not facilitate youths' entry into the labour market. For example, youths who were able to find jobs often found themselves working in an area for which they had not been trained. It is hard to determine whether this was due to problems with the training, or to labor market constraints. [59] Hence, it would be useful to develop monitoring mechanisms that track whether youths are actually entering the labour market, and are able to make use of the skills learned during the intervention.

Civil Societies' Involvement

Given the multifaceted nature and impact of crime, the IDB prioritizes the involvement of local communities in the development and implementation of crime prevention strategies. Therefore projects in both countries funded the delivery of violence prevention services by civil society organizations.

In Colombia, where access to formal legal services are financially out of the reach of the majority of the population, the IDB financed the creation of Conciliation and Mediation Centers that offer a variety of counselling services and legal advice for non-violent conflict resolution. This initiative has yielded significant results both at national and municipal levels by providing services to three times the target number of clients (30,000) set for the 1999–2002 period. The vast majority of cases that came before the centres were related to land, housing and property issues (55 percent), non-compliance with contracts (17 percent), and domestic disputes (11 percent).[60]

In Uruguay, the IDB funded two pilot conflict prevention centers, which were staffed by three police officers specializing in community policing, together with one lawyer, one psychologist and one social worker. Between 2000 and 2002 the two centres handled more than 1,000 cases relating to domestic violence, disputes with neighbours and family members, and other legal issues. Public trust in the performance of the centers prompted a more active participation of social organisations in neighbourhood safety.[61] In addition, 180 neighbourhood safety commissions were established. These commissions are comprised of various sectors of the population in a neighbourhood or area, such as residents, community leaders and business people, and their role is to provide input into the design of crime and violence prevention strategies. Their success is evident from the extension of the commission model to other areas of the country. This expansion indicates an increase in both community engagement and police-community cooperation in crime prevention.

Campaigns for Raising Public Awareness

IDB programs emphasize the need to change attitudes to violence through communication and outreach, not least because the dissemination of violence statistics makes citizens aware of both the problem and what the government is doing to reduce and prevent it. In Colombia, the focus of lending was on media campaigns to reduce crime and violence during local and national holidays. In Uruguay, campaigns highlighted initiatives to publicize programmes tackling domestic violence and substance abuse.

Although the results of public information campaigns in Colombia have been variable, they clearly demonstrate the potential of the media to change attitudes towards violence. Thus evaluations of campaigns geared toward the establishment of norms among schoolchildren such as *Ciudad de los Niños y las Niñas* (City of Boys and Girls) recorded positive outcomes. Some campaigns focused on reducing youth violence. In Cali a campaign called *Fiesta por la Vida* (Party for Life) was introduced in response to high levels of crime and violence observed during holiday periods, and has reduced the number of violent incidents.[62] However, other campaigns have been less successful, including a similar campaign launched in Bogotá – *Corresponsabilidad en la Rumba* (Shared Responsibility when Partying) – that did not yield the expected reduction in violence.[63] This campaign included too much symbolism and was too abstract for youths to understand and process. Moreover, citizens said that campaigns need to be sustained over time if they are to have an effect, and need to target the whole population, rather than just youth.

Despite being relatively short term, opinion polling suggests that the campaigns in Uruguay increased public awareness of government efforts to fight crime and violence.[64] This increased consciousness of violence reduction activities has translated into a decrease in citizens' perception of violence and an increase in their trust of the police.[65]

The comparatively small amount of resources allocated to this component of the programme, and the consequently short duration of the campaigns, limited what could be achieved.[66] However, the positive results achieved with limited funding suggests that the IDB should consider allocating more resources to awareness raising campaigns, and should urge local governments to assign greater importance to such activities. Future campaigns could also benefit from the inclusion of tools designed to measure the long-term impact of campaigns on violence reduction.

CONCLUSION

The IDB was the first development bank to invest directly in violence reduction, so this concluding section reflects on the successes it achieved, the challenges it encountered, and the lessons it identified when loans were provided for the explicit purpose of addressing violence and insecurity.

Overall, the programme experiences have been positive. In policy terms, IDB's work underscored the economic costs of violence and placed the linkage between insecurity and stunted development firmly on the region's development agenda. In practical terms, evaluation data suggest that many components of the loans are worth replicating: strengthening and unifying information systems on crime and violence; domestic violence treatment interventions; police training; interventions for youth at risk; 'one-stop shops' that provide social, judicial and mediation services; and targeted media campaigns – all appear to have produced positive outcomes.

The IDB's lending experience has revealed several lessons that will benefit future lending programmes. The first is that simple designs are more effective than complex ones with many parts. The complexity of the issues surrounding violence can lead to exceedingly ambitious programs being designed, but while the IDB recognizes the need for a multifaceted response to the many causes of violence, the involvement of multiple projects and different agencies can result in programmes that are too complex and elaborate for effective implementation. Although the Colombia and Uruguay projects successfully executed all or most of the planned activities, a more focused approach might have been more efficient and yielded more visible results. This is not to say that well-crafted, comprehensive violence reduction strategies cannot succeed. The dramatic decrease in annual homicide statistics in Bogotá in less than a decade attests to the contrary. However, given the limitations under which the IDB and borrowing countries operate, less ambitious designs warrant consideration, especially when critical conditions – such as long-term political commitment – are difficult to ensure.

The second lesson relates to the first. Ambitious projects that strive for long-term change may overlook the potential impact of short-term interventions that cost little and are known to be effective, such as restricting alcohol sales. The emphasis on social prevention (which yields results in the long- rather than the short-term) has probably taken attention from more immediate-impact interventions. Situational prevention initiatives, which seek to increase the perceived effort required to commit crime, may be more programmatically attractive because they deliver short-term results. It may therefore be appropriate to change programming design so as to expand the range of such interventions, especially those that can have immediate results, such as street surveillance systems, open phonelines for reporting domestic violence, and restrictions on the sale of alcohol.

Of course, violence reduction programs must not focus solely on short-term impact. Quick results are important but they have little lasting effect unless complemented by other investments that contribute to social prevention over the long term. Early childhood development programs, for example, are known to be a cost-effective strategy to reduce the probability of future criminal behaviour.[67] Social protection – insurance, social security etc. – and public works programs can also complement citizen security interventions especially in countries undergoing economic downturns, low growth and/or high unemployment.

The third lesson identified is the importance of information management. Project evaluations indicate that a unified system of data collection that provides reliable information on a timely basis is extremely helpful in developing adequate responses and cost-effective prevention strategies. The Colombian cities of Bogotá and Cali were able to successfully reduce levels of crime and violence during loan implementation in part because they set up reliable information and monitoring systems. Project experiences also indicate the value of collecting a broader range of statistics on crime and violence to inform programming choices, emphasizing previously hidden or underreported forms of violence such as violence against women, children and the elderly. Information must, however, be used, rather than just collected, and this requires strong partnerships among the array of actors involved in violence reduction: the municipality or other main coordinating agency must be involved, as must the police, other government agencies, service providers such as hospitals, and community groups.

The fourth lesson identified is the difficulty of measuring cause and effect. Measuring project impact, identifying cause and effect relationships, and assessing the cost-effectiveness of interventions and their impact on violent behaviour is crucial, but finding sufficiently attuned indicators to do so accurately is hard. It takes time for impact to filter down and results may be subject to external factors that are beyond project control, such as demographic change. Moreover, violence prevention projects typically will not yield reductions in homicide and violent crime rates until after project completion. The Uruguay project illustrates the different factors affecting violence rates and the need for suitable indicators to measure project results. Homicides rose by 20 percent and violent assaults rose by 100 percent in Uruguay during the project. The public's perception of insecurity, which was used along with homicides and assault rates as indicators of project impact, also climbed.[68] However, the fact that indicators behaved contrary to expectations does not automatically mean that the project was without positive impact. The rise in crime statistics was likely the result of the serious economic crisis and high unemployment rates that hit the country in the early part of the period, as well as improved police information systems, which led to increased recording of violent acts including, most dramatically, a 400 percent increase in domestic violence reporting.[69]

The fifth lesson is that demonstrable long-term political commitment at national and local levels is vital. It takes time to build community infrastructure, increase institutional capacity, change public perceptions of crime and violence, and alter individual behaviour. This cultural transformation, whether at the institutional or individual level, may take years to have effect, and requires sustained government engagement – the success of the Bogotá project is in large part attributable to the political commitment of successive municipal administrations. Sustained political commitment is an issue in all IDB operations, but is especially critical to citizen security projects because such projects are implemented through sub-national government agencies that are typically subject to a high turnover of leadership and principal staff. Mayors (who provide key leadership serve short tenures of two or three years), and new municipal administrations often bring new priorities and may seek to amend a project's scope or de-emphasize its importance.

Finally, project experience indicates the lack of institutional capacity among the agencies charged with designing and managing the proposed policies and projects. In the Colombia and Uruguay projects, this capacity deficit necessitated training at the outset so as to develop the human resources required to maintain and manage technical aspects of the new systems. The issue of managerial capacity is, therefore, critical to the design of future projects.

Given that the IDB has only recently become involved in violence reduction programming in Latin America, it is no surprise that there is significant room for further learning. Continued evaluations of ongoing programs will further identify and document the optimal and most cost-effective aspects of interventions to prevent and reduce violence. However, as the first development bank to issue loans for violence reduction programs, the IDB has provided a rich field of learning and much encouragement for other lending institutions considering involvement in similar programming.

NOTES

1. The opinions expressed herein are those of the authors and do not necessarily represent the official position of the Inter-American Development Bank (IDB). The authors wish to acknowledge the contributions made by Tracy Betts, Hugo Davrieux, Rafael Hernandez, Beatriz López, Andrew Morrison, Maria Teresa Traverso, Ana Lucia Muñoz, and Juana Salazar to this article, and to helping shape the Bank's violence prevention program.
2. Nicole Ball, 'Transforming Security Sectors: the IMF and World Bank Approaches', *Conflict, Security and Development* 1/1 (2001) pp.45–66.
3. Founded in 1959, the IDB is the oldest and largest regional development bank in the world and the primary source of multilateral funding in Latin America and the Caribbean. The IDB's mandate is to promote economic and social development in the region.
4. Mayra Buvinić and Andrew Morrison, 'Living in a more violent world', *Foreign Policy* 118 (2000) pp.58–72.
5. Andrew Morrison and María Loreto Biehl (eds.), *Too Close to Home: Domestic Violence in the Americas* (Washington DC: Inter-American Development Bank and Johns Hopkins UP 1999).
6. Soledad Larrain, Jeannette Vega and Iris Delgado, *Re Latín Americaiones Familiares y Maltrato Infantil* (Santiago, Chile: UNICEF 1997).
7. Mayra Buvinić, Andrew Morrison and Michael Shifter, *Violence in the Americas: A Framework for Action*, Technical Study (Washington DC: IDB 1999).
8. The Report of the United Nations (UN) Secretary General's High Level Panel on Threats, Challenges and Change backed up this assertion. See UN High Level Panel on Threats, Challenges and Change, *A More Secure World: Our Shared Responsibility* (NY: UN 2004) para. 44.
9. In Chile, children who stated that they had been seriously abused performed considerably poorer in school than did children who reported never being victims of physical abuse. See Larrain et al. (note 6); Buvinić and Morrison (note 4); Pablo Fajnzylber, *What Causes Crime and Violence?* (Washington DC: World Bank 1997).
10. K. E. Leonard, 'Drinking Patterns and Intoxication in Marital Violence: Review, Critique and Future Directions in Research', in S.E. Martin (eds.), *Alcohol and Interpersonal Violence: Fostering Multidisciplinary Perspectives* (Washington DC: US Dept. of Health and Human Services 1992).
11. Buvinić, Morrison and Shifter (note 7); UN High Level Panel on Threats, Challenges and Change (note 8) para. 45.
12. Andrew Morrison and María Beatriz Orlando, 'Social and Economic Costs of Domestic Violence: Chile and Nicaragua' in Morrison and Biehl (note 5).
13. Buvinić, Morrison, and Shifter (note 11).
14. Londoño, Juan Luis and Rodrigo Guerrero. 1999. Violencia en América Latina: Epidemiología y costos. Research Network Working Papers R-375. Washington, D.C.: Inter-American Development Bank.
15. The Disability Adjusted Life Year measures the burden of disease, and reflects the full amount of healthy life lost, to all causes, whether from premature mortality or from some degree of disability during a period of time. DALY is composite of five variables, which include: (1) years of life lost to premature mortality, (2) degrees of incapacity associated with different conditions, (3) age weights. (5) time reference (e.g. discount rates) and (5) the idea of adding health across individuals. < www.who.int/mental_health/management/depression/daly/en/> .

16. Andre Medici, 'Diagnóstico de la Situación de Salud en América Latina', unpublished manuscript. Washington DC: Inter-American Development Bank 2005.
17. Mayra Buvinić, and Andrew Morrison, *Economic and Social Consequences of Violence*, Technical Note 4, Technical Notes: Violence Prevention (Washington DC: Inter-American Development Bank 1999).
18. *Fundación Paz Ciudadana* (Santiago, Chile 1999) quoted in Buvinić and Morrison, Ibid. p.5.
19. Felicia Knaul and Miguel Ángel Ramírez, *Family Violence and Child Abuse in Latin America and the Caribbean: The Cases of Colombia and Mexico*, Social Development Division Technical Paper (Washington DC: Inter-American Development Bank 2005).
20. P.G. Jaffe, D.A. Wolfe, A. Telford and G. Austin, 'The Impact of Policy Changes on Wife Abuse'. *Journal of Family Violence* 1/1 (March 1986) pp.37–49; G.W. Holden, and K.L. Richie, 'Linking Extreme Marital Discord, Child Rearing, and Child Behavior Problems: Evidence from Battered Women', *Child Development* 62/2 (1991) pp.311–27; J.D. Coie, 'Toward a Theory of Peer Rejection' in S.R. Asher and J.D. Coie (eds.), *Peer Rejection in Childhood* (NY: Cambridge UP 1990) pp.365–401.
21. Anthony Bottoms, 'Crime Prevention Facing the 1990s', *Policing and Society* 1 (1990) pp.3–22.
22. Laura Chinchilla and Jose Maria Rico, *La Prevención Comunitaria del Delito: Perspectivas para América Latina* (Miami: Center for the Administration of Justice, Florida Int. Univ. 1997).
23. Rachel Neild, *The Role of the Police in Violence Prevention*, Technical Notes on Violence Prevention No.9 (Washington DC: IDB 1999) p.2.
24. IDB, *Guidelines for the Design of Violence Reduction Projects*, Sustainable Development Department Best Practices Series, No. SOC 135 (Washington DC: IDB 2003) < www.iadb.org/sds/ doc/SOC%2D135%2De.pdf>.
25. These restrictions are set out in a memorandum from the Legal Department, 'Limits on the Activities Which May Be Funded with IDB Resources' in accordance with the Bank's Charter 9 April 1998. Quoted in IDB (note 24) p.4.
26. Peter W. Greenwood, Karyn E. Model, Peter Rydell and James R. Chiesa, *Diverting Children from a Life of Crime: Measuring Costs and Benefits* (Santa Monica, CA: RAND 1998) < www.rand.org/ publications/MR/MR699/index.html>.
27. IDB (note 24).
28. Operations in Chile ($10 million), Honduras ($22 million) and Jamaica ($16 million) are in the early stages of execution; a loan for Nicaragua ($7.0 million) has recently been approved, and a Guatemala citizen security project ($27 million) is in the approval stage. Projects in Guyana, Peru, and Trinidad and Tobago are in different stages of preparation and the Bank is identifying additional possible citizen security programs in Brazil, the Dominican Republic, Ecuador, Panama, and Venezuela (data correct as of Feb. 2006).
29. Authors' calculation based on *Latinobarometer* data.
30. All citizen security operations incorporate the development of information, monitoring and evaluation systems. In the Colombia and Uruguay loans, a separate component solely financed this activity.
31. Ana María Sanjuán, 'Situación de los Cuerpos Policiales en Latinoamérica', unpublished manuscript. Washington DC: IDB 2004. Copy with author.
32. Paul Chevigny, *Edge of the Knife: Police Violence in the Americas* (NY: The New Press 1995); Rachel Neild, 'Confronting a Culture of Impunity' in Andrew Goldsmith and Colleen Lewis (eds.), *Civilian Oversight of Policing* (Oxford: Hart 2000).
33. John Bailey and Lucia Dammert, 'Public Security and Police Reform in the Americas: Introduction and Overview', in idem (eds.), *Public Security and Police Reform in the Americas* (Univ. of Pittsburgh Press 2005).
34. IDB (note 24) p.14.
35. Some of the key characteristics of community policing include community crime prevention; patrol deployment for non-emergency interaction with the community; active police solicitation of public service requests; and the provision of opportunities for community feedback regarding police performance. See Rachel Neild, 'Community Policing' in *Themes and Debates in Public Security Reform: A Guide for Civil Society* (Washington DC: Washington Office on Latin America 1998) p.7.
36. The Bank is starting to incorporate internal and external accountability mechanisms in the design of new operations in Guyana, Peru and Trinidad and Tobago.
37. $4 million was allocated for the project in Colombia and $1.03 for Uruguay.

38. María Victoria Llorente and Angela Rivas, 'La Caída del Crimen en Bogotá', unpublished manuscript, Bogotá, Colombia 2004. Copy with author.
39. For further information on COMPSTAT see Dennis C. Smith and William J. Bratton, 'Performance management in New York City: COMPSTAT and the Revolution in Police Management' in Dall Forsythe (eds.), *Quicker, Better, Cheaper? Managing Performance in American Government* (Albany, NY: Rockefeller Institute Press 2001).
40. Hugo Davrieux, 'Program for Citizen Safety: Crime and Violence Prevention', unpublished Project Completion Report Memorandum, Uruguay, 2004. Copy with author.
41. Mayra Buvinić and Andrew Morrison, *Causes of Violence*, Technical Notes: Violence Prevention, No.3 (Washington DC: IDB 1999).
42. Maria Lereto Biehl with Carla Ortiz, *Destic Violence Against Women*, Technical Notes: Violence Prevention, No. 7. (Washington DC: IDB 1999).
43. Jaffe et al. (note 20).
44. Greenwood *et al.* (note 26).
45. Centro de Proyectos para el Desarrollo (Cendex), 'Estudio de Impacto de las UMC desde l a perspectiva de los actores de convivencia', Documento Técnico AGDT/1038-03, unpublished manuscript, Bogotá, Colombia, 2003; Cendex, 'Conflictividad e Impacto de las UMC', Documento Técnico AGDT/1045-03, Bogotá, Colombia, unpublished manuscript; Cendex, 'Estudio de Impacto de las UMC desde la perspectiva de los actores locales', Documento Técnico AGDT/ 1036-03. Bogotá, Colombia, unpublished manuscript; Cendex, 'Componente Fortalecimiento Ciudadano. Categoría Inversión Jóvenes en Riesgo y Resocialización', Documento Técnico AGDT/ 1096-03. Bogotá, Colombia, unpublished manuscript; Cendex, 'Componente Fortalecimiento Ciudadano. Categoría Inversión Comunicación para la Convivencia. Resultado Final de la Evaluación de las Campañas.' Documento Técnico AGDT/1092-03, Bogotá, Colombia, unpublished manuscript; Cendex, 'Impacto de las Unidades de Mediación y Conciliación en la transformación de Actitudes y Comportamientos frente al abordaje del Conflicto', Documento Técnico AGDT/ 1084-03, Bogotá, Colombia, unpublished manuscript; Cendex, 'Evaluación de los cambios propiciados en las conductas y actitudes de los usuarios de las Comisarías de Familia de Bogotá en la solución de sus conflictos intra-familiares', Documento Técnico AGDT/ 1115-04, Bogotá, Colombia, unpublished manuscript. Copies of all documents with author.
46. Llorente and Rivas (note 38).
47. Cendex AGDT/1045-03 (note 45).
48. $75,000 and $70,000 were allocated to these activities, respectively.
49. $953,000 was allotted to this activity.
50. Davrieux (note 40).
51. Ibid.
52. Ibid.
53. Peter Witt and John Crompton, *Recreation programs that work for at-risk youth: The challenge of shaping the future* (State College, PA: Venture Publishing 1996).
54. Maria Loreto Biehl, *Youth Violence Prevention*, Technical Notes: Violence Prevention, No.10 (Washington DC: IDB 1999).
55. Davrieux (note 40).
56. Ana Lucía Muñoz, notes from audio conference interview at the IADB, Jan. 2005.
57. Cendex AGDT/1038-03 (note 45).
58. Cendex (please see documents in note 45)
59. Ibid.
60. Cendex AGDT/ 1084-03 (note 45).
61. Davrieux (note 40).
62. Muñoz (note 56).
63. Cendex AGDT/1092-03 (note 45).
64. Carlos Bastón, 'Programa de Seguridad Ciudadana: Prevención de la Violencia en Uruguay' (Washington DC 2004) unpublished manuscript, copy with author.
65. Davrieux (note 40).
66. The percentage of funds allocated for this component was four and nine percent of the total loans for Colombia and Uruguay respectively.
67. Greenwood *et al.* (note 26).
68. Bastón (note 64).
69. Davrieux (note 40).

Two Steps Forward, One and a Half Steps Back: Police Reform in Peru, 2001–2004

GINO COSTA

The transformation of the Peruvian police was one of the central reform projects in the administration of President Alejandro Toledo, who came to power amid high hopes in 2001, following decades of military and authoritarian rule. It was an ambitious goal and this article – told from the perspective of a minister at the center of the reform effort – shows the host of difficulties confronted in achieving it.

The Peru case indicates how the sheer number of changes that need to be instituted simultaneously or in parallel, and on multiple levels can quickly overwhelm even the best-intentioned reform efforts. It raises the issue of how a process of such density and complexity can be managed, especially if – as is usual in such circumstances – it takes place in an environment of uncertainty and instability and where reform to other public sector institutions is equally pressing. It emphasizes the challenges of overcoming the tenacious resistance of security institutions to changing established systems and practices. Although some important changes have been made, many of the changes impinging on the habits and practices of the police were resisted. The case also shows that reform is not a linear process nor, once initiated, can it expect to be consistently supported. Indeed, Peru's police reform process flip-flopped in political interest and support, with the consequence that although achievements were significant, they were much less than initially hoped.

AUTHORITARIAN LEGACY

Policing in Peru has an inauspicious history. The National Police of Peru (*Policía Nacional del Perú* or PNP) were, like many of their counterparts in Latin America, militaristic in image, approach and practice.[1] 'Policing' traditionally emphasized the security of those controlling the state, rather than provided security and safety to its citizens, and the past few decades have seen a pronounced militarization of the police.

Peru had an extended period of military government from 1968 to 1980 during which the military dominated policing. Even though there was a transition from military to civilian control during the 1980s, policing continued to have a heavily militarized accent, especially as the state fought the Shining Path and Tupac Amaru guerrilla movements. The police were both victimizers and victims during the conflict, being cited for systematic and egregious human rights violations but also the targets of terrorist violence.[2] The period left deep marks on the ethos of the organization, with the views of many officers profoundly shaped by the counter-terrorist experience; many conflated human rights with guerrillas and communists.

Even after the effective defeat of the guerrillas, the police (and the Ministry of Interior in which they worked) effectively remained subjugated to the military throughout the authoritarian rule of President Alberto Fujimori (1992–2000). Although formally a democracy, Fujimori's Peru was run in large part by the intelligence services, led by Vladimiro Montesinos. Fujimori used the intelligence services to control the armed forces, the Ministry of the Interior and the police, and made them the cornerstones of an authoritarian government.[3] To maintain power the regime bought off and blackmailed senior police and military officials as well as congressional representatives, businessmen, journalists and judges.

The Fujimori regime further tarnished the already poor public reputation of the police. As was later observed, the Fujimori administration's objective was 'to incorporate corruption as a structuring element of the various aspects of the police organization, which was to cross-section not only processes and systems, but also people and values, thus making it easier to subdue and dominate their members'. [4]

Fujimori's government collapsed in 2000 when he fled into exile following the leaking of videotapes that showed the systematic bribing of Peru's political and business elite. Following the eight-month caretaker presidency of Valentin Paniagua, Alejandro Toledo was sworn in as president on July 2001. Accompanied by perhaps unrealistically high expectations, Toledo faced the enormous task of rejuvenating the economy and restoring long-absent public trust in the institutions of the state.

Start-Stop Reform

In his inaugural speech, President Toledo announced that police reform would be a policy priority, but he was vague on how to achieve it.[5] Toledo's party had no specific proposals on what to do with the police and it was an issue little discussed during the election campaign. The nature of Peru's transition – sudden government collapse –had meant there was little time for discussion and agreement on the shape of institutional reforms.

In July 2001 an unlikely team formed in the Ministry of the Interior to conduct the police reform process. The tarnished image and politically weak position of many senior military and police officials in the Fujimori administration meant a window of opportunity had opened for a team of civilians with a background as human rights activists and journalists to come in with goals that included reforming an institution they had frequently referred to in their writings. The new interior minister, for example, was Fernando Rospigliosi, a prominent journalist specializing in civil-military relations and intelligence matters. His vice minister (later minister), Gino Costa, had headed the UN police reform unit in El Salvador and later worked at the Peruvian Human Rights Ombudsman's office. A key advisor (and later vice minister) was Carlos Basombrio, ex-director of one of Peru's foremost human rights organizations, the *Instituto de Defensa Legal* (IDL). Another was Susana Villarán, formerly minister for women's affairs under Paniagua, and, previously, head of a coalition of human rights non-government organizations (NGOs). They brought with them some 20 additional civilians advisors and managers. This team set about reforming Peru's second largest ministry (after the Ministry of Education). It had 93,000 sworn officers and 5,600 civilians who were used to running their own affairs with little to no oversight or civilian control, a situation that would be profoundly threatened by the reform.

The reform process alternated between progress and regress. It can be broken down into five distinct stages. The first phase took place in the eight months of Paniagua's caretaker presidency when important initial measures were taken, including the dismissal of 250 of the officials most deeply implicated in the structures of the former administration. During this period a small team of senior officers began to develop initial ideas for police reform.[6]

The second stage was the key period of reform under the Toledo government. It was led by minister of the interior Fernando Rospigliosi from July 2001, and then by the author, who replaced Rospigliosi as minister following the latter's resignation in June 2002.[7] During this stage, the foundations of police reform were established. However, the foundations were unstable, and Costa resigned in January 2003, after failing to receive political backing in a dispute with the chief of police over changes to the promotions process. (The chief of police also resigned.)

The entire reform team at the ministry departed with Costa, and the third phase saw a waning of previous achievements. Under a new interior minister, Alberto Sanabria, reform ground to a standstill and the ministry ceded ground to police officials. At the same time, public disappointment with the Toledo administration intensified. Furthermore, following the ministry's mismanagement of a public order crisis, which was of such magnitude that a nationwide state of emergency was declared, Sanabria resigned, the Cabinet was reshuffled, and ministerial control of the operational response to public disorder was dramatically reduced.[8]

The return of the reformist Rospigliosi as minister of the interior from July 2003 to May 2004, marking the fourth stage of reform, and a reenergizing of the program. It took considerable effort to overcome the effects of half a year's stagnation, but there was little time for consolidation. Rospigliosi was under almost continual pressure from different sources; he was attacked by members of Toledo's political party in parliament, and under pressure from resistance in the National Intelligence Office. In May 2004 the pressure became too much and Rospigliosi resigned once more.

The fifth and final stage in the process followed Rospigliosi's second resignation and the appointment of a new minister of the interior. This started another period of stagnation, followed by backsliding as both the new minister and his successor – a retired police general – attempted to dismantle aspects of the reform process.

The primary explanation for the 'two steps forward and one and a half steps back' nature of the reform process lies in the political dynamics of the Toledo administration. Although the president assumed office amid high hopes, his government was marked by constant political instability resulting from widespread and often massive and violent social protests and demonstrations. Social demands suppressed through years of economic recession emerged as electoral campaign issues in 2000 and 2001 and fostered unrealistic expectations. Political leadership in the legislature and executive was also found wanting; the president had difficulty in maintaining discipline over his own political party, and in muzzling the voracious appetites for political and personal profit of many of its members. Unfulfilled electoral promises, a constant whiff of corruption, and poor decision-making and the lack of judgment displayed by the president and political leaders undermined political stability. The increasing weakness of the government allowed the reform agenda to slip, allowing the PNP to resist reform and recover an important share of power lost.

GETTING STARTED

On arrival at the Ministry of the Interior in July 2001, the reform team had to determine the nature, scope and characteristics of the required restructuring. As well as the size of the task, they were aware that this was not the sole reform program initiated: reform faced competition for time and attention with operational imperatives in the ministry's agenda. To speed along the process, they took into account initiatives that had already begun under the interim government. A small team of respected (and untainted) senior police officials had worked on proposals for re-crafting a new police for Peru. Their document entitled 'Foundations of Police Reform' was published on 27 July 2001, the day before Toledo's inauguration as president.[9]

This document was a good foundation and the team agreed with many of its proposals. Its major shortcoming was procedural. Prepared by a small number of high-level officials, it neither incorporated any feedback from different sectors of the police or public nor meaningfully assessed the ability of the institution to absorb reform. The reform team at the ministry felt that an additional assessment of policing in Peru was necessary in order to establish which parts of the police worked well and which did not. The assessment process would serve another purpose too: it would enable the civilian staff to familiarize themselves with the state of policing, obtain all available information, and get to know the viewpoints of the relevant actors.

The need for further consultation and study baffled the police. Senior officials believed that the institution's strengths and weaknesses were evident, as were the necessary remedies: a budgetary increase, and a stronger constitutional and legal framework to enable them to carry out their work. They, like most of the leaders of Peru's public institutions, believed that institutional reform was simply a technical exercise consisting of infrastructural investment, equipment upgrading and salary increases. The reform team at the ministry explicitly recognized the need for both a revised budget and the modernization of policing's legal framework, but had to persuade the top ranks that these objectives could not be achieved without also repairing frayed public trust.

This difference in perception spoke to a fundamental philosophical difference between reformers and those facing reform, a difference that remained present throughout the attempted transformation process. There was no understanding by the police leadership that real reform entailed more than technical tinkering and in fact meant changing the very make-up of the institution. Their view ignored the need to change attitudes and explore ways to improve service delivery within the available budget, which in turn required expelling corrupt functionaries, training and motivating staff, and developing a professional ethic that would dignify the members of the institution and improve their performance and vocation. Without these steps, the reformers felt discredited public institutions would never recover lost legitimacy and trust.

Consultation

The main purpose of the police reform process was to regain public trust and the service's legitimacy. The process began with an attempt to involve a wide cross section of Peruvians in a process of consultation on the nine groups of issues identified as weakening the institution. These were police doctrine; regulatory framework; internal and external control systems; human, material and logistic resources management; police welfare and healthcare; organization and structure; education; and the role of women in the police.

This desire to be as inclusive as possible was reflected in the terms of reference of the Restructuring Commission, which was the principal information-gathering vehicle. Established in 2001, the Commission was created to carry out an institutional assessment and solicit feedback in order to define the objectives and timeline of the reform process, establishing objective goals and terms for the achievement thereof. The commission was encouraged to solicit the opinions of police staff of all levels, and of experts, civil authorities and the public. There were also attempts to ensure that the reform process did not center exclusively on the capital, Lima. Commissioners traveled to many cities in the country to receive feedback from local and judiciary authorities, regional police commanders, middle management and rank-and-file officers. It helped that private and public institutions supported this task. Thus a toll-free hotline to receive feedback was established, while the Peruvian bar association staffed helpdesks that received responses directly from the public. Opinion polls of the public and the police were conducted thanks to enthusiastic support from officials and sub-officials. This wide consultation provided the institutional change process with a base line of support and legitimacy within the police. It also allowed the public to participate.

The Restructuring Commission took five months to complete its work, and the resultant 'Report of the Special Commission for Restructuring the National Police of Peru' – better known as the Green Book – was submitted to the president in March 2002.[10] It identified a range of deep structural problems afflicting the police:

systematic corruption, particularly in the areas of benefits and procurements such as pensions, health care, gasoline distribution and meals for officers; excessive discretion and personal patronage in recruitment, evaluation, promotions and training; massive rank inflation; dysfunctional disciplinary systems; and poor working conditions for lower-ranking officers. The authors were careful to ensure that their report would not only diagnose symptoms but would also provide remedies, proposing objectives and a two-year action plan for achievement.[11]

The Commission believed that technical changes alone would not be enough to reorient the police. Nothing less than a new policing philosophy and the introduction of a model broadening the police mandate would enable the PNP to address neighborhood conflicts and community problems, enhance police accountability in the community, and guarantee managerial transparency. To realize this objective, major structural reform would be required, including a decentralization and devolution of responsibilities downward to local precincts.

Although the Green Book's recommendations were extensive, they were far from exhaustive or, indeed, the final word on the matter. The reformers conceptualized the process as a permanent process of institutional change, upgrading, and adjustment. The recommendations of the Restructuring Commission became embodied in Policy No. 7 – 'Eradicating violence and strengthening civism and public security' – of the National Agreement, an agenda for political reform agreed to by all political sectors and passed by Congress on 22 July 2002.[12]

Locally Owned and Low Cost

Unlike other police reform processes in Latin America – especially the Salvadorian, Guatemalan and even the Colombian ones – in which international cooperation played a crucial role, the Peruvian reform proceeded largely without external support. Other than some small grants from various international donors[13] and funding from the FEDADOI – a government fund created in 2001 with repatriated illegal money from the Fujimori-Montesinos era – to buy new uniforms and life insurance for police officers, the police budget remained static. Indeed, compared to the previous decade, it actually saw a significant reduction.

Outside funding was sometimes useful for funding potentially sensitive projects. The Open Society Institute (OSI), for example, gave US$333,000 to the ministry to support among other things, the new Internal Affairs Office in 2002.[14] The US government, through the Federal Bureau of Investigation, also advised and supported the office with a grant of US$100,000 awarded on 13 March 2002.[15]

External influences proved useful in providing a forum for the discussion of ideas too. Some of the senior civilian staff at the ministry (including the author) formed part of an international network of experts that discussed comparative police reform processes and were able to draw upon experiences gathered in the network.[16] Academic forums were useful spaces to think through potentially difficult issues. In November 2001, for example, the Washington DC-based Woodrow Wilson Center co-hosted with the ministry an international seminar targeting an audience of 250 high-ranking PNP officials to discuss comparative experiences of police reform elsewhere in the region.[17] In many ways, the most useful aspect of the seminar was the revelation of key objections from different sectors in the police, often aired through angry interjections from the conference floor.

Money did come later but, by that point, the impetus for reform was petering out. In January 2003, the government signed an agreement with the Inter American Development Bank (IDB) to start preliminary studies in a loan process for a US$20 million loan to update and streamline the public security system.[18] The Ministry of the Interior also started a project using the balance from a US$10 million loan from Japan, which was intended to provide the PNP with equipment. However, reform was stagnating at the time, and the funds have yet to be used.

Fitful Reform

Reform was also under way in other security sector institutions. These were less ambitious in vision and employed less consultative methods. Following the creation of the police restructuring commission in October 2001, for example, the Ministry of Defense created a commission to assess the armed forces and recommend relevant reform measures. The defense commission was composed of civilians, but unlike the broad composition of the police restructuring commission, it involved only retired, not serving officers. Its approach was generally far less participatory and transparent, and the outcomes of the two commissions differed. In contrast to police reform, which was carried out within the existing legal framework, the progress of military reform was based on an amendment of the legal framework for the Ministry of Defense. The defense commission proposed a new Ministry of Defense Act, which, for the first time, created a real Ministry of Defense permitting civilian leadership of the armed forces and approved in late 2002.[19] Following enactment of the Defense Act, some civilians were incorporated into the new structure, although with the ongoing presence of retired and active duty officials. President Toledo's decision in December 2003 to replace his second civilian minister of defense with an army general (who had to retire in order to assume the position) demonstrates that – as in the intelligence services – civilian leadership of the Ministry of Defense and the restructuring of the armed forces is a problematic endeavor.

There were also moves to reform the intelligence services, which had been so dominant under Fujimori, but these ran up against unbending institutional resistance. Successive changes of institutional leadership prevented the achievement of a real reform, and the president's appointment in 2004 of retired military officials to run the institution ended the brief effort to install civilian management.

Judicial reform was also sluggish. In early 2003, as the police reform process appeared to make significant progress, the new president of the Supreme Court, Hugo Sivina, announced the creation of a judicial reform commission. The Attorney-General's office followed suit. Previously, both institutions had argued that reform was impossible, as they had no funding for it. Much as was the case with the police, they understood reform in narrowly defined technical and institutional terms. Their prime focus was resource acquisition. Their agenda did not include fighting corruption effectively, training and motivating staff, or introducing modern administration techniques to improve performance. It is difficult to see how these discredited public institutions will recover public legitimacy and trust without first dealing effectively with corruption and bad management.

COMPLEX CHALLENGES

Once the restructuring commission's report was delivered, it was necessary to begin the more difficult task of implementing its suggestions. A Follow-up body called the modernization commission was created in March 2002 to supervise implementation of the recommendations. Organized under the same thematic sub-commissions, the body also tried to be as inclusive as possible: the sub-commissions comprised both civilian and police participation, including police from varied ranks.

In order to facilitate the coordination of such complex reform measures, a technical secretariat was created too; this consisted of high-ranking officials who served on the various sub-commissions. The technical secretariat had an additional function: to communicate progress of the reform and allay potential concerns within the police. Two communication mechanisms proved of particular value. First, the commissioners traveled throughout Peru in an effort to reach out to the regions, and second, a weekly television program discussed reform initiatives and progress, and took call-in questions from viewers.

The intricacy of implementation soon became clear, as did the fact that reform could not proceed without political support, which was, as indicated above, variable. In the early stages of the reform, the Modernization Commission played a critical role in facilitating change. However, over time an increasing number of decisions required ministerial action, which was inconsistent.[20] Sometimes, positive achievements in consultation actually had a negative effect on implementation.[21] The sub-commissions were so inclusive and represented so many opinions that they actually slowed reform down. Rather than facilitating change, in some cases the sub-commissions increased open contest and competition, while overt police reluctance caused stagnation in the decision-making process.

Reform Achievements

Despite its stop-start nature, the reform program left important achievements. The first area of improvement was in police professionalism. Previously, personal contact had been the main determinant of access to the police training academy whereas recruitment is now based on merit. In order to eliminate political influence, the team outsourced the admissions process temporarily to a private university[22] while the entire admissions and training system was reviewed and reformed. A new personnel law was drafted that defined standards, and regulated new processes for promotions and retirements that were based on competitive, fair, transparent, and merit based procedures.[23] Based upon the Restructuring Commission's recommendations, regulations governing admissions to specialized training were tightened, while levels of discretion concerning who should receive training and other benefits were reduced. Another example of increased professionalism was an agreement with a private university in Lima[24] to provide police cadets with the opportunity to study and obtain professional qualifications in addition to their police training.

Similarly, in the personnel system, political influence on operations at the station level and in promotions has eliminated. Demilitarization and a greater distinction between police and military functions have also helped. Constitutional amendments passed since 2001 have established the right of police to vote although the jurisdiction of military courts over police for disciplinary and criminal infractions is still in place.

The second improvement was in police welfare. The majority of police officers worked in abject conditions; changes in working conditions were introduced as part of an effort to increase respect for the profession and a sense of self among those who worked in it. Peruvian police, as in most of Latin America, cannot form trade unions and, as in most steeply hierarchical institutions, lower ranks had few channels through which to defend and negotiate their interests. The first step was to create an Ombudsman's Office to investigate complaints and grievance within the police. Pay rises improved morale too. Between 2001 and 2003, officer pay rose by 25 percent.

Third, after years of indifference the ministry recognized the outstanding debts owed to police personnel, and initiated the amortization of the debt. New uniforms were purchased and life insurance issued for each officer. Handicapped police officers and the widows of officers killed in the line of duty were also given benefits where previously they had been largely ignored.

An area of more partial achievement concerns a new office of internal affairs, which was created in July 2002 to deal with police abuse and corruption.[25] Rank-and-file officers said that they could not take such complaints to senior officers so, on their recommendation, Internal Affairs was staffed with civilians working in pairs with selected police officers. But the new office created deep resentment among senior officers who argued that its reporting procedures (which were to the minister) represented political interference in police matters.

Some success was also recorded in winning back long lost public trust. In Peru, as in many countries, the public is accustomed to bribe the police to get things done or to avoid a traffic fine. A new campaign called 'Respect the Police' (A la policía se la respeta) was launched with a major publicity campaign in an attempt to improve the police's public image. The campaign adopted relatively unusual methods to make its case. Internal Affairs officers, with a prosecutor present, videoed citizens offering the police bribes. Broadcast on TV, the video clips showed citizens of both sexes and all social strata attempting to bribe police, thus demonstrating the pervasive nature of corruption. Although the campaign displayed the co-responsibility of the public in police corruption, it was at first resisted by high-ranking police who felt that it drew unwanted attention to police corruption. Later, however, many officers came to appreciate and praise the initiative, for it showed that they were not entirely responsible for corruption.

Finally, police-community relations were improved by the creation of neighbourhood watches (juntas vecinales) and efforts to develop a new, collaborative relationship between the police and peasant patrols (rondas campesinas). More importantly, local security committee's headed by mayors were set up nationally to implement crime-prevention policies and to encourage coordination between local governments, the police, the judiciary, other public agencies and citizen organizations. Peruvian citizens today have a much greater say than in the past in influencing decisions relating to their own security.

Reform Difficulties

The list of necessary improvements was so long that little could be achieved in the short term. That said, police reform has yet to achieve the transformational change envisioned by its advocates; fundamental reform has not been achieved. The reasons for this include variable levels of political interest, institutional resistance, and the sheer difficulty of changing an institution and ensuring the buy-in of local stakeholders. The issues around ownership in the Peruvian case pertain to the dual problems of limited support: political support at the highest level of government, and police support from senior police managers and commanders. A clear pattern also emerges: when reform did not impact upon the interests of those in the police organization, it was welcomed; where it did, change was resisted.

At the level of police professionalism, progress toward restructuring advanced mainly through restricting the positions available for promotions, and by inviting police officials to retire early. Some progress was made with the drafting of new laws on policing – a new Disciplinary Statute was adopted in early 2004, and a new Police Career Act and labor framework (still pending presentation to Congress) was introduced that would limit the number of promotions to top positions to those actually needed to cover them. However, Rospigliosi's successors then undid progress towards achieving the new structure by again promoting large numbers of officers to high rank, and by changing the regulations that stated promotion should result from merit, rather than seniority. This indicates how transitory and fleeting reform can be.

Although there were important improvements in the personnel system, much still needs to be done. To this end, the entire educational system needs modernization to make learning more practical and critical. The system rewards tenure and rote learning, rather than possession of actual skills. In practice, this means that promotion usually goes to officers who are good at learning facts, who have been to more seminars, or who have performed administrative functions for long periods of time. The institution also urgently needs in-service training activities for all ranks (using a range of available methodologies such as distance-learning courses) in order to keep officers abreast of regulatory changes, new policing techniques and the principles of police reform so that each police member has the possibility of becoming an instrument for change.

At the station level, it is hard to see how reform has made much of a difference. Despite progress in identifying needed changes, few have actually taken place. The new policing model called for decentralization into district commands, involving the appointment of a head officer at every district, but this remains pending. Similarly, it has proved difficult to replicate the new organization and approach developed in the pilot police station of Surquillo, Lima,[26] where computerization has replaced dozens of manual logbooks, reduced processing time – citizens now receive copies of police reports in 15 minutes, rather than the former 72 hours – and produced crime maps and reports that support targeted interventions. The chief problem in replicating the pilot model nationwide was funding, for upgrading police stations into adequately equipped basic police units requires a significant investment, particularly in terms of the communications network giving access to the main national police databases, and this was not available. Police resistance was present too, for better information can contribute to a more accurate assessment of police performance, which is not necessarily in their interest.

At a higher structural level, the reform sought to improve police-community cooperation and accountability through the passage of a law in February 2003 creating a system of crime prevention committees at the national, regional, provincial and local level called the National Citizen Security System (*Sistema Nacional de Seguridad Ciudadana*, SINASEC), but implementation has stalled.[27] SINASEC was a strategic effort to generate closer police relations with the local communities and with other state agencies, but it received little financing and political support. The committees currently only function whereas the local elected or police authorities wish to engage with multisectoral crime prevention.[28]

The system of police management remains arcane. For example, the processes and procedures used by the human resource department are largely obsolete, requiring reams of paperwork and huge efforts on the part of officers to process almost any function, from requesting vacation and sick leave to applications for training, transfers and so forth. This oppressive bureaucracy drains police morale. The management system is also lacking in control mechanisms, with the result that it remains easy to get away with corruption. Lack of control in the purchasing and distribution of petrol for example, encourages corruption; petrol is siphoned off and sold on the private market at every step in the distribution chain. The large network of individuals benefiting from the system generates a degree of resistance that the reform team found impossible to surmount.

Although there were some important changes in police welfare, one of the aspirant reformers' greatest frustrations was to have achieved so little in the fields of police healthcare and housing. Every officer made a monthly five percent pay check contribution to the police housing system (FOVIPOL). Yet, in the 14 years of its existence, FOVIPOL, which amassed one million US dollars a month, provided housing to less than seven percent of the force.[29] To change this pattern of mismanagement, paycheck deductions were suspended (thus providing a salary boost) while the regulatory framework and the administration of the fund was reformed. FOVIPOL was then reoriented toward a promotional role, providing loans to officers (with support from other public and private entities) in order to give large numbers of police personnel access to decent housing.

Change was even more modest in the police healthcare system, which employs about 12 percent of police personnel.[30] The system was appallingly inefficient and provided almost no service beyond Lima, but the breadth and depth of vested interests in maintaining the status quo generated great resistance to change. In addition to corruption in the procurement side, medicines sent out to the regions never reached their intended beneficiaries, but were sold on the private market for the personal benefit of regional and district commanders. Rospigliosi's second period in charge saw the convening of a team of civil experts responsible for running, managing and leading the modernization of the healthcare division; they were committed to improving police access to system.[31] However, all such reform efforts ended with Rospigliosi's departure.

In these cases of administrative corruption, the degree of police resistance related directly to the number of beneficiaries involved. The web of vested interests meant progress was impossible, despite the clear knowledge of all concerned that a proper purchasing and distribution system would result in significant savings. As these examples make clear, the greatest anti-corruption challenge is cultural. The attitude that profiting from administrative systems is normal is widespread, and indeed, it is part of the police institution's unwritten code of conduct.

LESSONS

Peru's police reform was made possible thanks to the concurrence of at least three factors. First, police reform took place in the broad context of SSR. Second, the military and police role was delegitimized because of the part they played in the Fujimori regime. The reform was not led by either international organizations or the police, but was driven by a team of reform-minded civilians in the Ministry of the Interior. Despite these strengths, the process had many weaknesses and this conclusion reflects, with some benefit of retrospection, on the lessons identified during the process.

First, the institution that is to be reformed does not always welcome reform. The Peruvian reform process always encountered dogged police opposition. Some resistance was understandable in that ordinary officers often felt threatened by new rules and were afraid of change; this was compounded by the institution's innate conservatism. Senior officers, meanwhile, feared that demilitarization would result in indiscipline and the abandonment of institutional traditions. Many objections, however, had more to do with self-interest and officers protecting their own positions. The typical police strategy was to claim institutional autonomy, arguing that only they could make decisions on policing matters, and that external interventions were an inappropriate political interference.

This led to a second weakness in the reform process: the lack of the leadership within the police institution required to 'sell' and steer a reform package. The driving force of the reform process was always *outside* the police, which explains in part the lack of overall progress. In consequence, reform issues that depended directly on action at the ministerial level – such as the creation of the Police Ombudsman and the Internal Affairs Office – progressed quickly, as did reforms guided by officers advocating reform. In contrast, initiatives that depended directly on the police command (especially those related to the allocation of funds) either progressed very slowly or never materialized; examples include the reform of the procurement of goods and services, especially of petrol and medicines, and the modernization of management systems in general and of welfare funds in particular. While high-ranking officials did not openly challenge reform measures, they obstructed the implementation of proposals that harmed their interests. In these areas, officers with vested interests and time on their side sought to maintain the status quo, using a web of regulatory red tape that buttressed institutional autonomy and impeded ministerial intervention. In difficult periods, police claimed institutional autonomy for their actions, maintaining that external intervention was improper and constituted unwarranted political interference.

However, the greatest source of the processes' fragility related to the weakness of the government itself. Elected amid high hopes, President Toledo's popularity ratings fell to such low levels that many questioned whether his government would survive its term in office. The precariousness of the administration in turn weakened other public institutions, including political parties, and led to a failure to support the civilian reformers leading the Ministry of the Interior.

Another issue which significantly weakened reform was competition from the military. Although both the police and military were part of the security sector, the Ministries of the Interior and of Defense competed over budgetary allocations and political influence throughout the reform period. The military were reluctant to cooperate with the Ministry of the Interior, and, during crises in public order, displayed their unwillingness to support the police. As the country's security needs became less pressing with the near-complete defeat of the terrorist movements, the end of the state of emergency, the end of obligatory military service, resolution of border conflicts with Ecuador and Chile, and increased regional military cooperation, the military's previously dominant influence diminished, prompting a reduction in the military budget. The military – struggling for political influence – was unhappy that the influence of the police appeared to be in the ascendant, particularly as the demands placed on the Ministry of the Interior increased dramatically with the restoration of democratic government. The government's electoral promise had been to reduce military spending, but this should not, the military argued, have implied a parallel reduction in the budget allocated for public security. On the contrary, this should have been one of the new administration's public expense priorities, along with education, healthcare, social programs, and infrastructure. However, the two expenditures were treated equally despite each having very different threat and disorder scenarios.[32]

The military's unhappiness with the police resulted in their refusal to cooperate in joint actions. Although Peru's internal conflict had abated significantly, it had not petered out entirely and still required joint military and police action; the Armed Forces maintained 67 antiterrorist bases in the region (five were newly established in 2002), and had the experience and equipment the police lacked. The military again insisted that they could not carry out antiterrorist action without additional funds. They also argued that, without the declaration of a state of emergency, the task fell entirely to the PNP. However, they systematically prevented the police from receiving the resources they needed to undertake what the military refused to do.

The Ministry of the Interior made more progress than any other security sector institution in bringing about the changes that would enable it to use additional funding effectively. Yet, the Interior budget has been flat since 2001. In spite of repeated surveys indicating public demand for greater citizen security, and the government stating that this was a priority area, the Ministry of the Interior has not received the additional funds needed to support reform and policing effectiveness.

The case of Peru also raises some of the everyday dilemmas of institutional change that confront most reform efforts. One is how to manage the short-term and the long-term aspects of such a complex process. In Peru, the needs of reform were constantly pitted against the daily operational imperatives of police work, which were becoming increasingly onerous. It meant delicate balances had to be struck as public dissatisfaction with the Toledo regime increasingly took place on the streets.[33] In addition to social protests, there were scares about a resurgence of Shining Path and constant pressure from the United States for aggressive counternarcotics policies, such as coca eradication campaigns that had historically provoked social conflicts.[34]

These day-to-day operational priorities competed with reform initiatives for the ministry's time and attention. The minister and his team had to tread lightly in order to avoid antagonizing the senior police officials on whom they depended for public order operations. Additionally, they had to manage the conflicts that arose between high-ranking police officials as a result of reform processes. Public order crises forced them to soft pedal on reform issues too, for the Interior Ministry had to ensure that the police could respond effectively to challenges that might undermine the government's political credibility. The consequence of short-term problems, therefore, was that the reformers were unable to provide the attention required for long-term reform strategies, planning, and implementation.

One unresolved dilemma in the Peruvian case was the appropriate degree of government involvement required to guide reform. Costa and Rospigliosi adopted a policy of minimal involvement, especially on the part of the Congress, lest the process stagnate. Their non-involvement policy had certain advantages, including independent management and less political intervention. However, this approach linked the success of the reform to that of the team that managed it, rather than to the government more broadly, and it meant that the process lacked an important source of political support, which was reflected in the absence of financing. For example, in 2003 and 2004, external loans for security were exclusively allocated to Defense.

Political and financial limitations on the reform process, along with the slow progress in improving police welfare and working conditions, made it hard to achieve police buy-in to the process and thus increase the impetus for reform from within. It also meant that the public could see little change. Crime statistics in Peru are notoriously inaccurate, but survey data indicate no significant increase in reporting rates, and little evidence that the public's perception of service provided by local police stations has improved.[35] This data indicates that public awareness of, and support for reform did not translate into attitudinal change towards the police. It is reasonable to surmise that concrete improvements in police service delivery would be required to produce deeper and long-lasting changes in police-community relations – and to encourage active civilian participation in future reform.

With the benefit of hindsight, the scale of the challenges facing SSR becomes clear. While this article has shown that leadership, changes of attitude, improved management, and anticorruption initiatives play a more significant role than funding in the early stages of institutional transformation, the lesson of Peru is that all of these variables are insufficient to ensure reform. Additional resources and consistent political and institutional backing are necessary to foster and sustain transformation. Inadequate resources add to the challenge of reform, and, more particularly, impede the improvement of police services to the public within a reasonable period.

Although hard to detect, and despite the interrupted trajectory of police reform in Peru, the reforms initiative may still have a lasting legacy. Importantly, the achievements of the reform process, despite its short lifetime, were widely publicized and offered an alternative vision of policy-making and public management to the police, the public and opinion-makers in Peru. Police reform has been shown as an area in which effective management can produce important and relatively quick results. Most importantly, it must now be clear to senior officers that the writing is on the wall – reform has come and will return. What remains to be seen is when and in what form.

NOTES

1. The Peruvian National Police (*Policía Nacional del Peru*, PNP) was created in 1988 with the integration of three pre-existing forces: the Republican Guard (the most militarized of the three); the Civil Guard (which also had a military rank structure); and the Investigative Police (the most civilian). In the unification process, however, the most militarized traditions prevailed.
2. *Comisión de la Verdad y Reconciliación. Informe Final* (Lima: CVR 2003) < www.cverdad. org.pe > . All websites were accessed in Feb. 2006.
3. *Informe de la Comisión Especial de Reestructuración de la Policía Nacional del Perú* < www.pnp.gob.pe/especiales/modernizacion.asp > .
4. Ibid.
5. Gino Costa and Carlos Basombrío, *C. Liderazgo Civil en el Ministerio del Interior. Testimonio de una experiencia de reforma policial y gestión democrática de la seguridad en el Perú* (Lima: Instituto de Estudios Peruanos 2004) p.79 < www.seguridadidl.org.pe/institucional/liderazgocivil.doc > . For the inaugural speech see the *Diario Oficial 'El Peruano'*, 29 July 2001 < www.editoraperu.com.pe > .
6. Costa and Basombrío (note 5) pp.79–80.
7. Costa was previously vice-minister of the interior.
8. For further details on the public order crisis, see Costa and Basombrío (note 5) pp.50–4.
9. *Diario Oficial 'El Peruano'* (note 5).
10. *Informe de la Comisión Especial de Reestructuración de la Policía Nacional del Perú*
11. Ibid.
12. See < www.acuerdonacional.gob.pe > .
13. The UK also gave a grant of some US$300,000 to support the creation of the Police Ombudsman's Office. Germany financed some activities of the Peace and Development Commissioners, which were established in Ayacucho, Satipo and Tingo María as part of the anti-terrorist strategy. Spain funded the visit of some of its police experts during the work of the Restructuring Commission. Costa and Basombrío (note 5) pp.92–6.
14. Ibid. pp.94–5, 108–10.
15. This support complemented the regular police training programmes in drug enforcement and operational intelligence, as well as the exchange of drug enforcement agents in the Western Hemisphere within the context of the activities of the Lima-based School for Drug Enforcement Intelligence.
16. The Washington Office on Latin America (WOLA), the Center for Development Studies (CED) in Santiago, Chile, and the Institute of Legal Defense (IDL) in Lima, Peru were active members of the network.
17. For further information on the seminar see Costa and Basombrío (note 5) pp.92–4.
18. Ibid. pp.95–6, 216–22. In early 2006, two months before the presidential and parliamentary elections, only a few of the preliminary studies had been conducted.

19. As embodied in Law 27860.
20. Attempts to arrive at an agreement with the police on communications equipment needed were so elusive that a decision had to be taken by the ministry. Unfortunately changes of ministers made it impossible to purchase urgently needed communication equipment and resources have been used elsewhere, where investment was not a priority. Although difficult to prove, illegal economic gains from purchasing specific systems probably explains both the deadlock in discussions at the Modernization Commission and 2004's decision not to invest in communication systems. See Adolfo Gazzo Vega, 'Informática y telecomunicación policial. La historia interminable' in Carlos Basombrio *et al.*, *Manejo y Gestión de la Seguridad. De la Reforma al Inmovilismo* (Lima: Instituto de Defensa Legal 2004) pp.153–62 < www.seguridadidl.org.pe/libros/manejoygestion.pdf > .
21. For example, decisions about replacing the existing inefficient and corrupt systems for purchasing and distributing petrol and medicines were avoided. Compare Ricardo Valdes, 'Combustible y medicinas: la punta del iceberg (lecciones de las licitaciones)' in Basombrio *et al.* (note 20) pp.119–27.
22. Pontificia Universidad Católica del Perú.
23. As of Feb. 2006, the presentation of the law to Congress was still pending.
24. Universidad Particular San Martín de Porres.
25. For more on the Police Ombudsman's Office and the Internal Affairs Office see Costa and Basombrio (note 5) pp.139–44, 108–10. On the work of the Ombudsman's Office and efforts to promote respect for the human rights of the police, see also Carlos Basombrio, Gino Costa, Miguel Huerta and Susana Villaran, 'Activistas de derechos humanos a cargo de la seguridad y el orden en el Perú' (Lima: Instituto de Defensa Legal 2004) pp.179–219 < www.seguridadidl.org.pe/trabajos/activistasmininter.doc > . On the stagnation of the Ombudsman's Office, see S. Villarán, 'La Defensoría se desvanece', in Basombrio *et al.*, (note 20) pp.101–5. On the work of the Internal Affairs Office, see L. Caparros, 'OASI: una bien ganada mala fama' in Basombrio *et al.* (note 20) pp.106–12.
26. The Surquillo pilot project was established in Sept. 2002.
27. Law 27933. See E. Yépez Dávalos, *Seguridad Ciudadana. 14 Lecciones Fundamentales* (Lima: Instituto de Defensa Legal 2004) pp.112–20 < www.seguridadidl.org.pe/libros/yepez.htm > .
28. An Open Society Justice Initiative project supporting local committees in six pilot areas is demonstrating that in addition to political will on the part of the mayors and police, significant investments in education and capacity-building on the concept and strategic approaches to prevention are required to produce results. See < www.justiceinitiative.org > .
29. *Informe de la Comisión Especial de Reestructuración de la Policía Nacional del Perú.*
30. Valdes (note 21) in Basombrio *et al.* (note 20) pp.119–27.
31. Ibid.
32. There have been no serious external security threats in recent years. The possibility of the Colombian conflict spreading was never real, given the geographic characteristics of the dense jungle border area. It was not difficult for the armed forces to tackle sporadic incursions by the Colombian rebel movement FARC (Revolutionary Armed Forces of Colombia) into Peruvian territory, for they had excellent intelligence from Colombian and United States sources on FARC movements, and were used to handling small-scale deployments. The other important threat to the country's security, which had larger repercussions in the national psyche and political discourse than in reality, lay in the last remnants of terrorist groups, confined within the Alto Huallaga and Ene–Apurímac basins.
33. Costa and Basombrío (note 5) pp.228–9.
34. Eileen Rosin and Coletta Youngers (eds.), *Drugs and Democracy in Latin America: the Impact of U.S. Policy* (Boulder, CO: Lynne Rienner 2005).
35. See Carlos Basombrio's analysis of public perceptions of the police in *Percepciones, victimización, respuesta de la sociedad y actuación del Estado. Evolución de las tendencias de opinión pública en Lima Metropolitana 2001–2005* (Lima: Instituto de Defensa Legal 2005); Seguridad Ciudadana y Actuación del Estado, *Análisis de tendencias de opinión pública* (Lima: Instituto de Defensa Legal 2004); *Perú 2003: Inseguridad ciudadana y delito común. Percepciones y realidades* (Lima: Instituto de Defensa Legal 2003).

The Company We Keep: Private Contractors in Jamaica

FRANCESCO MANCINI

Private companies play an increasingly important role in security sector reform (SSR).[1] From Nigeria to India, the Balkans to the Caribbean, such companies (henceforth contractors) provide services to local governments, and to the donors and international organisations that design and implement the reform of security sector institutions.

A broad range of contractors is involved, including management consulting firms, risk consultancy companies, non-profit organisations, freelance consultants, and private military and security companies. All have different backgrounds and interests, pursue varying approaches, offer diverse benefits and bear different risks. Some transfer expertise developed in their military and police practices, while others approach reform from a public sector perspective. The range of activities offered spans everything from the reform of pay and grading systems to providing strategic advice about counter-terrorism.[2]

Mirroring the way that normal business outsourcing is categorised, contractor activities in SSR are best classified by the range of services they offer: training; management support, and diagnosis and policy review.[3]

The first group includes training for professional and operational development in myriad areas, such as in the use of new equipment, operation planning, human rights, and civil oversight.

The second relates to management. This may involve change and project management,[4] as well as strengthening financial and human resources, managerial processes, judicial case management, improving procurement, and budgeting systems.

The third service pertains to assistance in diagnosing the security sector (or a component of it), its operations and organisational structure, as well as providing advice to support national reviews of security policy.

This article investigates the role of one particular subset of contractors involved in SSR – management consultants. It takes as its case study the work of Atos Consulting (henceforth Atos), which was subcontracted to reform the Jamaican police by the United Kingdom (UK) Department for International Development (DfID).[5] DfID financed the Jamaica Constabulary Force Reform and Modernization Programme (JCFRMP), which ran from March 2001 to July 2005,[6] but relied on Atos to support the Jamaica police in carrying out the reform. Atos led a consortium of contractors and coordinated a variety of activities, while DfID provided policy and programme supervision.

The article is divided into five sections. The first outlines the severity of Jamaica's security challenges – murder is the leading cause of death for working-age males and rates of violence continue to escalate.[7] This section also introduces the police reform programme, the role of the Atos-led consortium, and the costs and results of the reform. The second section presents Atos' approach to reform. The third analyses the activities undertaken, while the fourth evaluates the programme. Finally, the article identifies lessons for contractors and donors.

Overall, it is clear that relying on contractors carries both benefits and downsides. The study demonstrates the Atos-led consortium's contribution to structural change in the Jamaica police, as well as its shortcomings. It highlights the fact that it is the responsibility of donors and reforming countries to define better the mandates under which contractors perform, and to improve their oversight and management. Effective coordination is crucial to the success of reform programmes.

BULLETS, POLICE AND CONTRACTORS

Having gained some degree of political control over its own affairs in the late 1930s, Jamaica held its first election under universal adult suffrage in 1944, when a national government was elected to work with the British-appointed governor. The country faced challenges of identity, economic development, social transformation and institutional re-engineering, all of which became increasingly pressing after independence from the UK in 1962. Today, Jamaica is confronted by a serious 'crisis of public safety'.[8]

Jamaica struggles with violent and organised crime, drug trafficking, extortion and corruption. The number of shootings and murders has reached a record high. In 2000, the last detailed data available recorded an annual homicide rate of 34 per 100,000 inhabitants, lower only than that of Colombia (63), South Africa (52) and Swaziland (88).[9] As of August 2005, there were already 1,028 murders that year, 25 per cent more than in the same period the previous year.[10] Inevitably, this disrupts the economy; the World Bank estimated that in 2001, criminal activities cost Jamaica as much as four per cent of its gross domestic product.[11] Although no external force threatens Jamaica, the personal security of citizens is under constant threat, and state institutions appear incapable of protecting people.

Patterns of violence have evolved over the last 40 years, and three main trends can be identified.[12] First, violence moved from being politically driven to being the result of drug trafficking and organised crime. Both of Jamaica's main political parties have their roots in political violence and sponsored criminal gangs, who control whole neighbourhoods.[13] This relationship between political violence and crime forged the so-called garrison phenomenon (where neighbourhoods are controlled by one political party), and has been one of the key factors in the upsurge in crime and violence.[14] The political control of major organised criminal networks thus combines with protection rackets and gang warfare to heighten insecurity.

Second, in 1976–77, Jamaica departed from the traditional pattern of high levels of property crime to one where crime against the person, especially murder, was pre-eminent.[15] The government responded by declaring a state of emergency and involving the military in policing. However, instead of curtailing the violence this led instead to considerable human rights abuse. Finally, inter-personal violence and property crime evolved into inter-group and inter-community conflicts, a significant number of which persist even though overt political conflict subsided in the 1980s.[16]

Jamaicans are very concerned about violent crime, but they are slowly developing a tolerance to high levels of lawbreaking.[17] Bribery is often seen as the norm when doing business with the government, and violence during electoral campaigns is commonplace. Citizens are increasingly insecure at the same time as corruption in the state limits its capacity to respond.[18]

Domestic insecurity has international implications too, for Jamaica's geo-strategic position as a bridge between Central America's drug producers and Western markets reinforces the power of the drug trade. Some of Jamaica's large diaspora facilitate the supply of drugs to major cities in Canada, the UK and the United States (US). Gang-related violent crime is a regular result of the trade.[19] Consequently, the British, Canadian and US governments offer investigative and other technical support to the Jamaican authorities; they have an interest in reforming security institutions, send their police as advisers, and provide technological and monetary assistance. From their perspective, Jamaica's law enforcement and community safety is directly related to their own domestic security.

JAMAICA CONSTABULARY FORCE

With a roster of 8,500, the Jamaica Constabulary Force (JCF) has an authoritarian police culture.[20] It is top-heavy, with only 19 per cent of the force available for work on the street.[21] The JCF Act, passed in 1939 and amended in 1977, established a hierarchical structure of 11 ranks, which reinforces the paramilitary style of the organisation.[22] Although the JCF's mission statement is to 'serve, protect and reassure the people in Jamaica through the delivery of impartial and professional services', corruption and political interference are major concerns.[23] Indeed, corruption has been highly institutionalised and is largely accepted and mostly unsanctioned.[24]

The police record on human rights and the lawful treatment of citizens is woeful. An average of 140 people per year have been shot and killed by the police over the last decade, one of the highest per capita rates in the world.[25] According to the non-governmental organisation (NGO) Jamaicans for Justice, the government also fails to provide 'speedy and efficient remedy to victims' families [...] and to prosecute police officials for the killing of civilians, despite overwhelming evidence'.[26] The United Nations Commission on Human Rights released a report in 2003, which stated that the country had 'an unacceptably high number of questionable police shootings, and should hold more policemen accountable for their actions'.[27]

Against this background, the government is committed to reforming Jamaica's security institutions, and strengthening their capacity to implement policies.[28] The Ministry of National Security (MNS), for instance, was recently reformed and separated from the Ministry of Justice, and in 2005 a Jamaican team, with Canadian, British and American advisory support, completed the first national security review. The review produced a National Security Strategy that was coordinated across all relevant security and justice institutions, including the courts, prosecution services and penal institutions. However, nothing has been done to reform the court and prison systems, which are overburdened, operate with inadequate resources, suffer from overly bureaucratic and corrupt administration, and are frequently cited for human rights violations.[29]

The JCFRMP was one of several reform projects, its aim being to reduce crime in order to 'sustain economic and social development through the establishment of a safe, just and secure society for all citizens'.[30] The programme was designed to focus on seven main outputs: greater transparency, integrity and service orientation; the restructuring of the organisation to enhance delivery of services to the public; the development of community-based policing to create confidence between the police and local communities; an improved performance of the Criminal Investigation Bureau (CIB) in preventing and solving crime; a reduction in the careless and dangerous use of public thoroughfares; a JCF equipped with professional personnel; and a more efficient use of material assets, including budgets.[31]

CONTRACTORS

Police reform is a crowded field in Jamaica. The Organization of American States (OAS) worked on drug demand reduction, while the US – through the Police Executive Research Foundation (PERF) – provided technical assistance for criminal investigation in specific pilot areas of Kingston. American consultants worked as mentors for the police commissioner while other contractors (mainly current or former UK police officers) worked on police reform. Officers from London's Metropolitan Police Service helped the JCF on an anti-corruption programme, and on improving crime scene preservation, investigative capacity and intelligence gathering.[32] One was appointed as assistant commissioner of police (ACP) for crime in March 2005.

DfID is a leading donor in Jamaica's police reform. In 2001 it hired Atos to fulfil two main tasks: to assist DfID in elaborating the terms of reference for programme implementation, and to coordinate the implementation of the programme.[33] DfID stated that their involvement in SSR represented 'an important advance in development thinking; i.e. that well-run security and justice sectors are essential "services" that responsible states should provide to their citizens, including poor people'.[34]

Atos led a consortium of three subcontractors: Ramesses,[35] Capital Eye[36] and Consort HR.[37] The team working under Atos comprised just 23 members, but nevertheless the structure was complex. Half the team members were management consultants (though only one was full-time on the project – the others were also engaged in various missions in other countries), while the remaining members were technical consultants. These were former UK police officers who brought expertise in community-based policing, crime investigation, traffic accident analysis and prevention, and professional standards.

The programme director was an Atos management consultant with expertise in change and project management. He visited Kingston every three months for a period of two weeks, during which he met with the project's two 'clients' (DfID and the JCF) and assessed the development of the programme. Atos also provided four other management consultants, with expertise in organisational change, human resources management and change management.

Three other firms worked under the Atos banner.[38] Consort HR, a network of independent management consultants, had two consultants on the project. One trained police officers in leadership and management, having worked in this field for many years at the UK National Police Training College, Bramshill (Hampshire) while the other was the programme manager and the only consultant based full-time in Kingston. His expertise included human resources management and programme management. He ran the programme and was the day-to-day point person for the clients. He also coordinated the contractors' team, which included two Jamaican consultants working on customer service training and raising public awareness.

Ramesses and Capital Eye had a total of 14 consultants on the ground. They provided technical training on a variety of topics, including community-based policing, transport management, crime management and finance. These consultants were generally former UK police officers with specific expertise. They came to the island for a period of two to three weeks every one or two months to deliver the training and/or support the execution of their respective activity or 'work-stream'.

The JCF reform programme was organised into seven broad work-streams, following the seven outputs mentioned above, each led by a JCF staff of the Corporate Strategy Coordination Unit (CSCU) created to carry out reform. Atos assigned a consultant to each work-stream, who was accountable for the execution of all activities included in that specific stream of the programme. The consultant worked as mentor for the JCF staff, although too often s/he had to assume a more interventionist role to move the work forward, that is, calling for meetings that the JCF should have organised, or preparing documents which the JCF should have written.

Effective coordination of all these activities and actors was a key factor for success. SSR programmes often struggle with coordination issues between donors and the recipient country, and Jamaica is no exception.[39] Further, donors subcontracting to private consultants made the task of coordinating donors more difficult. Coordinating the contractors thus became one of the main activities of the reform effort.

COSTS AND OUTCOMES

The JCFRMP had a DfID-provided budget of around US$6.5 million (UK£3.7 million), of which around $1.2 million (£700,000) was spent on capital acquisitions such as computers, office equipment, and the refurbishment of police station reception areas. The vast majority of the programme's cost was fees and other expenses. The average cost of a consultant was $1,150 (£650) per day. This price rose with the seniority of the consultant. Expenses, including travel and accommodation, also have to be added to the fee.[40]

The programme was revised in 2003 to enhance the impact of the reform. Therefore, at this stage only preliminary outcomes can be assessed. In terms of crime management, the JCF developed a crime and disorder strategy and trained 11 trainers in homicide techniques, who subsequently trained 145 detectives. Twenty-two new scene-of-crime officers received training, as well as 4,000 officers in basic crime-scene preservation.

Community-based policing was implemented in four pilot police divisions, with 67 community-based police advisers and over 3,000 officers trained. A community safety forum – a key element that included police officers and local representatives of the civil society – was established in each of the four pilot divisions.

The programme also published a Citizens' Charter and Code of Conduct for the JCF, and a new Corporate Strategy, 2005–2008. Training was delivered in customer service, and in values and ethics training. Police stations provided new reception areas, where, for instance, victims of rape can testify in private, and 3,000 staff were trained in customer service. Three road-accident investigation units and a traffic analysis unit were established and officers trained.

On the management side, the Atos-led consortium worked on a new decentralised budget model, including costing a model for budgeting and day-to-day operations, though this has yet to be implemented. A new model for motor vehicle fleet management was approved. The JCF reviewed the structure of senior management staff, and highlighted the importance of allowing divisional commanders greater freedom to manage human, physical and financial resources locally. Division officers were trained in leadership. A new competency framework to underpin human resource management was created, which will guide selection, recruitment, promotion and career development. This reflects the new emphasis on customer service, ethics and community relationship building.

A professional standards branch was created, which included an internal affairs and anti-corruption division, a performance, audit and monitoring bureau, a legal affairs unit and a corporate planning, research and development department. This new structure aimed to bring under one command responsibility for designing, implementing and monitoring professional and procedural standards throughout the JCF.

Notwithstanding these encouraging outputs, murders, human rights violations and corruption remain rife in Jamaica.[41] This calls for a closer analysis and evaluation of the reform.

DESIGNING REFORM

Atos developed a methodology for what it calls justice sector reform, which is based on four principles. [42]

First, Atos promotes a 'strategic' approach that acknowledges the complexities of security systems and aims to develop solutions that take interdependencies into account.

Second, the methodology focuses on the needs of individuals in the system and on the critical linkages between parts of the security sector.

Third, Atos promotes capacity-building and participative approaches, working closely with key decision-makers in each part of the sector to identify performance improvements and where specific reforms would have the most impact. Skills transfer and the training of counterparts who work alongside Atos consultants are promoted as regular features of a programme.

Finally, the approach stresses the importance of effective programme management. Atos typically develops a consortium for large projects in which Atos consultants are drawn together with smaller specialist firms, NGOs with expertise in particular sectoral areas, and local organisations to enhance sustainability and provide local context and language skills.

DfID, meanwhile, has published its own SSR guidelines.[43] However, this document does not refer to the use of contractors and is not known to either the contractors or the JCF. DfID did not promote its use by Atos or the Jamaican government, and there is no evidence that DfID in Jamaica, contractors or the JCF used the document as the basis for preparing the reform programme.[44]

However, DfID's SSR guideline offers a helpful tool for understanding the areas the JCFRMP's terms of reference focused upon.[45] Of the specific items that Atos had to implement, roughly 45 per cent related to 'improving human resource management,' including leadership and management training, change management, value and ethics, and broader activities such as establishing a professional standard unit at police headquarters, and a human resources director.

Nine per cent corresponded to 'strengthening financial management systems' (i.e., accounting system-user specification; new policies and procedures for the devolution of financial responsibilities to pilot divisions; planning and budgeting process), though only one activity related to 'strengthening civil oversight mechanisms' (i.e. community safety fora).

This was partially consistent with Atos' justice-sector reform approach, in which capacity building and effective programme management are main pillars. However, although central to the Atos methodology, much less attention was paid to a 'strategic approach which acknowledges the complexities and interdependencies of the security system', and to the 'individual citizen's needs'.

While on paper the programme seemed to be management-oriented, in reality resources were directed towards technical assistance. The programme was staffed with content consultants (advisers and training officers skilled in operational and technical policing skills) rather than process consultants (management consultants supporting JCF officers in the design, development and execution of the reform). Eight to ten former or current British police officers provided technical assistance, but only one management consultant was available full-time in Jamaica.

WHAT CONTRACTORS DO

In Jamaica, the Atos-led consortium oversaw a set of activities that can be grouped into three categories: planning, management, and ownership.

Planning

KPMG Consulting, bought by Atos in 2002, was involved with DfID in designing the reform plan in collaboration with the Jamaican Ministry of National Security and the Police Commissioner.[46] In 2001 KPMG Consulting interviewed senior police management and staff in headquarters and local offices to explore goals and objectives, evaluate operations and tasks. They also studied organisational charts, internal policies and practices, and decision-making processes. Following the interviews and analysis, KPMG Consulting proposed a comprehensive action plan setting out the activities identified as necessary for the modernisation of the JCF. The ministry and the commissioner approved the final action plan, while DfID provided the financial support. The JCF was directly involved in the planning phase.

The 2003 revision of the JCFRMP focused on the professionalism of the police, increasing its accountability and the application of ethical practices to fight corruption. The Commissioner and the Ministry of National Security specifically requested that the reform's effectiveness be strengthened, so in response Atos increased the degree of coordination among the seven work-streams of the reform and enhanced the project management assistance to the Corporate Strategy Coordination Unit (CSCU), which played a pivotal role in the implementation of reform.

In this sense, the planning process can be described as a concerted effort by DfID, Atos and the JCF to produce the project design that the JCF was to implement, Atos to support, and DfID to monitor and finance. Arguably, Atos, through interviews with JCF staff, enhanced JCF ownership of the programme, translating its perspective and priorities into a consistent action plan. This triangular relationship also reinforced DfID's capacity to provide assistance coherent with JCF needs.

Management

It was vital that the leadership of the JCF and the Ministry of National Security promoted and supported the modernisation programme, but given the demands on their time, the CSCU remained the nerve centre; the head of the CSCU, an assistant commissioner of police, was responsible for monitoring progress and reported directly to the Commissioner. Indeed, the programme was not sustainable without an effective CSCU, which was staffed with younger and motivated officers, located at headquarters, and tasked with implementing the reform programme and the corporate strategy. The CSCU was essentially a change agent, 'with one foot in the old world and one in the new, it acted as a bridge'. [47]

The Atos-led consortium provided the support the CSCU needed. This included maintaining the action plan; advising the Commissioner about donor funding requirements and potential sources of funding; monitoring and evaluating the action plan, and reporting on progress; supporting internal and external communication; supporting the operational and administrative boards, and the quarterly review process involving the Commissioner; project and programme management; and advising on change management.

The project also sought to address the central management concerns of the JCF by establishing a department dedicated to professional standards that could be used to introduce a series of managerial innovations. This new headquarters directorate was responsible for anti-corruption/internal affairs, corporate planning, research and development (incorporating the CSCU), legal affairs, and performance auditing and monitoring. Simultaneously, financial and asset management reform was undertaken.

The CSCU's capacity to manage the reform process was, however, weak. This affected human resources management, communication, project management, and financial planning and control. Thus the creation of a human resources division was delayed because it proved difficult to recruit a suitably qualified and experienced director. This mattered because in a labour-intensive hierarchical service such as the police, the director (who could be a civilian) plays a powerful role, hiring and allocating people. The new corporate culture promoting professionalism, ethics and customer service did not permeate the structure either, stopping at senior levels. Lastly, although the JCF was in 2004 given authority to manage its own budget (previously under the control of the Ministry of National Security), devolved functional accountability was minimal. Corruption concerns ensured that senior management resisted the delegation of budgets to JCF divisional commanders. [48]

Ownership

It is often asserted that local ownership is a prerequisite for implementing police reform. [49] Certainly, DfID and Atos paid great attention to the JCF's perspective and needs. However, while the JCF Commissioner was a persistent and vociferous proponent of reform, he did not always enjoy the support of his most senior officers, some of whom were resistant to change. Moreover, while politicians spoke enthusiastically about reform, their actions often fell significantly short of their rhetoric.

Such resistance was unsurprising, for the momentum of change is often slow in bureaucratic and politicised institutions like the JCF: 'Past reform processes encountered considerable resistance and were stymied, deflected or modified to fit the parameters set by the old guard conservatives of the Constabulary.'[50] Therefore, success depended on the ability of the Atos-led consortium, together with the JCF leadership and the CSCU, to ensure that officers at all levels, and civil society more generally, accepted ownership of the process.

Civil society's involvement in police reform was mentioned in documentation, but very few activities focused on it. The programme's main activity was to introduce 'community safety fora', the aim of which was to help the JCF better understand the needs of the local community. A contractor (a former UK police officer with expertise in community-based policing) assisted the JCF to organise and facilitate the fora. Four pilot divisions — Manchester (Mandeville), St. Andrew South (Kingston), St. Catherine South (Portmore) and St. James (Montego Bay) — started their own fora, and others were planned for the 15 remaining divisions. The key factor for their success was the leadership of the divisional commander and the relationships s/he developed with local community representatives, while a factor for failure was that most local communities did not trust the police. The police were seen as highly inefficient and corrupt. Also, in certain neighbourhoods, 'garrisons' or local 'dons', rather than the JCF provided security.[51]

Documents relating to the next phase of the reform noted that programming should be more citizen-focused, that the community's safety needs should be identified, and that the JCF should be more accessible. [52]

EVALUATING REFORM

It is too soon to gauge the effects of the JCFRMP. The lack of performance indicators complicates the task further. The JCF reform programme did not include an assessment methodology or performance indicators (either quantitative or qualitative) to measure the impact of the reform on the police organisation, or its progress toward the stated mission of 'serving, protecting and reassuring the people of Jamaica through the delivery of impartial and professional services'.[53]

However, the reform programme did not suffer from a lack of paper outputs; every six months DfID produced project progress reports monitoring its implementation and also the work of the contractors. Outputs were comprehensively listed and assessed; each report scored from one to five the likelihood of an outcome being achieved. This essentially internal reporting system allowed DfID to track the execution of the reform, and take corrective initiatives where necessary. However, it took no measure of the effectiveness of reform, and reports were not available to JCF staff.

To Jamaican citizens, the JCFRMP brought little change. The programme's objective was to reduce violent crime and serious traffic accidents, yet crime statistics showed few signs of improvement.[54] Although robbery decreased by over 40 per cent between 1998 and 2003, the number of shootings and murders increased.[55] Similarly, the JCF developed and disseminated a new traffic management strategy which addressed issues such as the deployment of traffic patrols, the targeting of accident hot spots, and the identification of those presenting the greatest risk on the roads. The JCF also started to work closely with other public and private organisations on public education programmes on road safety. Yet this achieved little substantive; the only data available showed a slight decrease (5 per cent) in the number of serious and fatal accidents, 2002–2003.[56]

Internally and organisationally, reform has been effective, particularly in improving the management structure of the JCF. The CSCU is operational, and a corporate strategy has been drawn up and implemented. The CSCU's management skills may be weak, but the production of a written strategy represents a major change for a society accustomed to unwritten norms; it serves as a standard and starting point for a more uniform style of management. Even so, corruption remains pervasive, especially in units such as intelligence and investigation.[57] Exemplary punishments have yet to be imposed.[58]

At the national level, the Ministry of National Security was separated from the Ministry of Justice, thus creating a dedicated administration managing both the Jamaica Defence Force (JDF) and the JCF. However, the lack of linkages between the various institutions in the security sector remained a weak point of the reform. The new National Security Strategy promised to address this, but the next phase of police reform still needs to create linkages between the police and other institutions, such as the judiciary and prison system, which are also in need of reform.

No Numbers, No Cry

Measuring the impact of the reform is challenging because the programmes did not include indicators for measuring success. Although an early draft of the new Corporate Strategy 2005–2008 presented seven strategic objectives, each to be matched with performance indicators, the final version did not include those indicators.[59] The JCF probably considered the numbers a step too far and opted for a more prudent description of 'expected benefits'.

The ways in which progress could have been evaluated include the following. Objective one, to 'improve quality of service and ethics of the JCF', included indicators such as the percentage of inspections indicating satisfactory performance, and the number of police stations renovated. The objective of reducing 'crime, disorder, and fear of crime' was originally meant to be measured by such indicators as: the introduction of crime recording and reporting systems at headquarters and divisional levels; a comparison of the percentage of crime against rate recorded the previous year; and the percentage of citizens surveyed who perceived the overall level of disorder as high.

Another objective, 'achieve better value for money in the service', was to be evaluated by the following indicators: percentage increase in the number of crimes detected at the divisional level per Jamaican $10m spent, percentage reduction of divisional budgets spent on utilities, goods and services; and percentage of divisions using financial information in planning and staff deployment decisions.[60]

In 2004–2005 Atos, with the support of one Jamaican social scientist, conducted an opinion survey among the community living in the pilot areas (Kingston, Montego Bay, Manchester, and Portmore) to gauge the impact of the reform. The survey consisted of a questionnaire, the outcome of which will (when it is available) influence the next phase of the reform programme.

LEARNING BY DOING

Atos' experience produced a number of valuable lessons, which can be applied to Jamaica but also have wider value for contractors and donors engaging in SSR in violent societies. Strengthening democratic governance in the security sector requires, among other things, changes in the structure and the processes of institutions, its financial and human resources management, and in personnel culture and skills. The human factor is the central variable that translates 'national priorities into specific institutional arrangements, policies and practices'.[61] To succeed, it is therefore necessary but not sufficient to formulate strategic objectives. Rather, it is critical to manage effectively the process of change. A poorly managed change process may result in institutions thinking about but not delivering safety and justice. Hiring management consultants can avert this risk.

Moreover, consultants are more likely to promote client ownership because they can adapt their services to local needs during implementation. The mid-term revision in 2003 of the JCF reform programme is a case in point. Day-to-day relations with the client allow consultants to adapt the sequencing and execution of reform. Provided their activities reflect the terms of reference, donors should give contractors latitude in implementing the reform programme.

Lessons for Contractors

The first set of lessons learned concerns the work of Atos in Jamaica, and also that of other contractors working in SSR. They can be grouped under the following five headings:

Focus on Citizens.   The nature of management consultancy risks shifting the focus of reform onto the organisation, its structures and processes, rather than the safety needs of the community. The JCF reform programme is very police-focused, but although the efficiency of the organisation is important, ultimately the client receiving the service is the Jamaican citizen. In the event, by the end of the programme community safety fora were established in the four pilot divisions. They met periodically and included members of the JCF and local representatives of civil society.

Measurement.   Performance indicators should measure the outcomes of reform, rather than outputs. Although indicators were excluded from the new corporate strategy, the JCF needs to create a set of appropriate performance indicators. Current measures are insufficient; DfID's project progress reports, for example, are an internal reporting system, rather than an assessment tool for measuring the impact of reform on the JCF and Jamaican society. Indicators should consider short-term wins (thereby providing evidence that change is worthwhile), and long-term impacts.

These could be extrapolated from crime trend analysis and public perception surveys.

It is difficult to link the introduction of management innovation (e.g. a code of ethics) with a reduction in violent crime. In Jamaica, everyone knows that criminality is an issue, but the problem is not quantified, and detailed data on the effectiveness (or lack thereof) of reform programmes are rarely offered. Only the divisional commander of Montego Bay periodically presented monthly data on crime in his area. This allowed the public – and the JCF – to link progress in police reform with crime trends.

Communication. Good internal communication improves management transparency and boosts morale, while effective external communication improves public understanding of reform, supports the institutional image, and increases transparency with civil oversight institutions.[62] The JCF reform programme, however, failed to communicate reform outcomes, for example, crime statistics, or achievements. Although the Atos-led consortium helped develop a communication strategy, the high command did not appoint a communications director to implement it. The new *Corporate Strategy 2005–2008* does not stress the importance of internal and external communication.

Presence and Dedication. The success of any outsourced reform depends on reliable contractors able to make a long-term commitment to a client; a rotating band of consultants works against continuity and effectiveness, but in practice this is usual. JCF officers may have expected to develop a continuous relationship with the consultants,[63] but most (with the exception of the programme manager) visited the island for only two and three weeks every one or two months. As a result, initiative often stalled.

Additionally, contractor turnover tends to be high. Not only is SSR usually undertaken in insecure environments, but also frequent travelling and uncomfortable accommodation disillusions consultants used to business-class travel. The JCF programme, for example, had three programme managers in four years. This creates problems of continuity and institutional memory that confused the client and weakened the reform process.

Understanding Local Culture. International consultants usually have limited knowledge of local culture, and often fail to appreciate the attitudes, perceptions and habits of the organisation to be reformed. Many consultants, with only 'limited international experience or a development background ... fall back on [the] models, processes and structures with which they are familiar back home without validating them in the local context'.[64] For example, a model of community-based policing that works in London will not necessarily work in Jamaica.[65] Style matters too, for business habits vary. In Jamaica, socialisation at the beginning of a meeting is a more effective means of expediting reform than an anonymous business approach.

Lessons for Donors. Atos' experience in Jamaica offers lessons for donors planning to hire management consultants to lead SSR in developing countries in other regions. Such lessons can be grouped under six headings:

Contract. DfID experience in Jamaica suggests that donors need to manage their contractors better. The mandate that contractors receive from government agencies and international organisations is critical for this because it determines what will be done. Terms of reference have to solve the complex equation of developing coherent approaches, show quick wins to core constituencies and engage in long-term activities on the ground.

Shortcomings arise when contracts focus on easily achievable outputs. For instance, training is a favourite activity of donors, recipient governments and contractors because is relatively straightforward to implement, easily measurable, and conveys an immediate sense of change to the trainees and the public. The reform programme tended to focus too much and too early on personnel training before addressing the JCF's institutional capacity to absorb new skills.

Contracts must balance ambitious goals against realistic outcomes; donors should be aware of the point of departure. SSR frameworks invariably propose ambitious objectives such as democracy, accountability, transparency, harmonisation of governments' security and development policies, local ownership and cost-effective management.[66] Some of these principles would be hard to implement in an industrialised, stable and mature democracy.

Coordination. An arduous task for donors is coordinating not only the various activities that occur under the banner of SSR, but also the competing or different national interests of bilateral donors. Lack of coordination duplicates interventions, wastes resources and sends mixed messages to the recipient institution. In Jamaica, the numerous contractors collaborate with Atos through informal meetings, sharing documents, exchanging ideas, and de facto allowing the coordination of the different activities. A first donors' conference was held in July 2004, after several years of donors' involvement on the ground.

However, the difficult role of coordination belongs to donors and international organisations, as the recipient government often attempts to obtain resources from many different donors simultaneously. There are ways to facilitate coordination among the many actors supporting SSR. The Organization for Economic Cooperation and Development (OECD) suggested trust funds, joint assessments and joint evaluations/lesson learning studies as methods to enhance SSR coordination.[67] Additionally, donors can hire one contractor as project coordinator, following the model of Atos in Jamaica.

Vision and Strategy. Strategic vision in a reform programme has three main goals.[68] First, vision clarifies the general direction for change. Second, it motivates people to take action in the right direction. And third, it helps coordinate the actions of different people.[69] Donors should ensure that first, the vision and strategy of the programme is clear, and second, that the client receives uniform and coherent messages. In Jamaica, the philosophy of the public sector reform can be summarised as 'from policy makers to policy implementers,' while the philosophy of the JCF reform is 'from police force to police service'.[70] Fine words, but this researcher discovered that most JCF officers seemed unaware of the philosophy and principles guiding reform.[71]

Client Education.   Donors need to strengthen the way the recipient institution makes use of the contractors. Although this capacity can be double-edged, donors should train their client to work with contractors. Too often the reforming institution assumes a passive approach to reform.[72] The JCF, for instance, relied on contractors' input and rarely requested services or initiated a meeting. Also, consultancy is supply-driven, and there is always a risk that recipients will become overly dependent when contractors drive reform. Donors should encourage their clients to be more proactive, and learn how to benefit from their access to costly resources.

Knowledge Management.   'The importance of knowledge management is increasingly recognised.'[73] Management consultants generally have systems and mechanisms in place that optimise the corporate knowledge needed to improve organisational performance.[74] In Jamaica, Atos' knowledge management enhanced DfID's understanding of how to identify, organise and disseminate information and expertise on SSR programmes more broadly. DfID should ask contractors to formally identify, explain and share relevant knowledge.

Capital Budget.   Police reform also require funds to buy computers, cars and uniforms. There are two main reasons for this. First, improving the means at the disposal of the police helps to develop capacity and sustain long-term reform. Second, reform needs signals of change. A new computer on a desk, for example, boosts staff morale, just as a new reception area in a police station can improve relations with the public. The benefits offered by managerial support are less visible.

CONCLUSION

Every actor brings specific added value, as well as challenges, to SSR programming. Contractors are no exception, as the case of Jamaica shows. The Atos-led consortium brought proven expertise to an ambitious programme for identifying and managing structural change within the JCF. However, the overall impact of their work – and of reform more generally – proved ephemeral.

This study highlights the key role played by donors and recipient in defining the mandates under which contractors perform, and in improving oversight. At the same time, while police reform is part of a larger effort aimed at modernising Jamaica's public services and improving the quality of governance, no initiative has been undertaken to reform other security institutions, such as oversight bodies, judiciary and correctional services. The case of Jamaica emphasises the importance of coherent and comprehensive programmes for successful governance reform.

Although contractors' involvement in SSR is increasingly common (and shows no sign of slowing in near the future), SSR literature mostly ignores the phenomenon.[75] Scholars focus on a wide range of governance objectives, including professional security forces, capable civil authorities, human rights, responsible civil society, transparency, conformity with international and internal law.[76] More analysis should be done on the relationship between donors and contractors, its benefits and risks, and the comparative advantage of using private services instead of public ones. The experience of the Atos-led consortium emphasises that security is a demanding and ambitious activity, which requires coherent strategies, solid management skills and sound financial investments to achieve success in crime control. More integrated research in organisational theory, change management, leadership and knowledge management will harness the knowledge of the diverse fields that SSR straddles.

NOTES

1. This article is based on field research and interviews conducted in Jamaica in Nov. 2004. For their critical advice and guidance through the research, the author would like to thank Assheton Bogg, Claire Howard, Gordon Peake and Eric Scheye. The author is indebted to the JCF officers and staff who provided insight on the reform, together with their external consultants. Special thanks go to Assistant Commissioner (ACP) Blake, ACP Novelette Grant, George Briggs (head of the Government of Jamaica Public Sector Reform Unit), and Phil Sinkinson (UK Deputy High Commissioner in Kingston). For their valuable comments, the author is grateful to David Kendrick, Mark James, Otwin Marenin, Graham Mathias, Graham Thompson, and Christoph Wilcke. Finally, the author would like to thank Clara Lee, Reyko Huang and Kaysie Studdard for their suggestions in improving the text.
2. For more details on contractors' role in SSR, see Francesco Mancini, *In Good Company? The Role of Business in Security Sector Reform* (NY: Demos and Int. Peace Academy 2005) < www.ipacademy. org/PDF_Reports/Good_company.pdf > .
3. Peter Singer uses this approach to typologise the private military industry. Peter W. Singer, *Corporate Warriors: The Rise of the Privatized Military Industry* (Ithaca, NY: Cornell UP 2003) p.91.
4. Change management includes programmes that deal with (1) structural change (how the organisation is structured); (2) cost cutting (how much the organisation costs); (3) process change (how things get done); and (4) cultural change (how human resources think). See Richard Luecke, *Managing Change and Transition* (Boston, MA: Harvard Business School Press 2003) pp.8–9. Project management includes a broad range of activities to meet the requirements of the particular project, such as planning, cost, human resources, quality control, and communication management.
5. Atos Consulting is a global business and technology consulting practice. It provides consulting advice and services in business and information technology (IT) strategy, operational transformation, change management and financial management. Atos Consulting is part of the Group Atos Origin, a leading IT services provider, which operates in 40 countries, has combined annual revenues of €5 billion ($6.3 billion) and employs over 46,000 staff < http://www.atosorigin.com/corporate/about_us/consulting/default.htm > .
6. Police reform is part of a larger effort that aims at modernising Jamaica's public services and improving the quality of governance. Several donors are involved in this broad effort. The British High Commission is directly involved at the prime-ministerial level with issues of governance, while the United Nations Development Programme (UNDP), DfID and the US Agency for International Development (USAID) work on governance and values and principles and regeneration of the public service. The Inter-American Development Bank (IADB) supports the reform of the Ministry of Finance and Planning, and the World Bank finances the restructuring of the Ministry of Industry, Commerce and Technology. The Canadian International Development Agency (CIDA) works on sustainable development for the Ministry of Land and Environment. See Public Sector Reform Unit's website, < www.cabinet.gov.jm/psru/partners.asp > .

7. 'Calling Scotland Yard', *The Economist*, 13 Aug. 2005, p.32.
8. Anthony Harriott, 'The Crisis of Public Safety in Jamaica and the Prospects for Change', *Souls* 3/4 (2001) p.57.
9. United Nations Office on Drugs and Crime, Centre for International Crime Prevention <www.unodc. org/unodc/crime_cicp_survey_seventh.html > .
10. During the author's eight-day visit in Nov. 2004, the total number of killings for the year increased from 1,230 to 1,255. See 'It Must Be a Duppy or a Gunman', *The Gleaner* (Kingston, Jamaica, 16 Nov. 2004) p.A4; 'Calling Scotland Yard' (note 7) p.32.
11. World Bank, *Jamaica: The Road to Sustained Growth* (Washington DC: World Bank 2004) p. xv. <http://wbln0018.worldbank.org/LAC/LAC.nsf/0/ 12C128BA971C348A85256E0400684CB9?Opendocument > .
12. For a more detailed overview of the Jamaican crime problem see Anthony Harriott, 'The Jamaican Crime Problem: New Developments and New Challenges for Public Policy', in idem (ed.), *Understanding Crime in Jamaica* (Kingston, Jamaica: Univ. of the West Indies Press 2003) pp.1–12.
13. The Jamaican political scene is dominated by the right-wing Jamaica Labour Party (JLP) founded in 1943 and the left-wing People's National Party (PNP) founded in 1938. 'By 1949, both political parties were engaged in violence to achieve political goals.' Amanda Sives, 'The Historical Roots of Violence in Jamaica' in Harriott, *Understanding Crime* (note 12) p.59.
14. 'A garrison is a political stronghold, a veritable fortress completely controlled by a party. Located in the heart of the urban areas, and created by the sharp political divisions of the 1960s and 1970s, the garrisons have fostered the escalation of political violence and nurtured the growth of gun and drug crime. [...] On election day, the garrisons are major sites for crime which are rarely prosecuted.' Mark Figueroa and Amanda Sives, 'Garrison Politics and Criminality in Jamaica' in Harriott (note 12) p.65.
15. Harriott, 'The Jamaican Crime Problem' (note 12) p.6.
16. An episode of inter-community violence in Sept. 2001 in western Kingston, a district of the capital, which was precipitated by the murder of an alleged drug boss ('don'), is a case in point: tensions within a highly cohesive group were projected onto an old political enemy, leading to killings and urban war between communities along the lines of the party–political divide. *Daily Gleaner* (19 April 2001) cited in Anthony Harriott, 'Social Identities and the Escalation of Homicidal Violence in Jamaica' in Harriott, *Understanding Crime* (note 12) p.95.
17. Harriott (note 12) p.4.
18. Ibid. p.5.
19. See, for example, 'Calling Scotland Yard' (note 7) p.32.
20. The JCF, founded in 1866 under the management of an inspector general appointed by the British government, was designed to 'keep the lid on' disorder in a hostile environment, and to 'suppress mass outbreaks against the peace'. Charles Jeffries, *The Colonial Police* (London: M. Parrish 1952) p.30.
21. Anthony Harriott, *Police and Crime Control in Jamaica: Problems of Reforming Ex-Colonial Constabularies* (Kingston, Jamaica: Univ. of the West Indies Press 2000) pp.36–7.
22. The colonial model usually has a higher number of ranks (8–13) than metropolitan police, which tend to have 6–13 ranks. See David Bayley, 'Comparative organisation of the police in the English speaking countries', in Michael Tonry and Norval Morris (eds.), *Modern Policing* (Univ. of Chicago Press 1992) p.527.
23. In 2001 Amnesty International reported many instances of police violence and abuse, including the case of a mentally ill detainee beaten to death by at least 14 members of the security forces in 1999. No one has been charged or disciplined. Amnesty International, *Jamaica: Killings and Violence by Police: How Many More Victims?* (Amnesty International 2001) <http://web.amnesty.org/library/ index/engamr380032001 > .
24. Local and international press often report on corruption in the JCF. See, for example, 'Commissioner Thomas, Transparency and Trust', *Jamaica Observer*, 17 Jan. 2006. <www.jamaicaobserver. com/editorial/html/20060116T210000-0500_96747_OBS_COMMISSIONER_THOMAS__TRAN-SPARENCY_AND_TRUST_.asp > .; 'Calling Scotland Yard' (note 7) p.32. For a detailed analysis of corruption in the JCF see Anthony Harriott, 'Rank and Money in the Bank: Corruption in the JCF', in Harriott, *Police* (note 21) pp. 47–71. For crime, political exploitation and corruption in Jamaica see Laurie Gunst, *Born Fi' Dead: A Journey Through The Jamaican Posse Underworld* (NY: Owl Books 1996); Duane Blake, *Shower Posse: The Most Notorious Jamaican Crime Organisation* (NY: Diamond Publishing 2003). I thank Ron West for bringing these two books to my attention.

25. Lynford Simpson, 'Police blasted for deadly force, *Jamaica Gleaner*, 11 April 2001, < www.jamaica-gleaner.com/gleaner/20010411/news/news1.html > .
26. Jamaicans For Justice, *Pattern of Impunity* (Kingston, Jamaica 2004) p.4 < www.jamaicansforjustice. org/archives/jw_archives.htm#writes > .
27. United Nations High Commissioner for Human Rights, *Report of the UN Special Rapporteur on Extrajudicial, Summary, or Arbitrary Executions* (Geneva: OHCHR 2003) < www.ohchr.org/english/ issues/executions/ > . See also US State Dept., *Jamaica: Country Report on Human Rights Practice – 2003* (Washington DC: US State Dept. 2004) < www.state.gov/g/drl/rls/hrrpt/2003/27904.htm > .
28. Interview with the director of the Public Sector Reform Unit, Government of Jamaica, 18 Nov. 2004, Kingston, Jamaica.
29. US State Dept., *Jamaica* (note 27).
30. Atos Consulting, *Jamaica Constabulary Force Reform and Modernization Project*, Revised Action Plan (31 March 2003) p.2. Document with author.
31. Ibid.
32. Interviews with JCFRMP Program Manager and JCF staff, 14–20 Nov. 2004, Kingston, Jamaica.
33. In recent years, Atos has been involved in several SSR projects. In the Balkans Atos worked on 11 projects in five countries (Balkans Safety, Security and Access to Justice), supporting ministries so as to increase policy-making capacity and develop community policing. In India, it carried out a police reform programme in the context of a wider governance reform initiative, while in Nigeria it focused on integrating justice reform at state and federal levels. Also, in Afghanistan Atos coordinated the actors involved in anti-narcotics. Interview with Atos Consulting Manager, 22 Oct. 2004, London.
34. DfID, *Fighting Poverty to Build a Safer World. A Strategy for Security and Development* (London, March 2005) p.11.
35. The Ramesses Group, formed in 2000, is a UK-based management and training consultancy, focusing on criminal justice reform, and modernisation and security in both the public and private sectors. Ramesses currently works in the Balkans and Nigeria on the reform and modernisation of criminal justice through the DfID Safety, Security and Access to Justice Programme (SSAJP) in partnership with Atos; and in Sri Lanka on training in anti-terrorism and major crime (in partnership with the Foreign and Commonwealth Office) < www.ramesses-group.com/index.php > .
36. Capital Eye is a specialist security consultancy set up by a former commissioner of the London Metropolitan Police in 1993. It provides consultancy and training services, including police review, security assessment, project management, investigations, and crisis management. < www.capitaleye.com > .
37. Interview with JCFRMP programme manager, 15 Nov. 2004, Kingston, Jamaica.
38. Ibid.
39. See, for example, Nicole Ball, 'Good Practice in Security Sector Reform', in Herbert Wulf (ed.), *Security Sector Reform* (Bonn, Germany: Bonn International Centre for Conversion 2000) p.20; Chris Ferguson, *UNDP: Conference on Justice and Security Sector Reform: Coherence, Cooperation, and Comparative Strengths* (Shrivenham, UK: Cranfield Univ. 2003); Albrecht Schnabel and Hans-Georg Ehrhart (eds.), *Security Sector Reform and Post-Conflict Peacebuilding* (Tokyo: UN UP 2005) p.320.
40. The figures throughout this section are taken from interviews with a JCFRMP programme manager and DfID policy adviser, 15–17 Nov. 2004, Kingston, Jamaica.
41. In Aug. 2005 the murder rate was 25 per cent higher than in the same month in 2004. More than 60 police officers were suspended or sacked in the first eight months of 2005. 'Calling Scotland Yard' (note 7) p.32.
42. Atos' use of 'justice sector' is broadly what most of the relevant literature refers to as the 'security sector'. Atos KPMG Consulting, *Work in Justice Sector Reform and Conflict Prevention* (6 June 2004). Document with author.
43. Department for International Development (DfID), *Understanding and Supporting Security Sector Reform* (London, UK: DfID 2002) < www.dfid.gov.uk/pubs/files/supportingsecurity.pdf > .
44. Interviews with DfID policy adviser and JCF staff, 17–20 Nov. 2004, Kingston, Jamaica.
45. DfID's SSR guidelines mention seven entry points which can vary according to local circumstances: (1) building public awareness and engagement; (2) building strategic planning capacity; (3) strengthening legal and constitutional frameworks; (4) strengthening civil oversight mechanisms; (5) strengthening financial management systems; (6) facilitating war-to-peace transitions; and (7) improving human resource management. DfID (note 43) p.19.
46. KPMG Consulting was formerly part of KPMG, one of the largest audit, tax and advisory services firms in the world. See < www.kpmg.com/ > .

47. See Everett M. Rogers, *Diffusion of Innovation* (NY: The Free Press 1983) pp.315–16, quoted in Richard Luecke, *Managing Change and Transition* (Boston, MA: Harvard Business School Press 2003) p.77.
48. Interview with JCFRMP programme manager, 15 Nov. 2004, Kingston, Jamaica.
49. William O'Neill, *Police Reform in Post-Conflict Societies: What We Know and What We Still Need to Know*, Policy Paper (NY: International Peace Academy 2005) p.5 <www.ipacademy.org/ PDF_Reports/PolRefERpt.pdf > .
50. See Anthony Harriott, 'Resistance to Reform', in Harriott, *Police* (note 21) p.160.
51. See John Rapley, *Jamaica: Negotiating Law and Order with the Dons*, North American Congress on Latin America (NACLA) Report on the Americas, New York, 37/2 (2003) pp.25–9.
52. Interview with JCFRMP programme manager, 17 Nov. 2004, Kingston, Jamaica.
53. See Jamaica Constabulary Force, *Corporate Strategy 2005–2008* (JCF Office of the Commissioner of Police 2005) p.1.
54. By 2004 more than 3,000 front-line officers had been trained in crime scene preservation, and over 100 detectives in investigative techniques. Interview with JCFRMP programme manager, 17 Nov. 2004, Kingston, Jamaica.
55. Jamaica Constabulary Force (note 53) p.8; 'Calling Scotland Yard' (note 7) p.32.
56. Jamaica Constabulary Force (note 53) p.8.
57. See Harriott, 'Rank and Money in the Bank: Corruption in the JCF', in Harriott, *Police* (note 21) p.61.
58. Interviews with JCF staff, 15–20 Nov. 2004, Kingston, Jamaica.
59. The seven strategic objectives are: (1) To improve the quality of service and ethics of the JCF by developing a culture of accountability, integrity, and performance; (2) To reduce crime, disorder and fear of crime by developing a proactive, intelligence-led approach to policing [...]; (3) To build safer communities by developing community-based policing as the model for Jamaica; (4) To reduce death and injury on Jamaica's road by improving the effectiveness of traffic policing; (5) To continue with the modernisation and restructuring of the JCF so that it can provide an enhanced quality of service to the public in an effective and efficient manner; (6) To improve the competence, professionalism and motivation of our staff by strengthening the JCF's human resources management system; (7) To achieve better value for money in the service we deliver by strengthening the JCF's financial and asset management. See Jamaica Constabulary Force (note 53) p.13.
60. Jamaica Constabulary *Force, Corporate Strategy 2005–2008*, First Draft (2004). Document with author.
61. Otwin Marenin, *Restoring Policing Systems in Conflict Torn Nations: Process, Problems, Prospects* (Geneva: Geneva Centre for the Democratic Control of Armed Forces (DCAF) 2005) p.22.
62. Change management literature underlines the role of communication. See Richard Luecke, *Managing Change and Transition* (Boston, MA: Harvard Business School 2003) p.60; John Kotter, *Leading Change* (Boston, MA: Harvard Business School 1996) pp.85–100; T.J. Larkin and Sandar Larkin, 'Reaching and Changing Frontline Employees', *Harvard Business Review* 74/3 (1996) pp. 95–104.
63. Interviews with JCF staff, Nov. 2004, Kingston and Mandeville, Jamaica.
64. Roderick Evans, 'Security Sector Transformation from a Development Donor Perspective' in *Security Sector Reform: Its Relevance for Conflict Prevention, Peace Building and Development* (Geneva: UN Office and DCAF 2003) p.39.
65. Hesta Groenewald and Gordon Peake, *Police Reform through Community-Based Policing: Philosophy and Guidelines for Implementation* (NY: International Peace Academy Sept. 2004) p.9 <www.ipacademy.org/PDF_Reports/POLICE_REFORM.pdf > .
66. See, for example, OECD, *Security System Reform and Governance*, DAC Guidelines and Reference Series (2005) <www.oecd.org/dataoecd/8/39/31785288.pdf > .
67. Ibid. p.29.
68. John Kotter refers to vision as 'a picture of the future with some implicit or explicit commentary on why people should strive to create that future'. See Kotter (note 62) p.68.
69. Ibid. pp.68–9.
70. Interviews with the director of the Public Sector Reform Unit, Government of Jamaica, DfID policy adviser, and JCFRMP programme manager, Nov. 2004, Kingston, Jamaica.
71. Interviews with JCF staff, Nov. 2004, Kingston, Jamaica.
72. Interview with Atos-led consortium's consultants, Nov. 2004, Kingston, Jamaica.
73. Fareed Hussain, Caro Lucas and M. Asif Ali, 'Managing Knowledge Effectively', *Knowledge Management Practice* 5 (May 2004) accessed online at <www.tlainc.com/articl66.htm > .

74. KPMG Consulting, *The Power of Knowledge: A Business Guide to Knowledge Management* (London 1988) <http://dmsweb.badm.sc.edu/798mis/papers/KPMG%20Power%20of%20 Knowledge% 201998.pdf > .
75. Rita Abrahamsen and Michael C. Williams, 'Security Sector Reform: Bringing the private in', *Conflict, Security & Development* 6/1 (April 2006) pp.1–23.
76. See Dylan Hendrickson and Andrzej Karkoszka, 'Security Sector Reform and Donor Policies', in Schnabel and Ehrhart (note 39) p.23.

Conclusions

GORDON PEAKE, ERIC SCHEYE AND ALICE HILLS

Despite differences in approach and circumstances, the cases discussed here reveal the gulf that exists between policy prescription and operational reality. They suggest that obstacles to implementing security sector reform or SSR can be grouped into two broad categories: managerial deficiencies, and insufficient awareness on the part of international organisations of the political context in which SSR programmes are designed and implemented.

MANAGERIAL CHALLENGES

Security sector reform in the aftermath of conflict or in violent societies is a task of daunting managerial complexity. The organisations charged with implementing reform usually lack appropriate structures and capacity, while many of the international personnel engaging in field-based activities – the link between policy goals and policy achievement – do not possess the necessary skills. The implication is that organisations such as the British DfID and the OSCE must be better organised if they are to improve, let alone reform, indigenous management practices: good management begins at home.

At least four related managerial issues emerge from the case studies.

First, the implementation of SSR programmes is usually badly managed. Programmes are rarely coordinated, and short-term activities are seldom reconciled with long-term goals. This means that the multiple and often simultaneous tasks involved in changing the structure, purpose and practice of a security institution can engulf other reforms in the sector. Alternatively, it often means that the effort involved in improving basic operational capacity prevents consideration of long-range issues, such as the creation of functioning oversight institutions.

Second, weak management manifests itself in flawed communications within the institution carrying out reform. Many of the cases here reveal an anemic relationship between headquarters and field personnel. In Iraq as in Sierra Leone and Papua New Guinea, policy guidance on SSR either did not exist at headquarters or, when it did, was not communicated to practitioners who improvised instead. This situation owed much to the manner in which donors are organised; high personnel turnover causes information to hemorrhage. It also resulted from the form in which advice was presented by headquarters staff; it was usually non-specific and unrelated to the practical challenges of fieldwork.

Third, many of the programmes described are of questionable durability. Too many make unwarranted assumptions about the financial and institutional capacity of the institutions concerned. In fact, the upkeep of newly reformed institutions is beyond the revenue-generating capacity of most host countries, while few have personnel capable of staffing the new institutions.

Fourth, the meaningful evaluation and measurement of field practice is missing in all the case studies discussed. Few programmes use discernible, reliable, or valid metrics, and the measures that are used tend to quantify outputs (officers trained, number of courses attended) rather than demonstrate the impact or outcome of specific activities. This has profound implications for programme refinement; it means that cost/benefit analyses cannot be carried out, and flawed institutional memories stand uncorrected.

POLITICS IN FORMULATION AND IMPLEMENTATION

Although the relevant literature asserts that SSR is an inherently political process, many of the programmes considered here appear to have been designed and conducted in technocratic and non-specific terms at the expense of their political context.

The importance of context – and its implications for implementation – manifests itself in three general ways. The first is the inertia and resistance to reform that exists within security institutions. Most see change as a direct challenge to their power, livelihood and working practices. The best way for international organisations to overcome or mitigate institutional resistance in the South remains controversial.

Second, current SSR policies and programming pays insufficient attention to the role of non-state actors in security provision. International support is overly state-centric; it invariably focuses on building the capacity of formal institutions even when the informal sector enjoys greater authority and legitimacy. Not only does this mean that state-based SSR programmes may be politically unrealistic, but also it suggests that they may be financially unsustainable in states with weak revenue-generating capacity or heavily reliant on foreign aid.

Finally, the case studies illustrate the overly-ambitious nature of international attempts to use SSR as a conflict management tool. In large part prompted by the politics of short-term donor cycles, international institutions attempt to do too much too quickly; there is too much governance and not enough management. However, the case studies also suggest that more effective management practices offer a key to developing a realistic reform agenda, among donors as well as among indigenous security institutions.

INDEX

Page numbers in *italics* represent tables.

Lightning Source UK Ltd.
Milton Keynes UK
UKHW020804070321
379882UK00004B/1165